Multicultural Competence in Student Affairs

Raechele L. Pope

Amy L. Reynolds

John A. Mueller

Foreword by Harold E. Cheatham

JOSSEY-BASS
A Wiley Imprint
www.josseybass.com

Published by Jossey-Bass
A Wiley Imprint
989 Market Street, San Francisco, CA 94103-1741   www.josseybass.com

Jossey-Bass books and products are available through most bookstores. To contact Jossey-Bass directly
call our Customer Care Department within the U.S. at 800-956-7739, outside the U.S. at 317-572-3986
or fax 317-572-4002.

Jossey-Bass also publishes its books in a variety of electronic formats. Some content that appears in
print may not be available in electronic books.

Library of Congress Cataloging-in-Publication Data

Pope, Raechele L., 1958-
  Multicultural competence in student affairs / Raechele L. Pope, Amy L.
Reynolds, John A. Mueller.— 1st ed.
      p. cm. — (The Jossey-Bass higher and adult education series)
Includes bibliographical references and index.
  ISBN 0-7879-6207-4 (alk. paper)
  1. Student affairs services—United States. 2. Multicultural
education—United States. I. Reynolds, Amy L. II. Mueller, John A.,
1961- III. Title. IV. Series.
  LB2342.92.P66 2004
  378.1'94—dc22
                                        2003023207

Printed in the United States of America
FIRST EDITION
HB Printing 10 9 8 7 6 5

Contents

List of Figures and Tables

The Jossey-Bass Higher and Adult Education Series

Foreword

It hardly seems possible that our profession is into the third decade (or the fourth, for those accepting the tumultuous sixties as the starting point) of the transformation that accommodates multiculturalism. Whatever the agreed-upon date, clearly the intervening years have brought added professional maturity as our research, theory, and practice respond to observations and some notable demonstrations that earlier models for intervention were inadequate to serve all of our students.

This is a fine day to consummate my blithe commitment of yesteryear to write this Foreword to what has emerged as a superior contribution to college student affairs and related professions. This is a fine day, because I have just returned from a cultural immersion of the sort that we envision for ourselves and for our students. Following more than two decades of teaching multicultural counseling and theory, and recent service on church-related medical mission teams to Zambia and to Ghana, I had the opportunity to return last month to Ghana solely as a *student*. A weeklong structured program of offerings in Ghanaian language(s), history, culture, art, and customs presented by faculty of a university campus was an elegant preface to the "study tour." Our questions, observations, and praise were tempered and guided by heightened self-knowledge and by our deepened appreciation of the Ghanaian perspective. So it will be, for readers of this volume as they are guided in capturing the perspective of "the other."

As education institutions continue pursuit of their stated and implied mission to recognize and infuse the curriculum and cocurriculum with the truths and values of all of their publics, they will be served now by the truths and values that make up *Multicultural Competence in Student Affairs*. This latest contribution to the growing literature is a primer for students, teachers, and administrators who, in their appointments and roles in student affairs, intend to serve the development of individuals who are members of the diverse cultures represented on campuses. The authors, our valued colleagues Raechele Pope, Amy Reynolds, and John Mueller, continue and extend the challenge to the normative system or paradigm. They offer grounded insights, syntheses, and practice exercises that serve to purge pessimistic, truncated, and sometimes pejorative perspectives, replacing them with balanced perspectives as represented in and drawn from current research and practice on human functioning.

This volume is about our individual and collective (professional) commitment to working with and for those functioning at the margins of the normative culture. Its central purpose is to contribute to the continuing development, understanding, and gracious accommodation of diversity not solely in cultural and ethnic dimensions but in all of its manifestations. The authors make this contribution through an exploration that adds to the self-assessment and self-knowledge that precede one's gaining accurate knowledge of others.

Their work in the opening chapter serves well to remove the edge, or "inny/outy," legacy of the early (late 1960s, early 1970s) multicultural counseling and therapy literature—which sometimes asserted unequivocally and unapologetically that one's ability to provide effective interpersonal interventions was constrained by or restricted to one's membership within the group served. Some writers asserted that only those who had come through the fire could serve the uninitiated or the naïve, and never could the opposite proposition prevail. Without even a hint of awareness of such ancient "truths," Pope, Reynolds, and Mueller implore, guide, and reassure the reader that no one is free of prejudice; each of us has the capacity to provide principled, competent, cross-cultural and multicultural interventions. In one's pursuit of multicultural competence, they offer and encourage use of diverse sources and experiences in formulating one's preliminary or tentative knowledge, skills, and awareness base. They offer postulates and the sage note that comprehension of the complexity inhering in an individual self is the first, elementary step toward achieving competence.

Chapter Two likewise is foundational and presents an excursus of theory and models, a critique of their origins and limitations for use with broader or diverse clientele, and the notation that a measure of competence is one's ability to distinguish between universals and particulars.

The remaining chapters adhere to a well-conceived model that presents first the issue and then review and discussion of the relevant older (and then the newer) literature, followed by infused or revised models and exemplars. Each chapter is directly (or else indirectly but clearly) related to a functional area of student affairs practice or administration, addressing multicultural competence from a singular perspective or model.

A unique value of *Multicultural Competence in Student Affairs* is its unusual focus and integration. It is a handbook of relevant critical information and how-to instruction for the professions, and it is a volume of thematic and comprehensive chapters that each can stand alone. While reading this work, I praised the accessibility and utility of some chapters for folks who are outside our profession but who serve students in particular. Here, I am thinking of "downtown" merchants, religious and social agencies, and others in the broader college and university community.

Through this pathbreaking contribution, Pope, Reynolds, and Mueller may not have eradicated the dated bromide regarding who can effectively serve whom, but they have through their excellent scholarship succeeded enviably in hastening its demise. For this seminal publication that advances our profession, I extend gratitude and congratulations. I am deeply appreciative of their regard for me as a colleague, from which came the honor of writing this Foreword.

Harold E. Cheatham
Dean Emeritus
Professor Emeritus of Counseling and Education Leadership
Clemson University
Clemson, South Carolina

Preface

In *Multicultural Competence in Student Affairs,* we have assembled our learnings from years of practice, teaching, research, and consulting on multicultural issues. We are confident that this book will be an additional and important resource for those attempting to create a multicultural campus. Further, we hope to offer a deeper appreciation of the multicultural awareness, knowledge, and skills necessary to be effective and ethical professionals by offering both theory and applied understanding to the dynamic and challenging responsibility of providing meaningful and relevant services to students. Although most books on multiculturalism in higher education focus on college students or the services and programs provided to them, this book is designed to focus on the awareness, knowledge, and skills of student affairs educators (both practitioners and faculty) to help them in their quest to become more multiculturally competent.

It is important to be explicit about the assumptions underlying this book and to define key terms. One of the barriers to developing a multicultural campus is that there is no broadly accepted definition of the term *multicultural* and no clear vision of what a multicultural campus looks like (Cheatham, 1991). Multicultural scholars have often disagreed about the definition of multiculturalism. Some argue for a more inclusive definition that would include race, gender, sexual orientation, social class, and religion (Pedersen, 1988; Speight, Myers, Cox, & Highlen, 1991), while others express concern that broader definitions undermine efforts to eliminate racism (Carter & Qureshi, 1995; Helms & Richardson, 1997).

Some multicultural scholars believe that efforts to broaden the definition of multiculturalism are fueled by conscious or unconscious discomfort in openly facing issues of race (Helms & Richardson, 1997). This discomfort is real, and the history and current race relations of the United States have created a reality in which "race, racial identity, and racism are central to how we view ourselves, each other, and the relationships and community that we are able to create" (Reynolds, 2001a, p. 104). If we scratch the surface of any significant issue in higher education, such as curriculum, admissions, violence on campus, or retention, it is almost impossible to ignore how racial dynamics influence solutions and strategies for resolving or addressing those issues. Whether the examination involves a predominantly White institution, a tribal college, or a historically Black college, racial issues affect the experiences of college students and the student affairs professionals who attempt to meet their needs.

We believe it is important to acknowledge that all of our social identities (race, class, religion, gender, sexual orientation, age, and abilities) influence who we are and how we view the world. Reynolds (2001a) suggests, "because of the complexity of diversity, we all experience life from the perspective of those social identities (from either the dominant or target group point of view) whether we realize it or not" (p. 104). Although most of us view ourselves in terms of one or two identities, nonetheless our other multidimensional experiences and identities shape our relationships with others who are similar to and different from us.

Although it may seem contradictory to some, we believe that it is possible *and* necessary to embrace race-based and more universal definitions of multiculturalism simultaneously. Such multidimensional definitions and conceptualizations of multiculturalism more accurately reflect the complexity of diversity and demand that we transform our assumptions about race, multiculturalism, and differences. In addition to identifying the key definitions that underlie this book, it is vital to acknowledge the assumptions on which we base this work. Without insight into the belief system of the authors, the reader is sometimes encouraged to view academic works as neutral or value-free. They never are. Instead, it is our intention to be clear and concrete about the core beliefs upon which the very idea for this book was created. First and foremost, multicultural competence—those awareness, knowledge, and skills that are needed to work effectively across cultural groups and to work with complex diversity issues—can no longer be viewed as a specialty or area of expertise for a limited few. It is no longer reasonable to assume that a few student affairs educators with deep interest or strong commitment to these issues should carry the bulk of the responsibility in addressing multiculturalism. As the complexity of the world permeates every corner, it becomes increasingly important that *all* student affairs professionals develop multicultural competence to better meet the needs of all students.

Secondly, multiculturalism must be woven into all aspects of the profession, from the curriculum (for example, courses offered, books used, theories cited) to academic standards (such as the Counsel for the Advancement of Standards) to job evaluation criteria, to mention just a few. When multiculturalism remains a separate domain and is not infused into all aspects of a profession, it becomes isolated, less meaningful, and without influence. The more multiculturalism is integrated into the very center of student affairs work instead of merely added on, the more the profession changes and transforms itself into one that is truly meeting the needs of *all* students and is contributing to the creation of multicultural campuses. Finally, to infuse multiculturalism, we must first question and possibly deconstruct our underlying beliefs and values as a profession. For example, is individuation (the process of young adults emotionally separating from their parents) as it is defined in student development theories a reasonable or culturally relevant developmental goal for all students, given that such a process would be alien to many cultures? Another example involves our conceptualization of quality; how do we define a "good" resident assistant? On what assumptions and upon whose culture do we base such definitions? What will it take to transform the fundamental beliefs, theories, and practices of student affairs so that all students regardless of age, race, nationality, gender, religion, or other significant social identity feel welcomed and affirmed on campus?

In essence, we believe that multicultural issues and the development of multicultural competence are, at once, enormously complex and deceptively simple. We need to see people as individuals, and at the same time we need to recognize that a person's core being may rest in his or her social group membership. The late Pat Parker, a much-revered Black lesbian poet, wrote a poem that captures this difficulty well. The poem was titled *For the white person who wants to know how to be my friend*. The opening lines are "The first thing you do is to forget that I'm Black. Second, you must never forget that I'm Black." Perhaps it is through our recognizing and embracing this diunital (the union of opposites) reasoning that fertile ground is prepared for multicultural competence.

The primary purpose of this book is to fill a void in the student affairs literature. Specifically it (1) offers a model of core competencies for student affairs professionals (both practitioners and faculty) that infuses multicultural issues, (2) extends the significant work in the counseling psychology multicultural literature to the student affairs profession, and (3) presents specific examples of effective practice as well as useful case studies that help professionals apply vital multicultural awareness and knowledge. The book gives the reader a substantive and fairly comprehensive approach to the topic, applying information collected from several fields of study to the college environment. Although several of the chapters may stand alone, the book builds upon and assumes the reader has knowledge presented in previous chapters. We believe that, bolstered with theory, models, research, and practice opportunities, readers will be able to integrate new insights into their practice.

Audience

This book aims to speak to student affairs and higher education professionals who work on college and university campuses across the country. It is meant to be a practical book that enhances the awareness, knowledge, and skill level of the countless practitioners who work in diverse campus settings or with complex diversity issues on a daily basis. This book may also prove useful to graduate students enrolled in a higher education administration or student affairs preparation program. It can be used as a text in introductory higher education or a student affairs administration course attempting to infuse multicultural subject matter into course content, or in one of the specific multicultural courses that are increasingly being offered in student affairs and higher education administration programs.

Overview of the Contents

This book is divided into two parts. Part One is primarily structured around a model of student affairs practice proposed by Pope and Reynolds (1997) in which they describe seven core competencies needed for effective and ethical practice (Chapters One through Seven). Each chapter begins with some brief scenarios meant to illustrate how multicultural issues affect the core competencies. In addition to thoroughly examining each of the core competencies, each chapter offers good-practice examples. These exemplars are intended to convey to higher education professionals a more concrete and meaningful understanding of what it takes to be effective in their work with students who are culturally different from them, and in their work with the complex issues related to diversity.

Chapter One describes multiculturalism as a unique category of awareness, knowledge, and skills necessary for effective student affairs work; it serves as a foundation for the succeeding chapters. Chapter Two explores the theory bases of the student affairs profession (student development, group dynamics, management). The chapter addresses how historically these theories have excluded multicultural issues and knowledge and how such omission has affected both students and student affairs professionals. In Chapter Three, the administration, management, and leadership skills that professionals need to manage effectively in a multicultural context are explored. The focus of Chapter Four is on the core helping relationships and interpersonal awareness, knowledge, and skills that all student affairs practitioners need if they are to work effectively with students and other professionals who are culturally different from them. Chapter Five explores what kind of awareness, knowledge, and skills student affairs practitioners need in order to effectively assess students and evaluate important programs, activities, and services. In Chapter Six, the key ethical considerations related to multicultural issues in the student affairs profession are addressed. In Chapter Seven, teaching and training as a core competency of student affairs practice is explored. Since a significant portion of student and practitioner learning takes place in teaching and training contexts, it is important that we understand how the dynamics of diversity can influence these environments and how teachers and trainers can maximize the diversity in their classrooms and workshops.

In Part Two we turn our attention to the implications of this model for research and practice. In Chapter Eight, multicultural competence research is reviewed, with an emphasis on what implications it has for student affairs practice. Chapter Nine focuses on more practical applications of the core competency model through presentation of case studies. These case studies describe a campus dilemma or issue, allow readers an opportunity to examine how the seven core competencies can be used as a framework to analyze and address the situation, and offer readers some ideas and insights they might consider in their analyses of the case studies. Chapter Ten concludes this book and reemphasizes the key points of the book, while addressing what the profession needs to do, formally and informally, to ensure that multicultural competence becomes a key area of interest and concern within the field. Thus the second part of this book has significance for practitioners who wish to have an understanding of how application of the core competency model can assist them in fulfilling their personal, institutional, and professional objectives to create and maintain a more multicultural campus environment.

Acknowledgments

Although the completion of this book is an exciting life event for us, we realize that we could not have accomplished this goal without the hard work and support of many important people. First, we would like to thank David Brightman, our editor at Jossey-Bass, for his ongoing encouragement and his firm belief in the importance of this book. He answered our endless technical questions and gave us the resources we needed to complete the book. We are also grateful to the three reviewers of our book, Jane Fried, Nancy Evans, and Larry Roper. Their keen insight and helpful suggestions have surely strengthened the quality of this book. Harold Cheatham, a pioneer in the field of multicultural issues in student affairs and counseling, took time from his retirement to offer support and the Foreword to this book, and he offered cogent and inspirational words that, as always, set the right tone for this important journey.

This book is the result of many years of professional experience, which include teaching, working, consulting, and doing research on multicultural issues in student affairs. Along the way, many individuals, both colleagues and students, have contributed to our understanding of multicultural issues. Without the opportunity to learn from their ideas, experiences, and even their challenges, we would have much less to say on this important topic. To all of the students we have taught at the State University of New York at Buffalo, Buffalo State College, Indiana University of Pennsylvania, Teachers College, and Fordham University, we say thank you for sharing so much with us. In particular, we want to thank our research teams from those institutions for their endless hours of work and dedication to this important area of study. You have truly made a difference in our lives—and in the field of student affairs. Thank you for your generosity and commitment. It feels unfair not to list all of these amazing and dedicated students by name, but space limitations and a deep fear that we might inadvertently fail to mention someone prevents us from attempting it. Please know that your contribution will never be forgotten.

We sincerely appreciate all of the students who have served on our research teams over the years, and we also feel strongly that we need to acknowledge the immense gratitude we feel for the research team coordinators who helped to guide and support these scholarly efforts. For all of their dedication, commitment, time, and hard work, a special thank you is sent to Jayne Brownell, Debra Howard-Stern, Qi Jiang, Terri Miklitsch, Radhika Suresh, Corlisse Thomas, and Matt Weigand. When thanking important student contributors, it is crucial that we highlight the work of Richele Jordan-Davis, who was an equal participant in our early discussions of multicultural competence in student affairs and a coauthor of the initial version of the Multicultural Competence in Student Affairs (MCSA) instrument. Finally, a special note of thanks to Sara Adams, whose efficiency and attention to detail were essential to editing and preparing the final manuscript.

Just as it is impossible to name the many students who have contributed to the creation of this book, it is also difficult to name all of the important colleagues who have given their ongoing support and endless encouragement. In particular we want to thank our colleagues and friends from Teachers College, Columbia University, Fordham University, Indiana University of Pennsylvania, the State University of New York at Buffalo, and Buffalo State

College. In addition we are grateful for our colleagues and friends at the American College Personnel Association (ACPA), who have supported and challenged us throughout our careers.

Finally, we are forever grateful to our families and friends, who have supported and encouraged us along the way. They have tolerated how it has taken us away in body and spirit yet never hesitated to support and encourage our efforts.

We humbly put forth our ideas, beliefs, and ideals in this book in the hope that it will make a difference. We hope that the ideas and suggestions presented here encourage many conversations, debates, and a general increase in the visibility of multiculturalism in student affairs and higher education.

We dedicate this book to the children in our lives,
who remind us daily of the joy in celebrating diversity
and the importance of truly embracing multiculturalism.
Thank you, Justice, Mandela, Keenan, Kellyn, Dayle,
McKenzie, and Kate!

About the Authors

Raechele L. Pope is an associate professor of higher education and student affairs administration in the Department of Education, Leadership, and Policy at the University at Buffalo. Prior to her work at the University at Buffalo, she was an assistant professor in the Higher and Postsecondary Education Program at Teachers College, Columbia University. She earned her doctorate in organization development from the University of Massachusetts at Amherst and her M.A. in student personnel administration from Indiana University of Pennsylvania. With more than twenty years of experience in college student affairs, she has worked at several institutions in a variety of functional areas, including residential life, academic advising, and diversity education and training. Her principal teaching and research interests and publications are focused on the creation of multicultural campus environments. She has published several book chapters and refereed journal articles on multicultural organization development, multicultural competence, and psychosocial development of students of color. She has served as a reviewer or as a member of the editorial boards of the *Journal of College Student Development, ACPA Media,* and the *Journal of College Student Retention: Research, Theory, and Practice.* She has also presented numerous programs at local, regional, and national conferences on these and other issues. She remains active in several higher education professional organizations, among them the American College Personnel Association (ACPA), where she has held several leadership positions, including affirmative action chair and chair of the Committee for Multicultural Affairs.

Amy L. Reynolds is a staff psychologist at Buffalo State College Counseling Center. She received her doctorate in counseling psychology from Ohio State University. She has been working in higher education as a psychologist and professor for more than fifteen years. Her work as a scholar and teacher focuses on multicultural counseling and training; multicultural competence in counseling and student affairs; as well as feminist and lesbian, gay, bisexual, and transgender issues. She has published numerous journal articles and book chapters addressing multicultural issues, including race and ethnicity, gender, and sexual orientation, in counseling or student affairs. She has also presented more than twenty-five programs at regional or national conferences on a variety of topics. In addition, she has been actively involved in several professional organizations, notably the American College Personnel Association, where she has served as a national trainer for Campus Violence and Culture Diversity road shows; a member of the Fund Management Group; program cochair of the 1995 national convention in Boston; chair of the Standing Committee for Lesbian, Gay, Bisexual, and Transgender Awareness; and secretary of the association.

John A. Mueller is an assistant professor in the Department of Student Affairs in Higher Education at Indiana University of Pennsylvania. He earned his doctorate in higher education at Teachers College, Columbia University. He received his M.A. in counseling psychology from Illinois State University. He has been working in higher education for more than fifteen years. Prior to becoming a faculty member, he worked in residence life at four institutions. He has presented at numerous national and regional student affairs conferences on a range of topics, with special emphasis on multicultural issues. His primary research interest is in the measurement and prediction of multicultural competence. He is an active member of the American College Personnel Association, where he has served on the directorate of the Standing Committee for Lesbian, Gay, Bisexual, and Transgender Awareness as well as the Core Council for Member Services and Interests, as chair of the ACPA Awards Committee. He also served as a trainer for the association's Cultural Diversity, Campus Violence, and Beyond Tolerance road shows. In 2003, Mueller received the Annuit Coeptis Emerging Professional Award from ACPA.

Multicultural Competence
in Student Affairs

Part One

The Dynamic Model of Student Affairs Competence

Part One of this book is primarily structured around the Dynamic Model of Student Affairs, initially proposed by Pope and Reynolds (1997). This model identifies and describes seven core competencies needed for effective and ethical student affairs practice. To develop multicultural competence, one must have a thorough understanding of each core competency and how it applies to practice. Each chapter in Part One addresses theoretical concerns and dynamics and offers examples of how to effectively apply them within a multicultural context.

Chapter One

Multicultural Competence in Student Affairs

I teach in a master's level student personnel program at a Research I university. I teach about college students and social conditions affecting higher education and try to do so from a fair and objective perspective. My goal is to be "color-blind" and understand our society from all points of view. I don't ignore race, but it really isn't the focus of my class. That's why we have a Cultural Diversity in Higher Education class. I just can't figure out why some students of color express frustration with the readings I have assigned and the examples I use in class. I really just don't understand what they expect of me. (White male faculty member teaching at a predominantly White university)

I work in the Office of Student Activities (OSA) and I am really good at what I do. Recently I was accused of showing favoritism towards students of color by some White students because of the types of programs that OSA sponsors. The fact is, OSA supports all student groups—and we try to ensure that they all have the opportunity to succeed. But some of these groups—especially the students-of-color groups—really struggle to survive on this predominantly White campus. I know from my own undergraduate experience that if students-of-color groups are really visible and powerful on campus, they will, in turn, help individual students of color feel less marginal and stick around to graduate. OAS does target specific types of programs for these student groups. But when it is all added up, the students of color still get far less than the White students both from this office and this campus. Yet, I'm accused of favoritism! Have these White students looked around this campus at all? (Latina assistant director of student activities)

I am completing one of my student affairs internships in the residence halls on my campus. My graduate program is located on an urban campus and since the resident population of the halls is almost 25 percent students of color, there is a lot of attention focused on multicultural issues in resident advisor and resident director training. My concern is that the only multicultural issue that ever gets attention is race. Don't get me wrong, I honestly believe that racism is a problem and that we should focus on it. But it bothers me that we don't even discuss other issues that affect the residents and the staff like sexual orientation or disability. I feel uncomfortable bringing up the issue because I haven't told anyone here that I am a lesbian. At the same time, I also don't like feeling invisible. (White lesbian graduate student in student personnel)

These statements and numerous others like them are all too familiar on college campuses today. Many student affairs practitioners, faculty, and graduate students are striving to create a campus that is welcoming for all students, yet they are often perplexed and frustrated with the results. The increasingly complex cultural dynamics on college and university campuses across the country are making the work of student affairs professionals more challenging than ever. Some of the most controversial and demanding cultural issues and concerns have included the changing makeup of the student body in terms of race, age, income, and other significant social variables; the increase in the reporting of discrimination and bias crimes; affirmative action policies that are either legally challenged or dismantled; and redefining and exploring core curriculum requirements in a multicultural context. These complicated and difficult issues necessitate a new collection of knowledge and skills. In addition, innovative approaches are needed to address the individual needs of a diverse student body and the organizational demands of changing campuses. Cheatham (1991) suggested that colleges and universities have responded to cultural diversity issues in a variety of ways over the years and that the results have been, at best, inconsistent. There is little evidence to suggest that much has changed in the last ten years.

Student affairs professionals have always played an important role in addressing multicultural issues in higher education. According to Pope, "student affairs professionals have been in the forefront of the quest to create more welcoming and affirming campus environments and have often been called upon to address the discontent and outrage of students who have experienced an alienating and hostile campus climate" (1993b, p. 3).

These efforts are consistent with the expectations of the role of student affairs on a college campus that has always been to address the needs of students outside the classroom (Hood & Arceneaux, 1990). Despite the significant role that the student affairs profession has played in responding to multicultural issues on campus, there is limited student affairs literature that specifically addresses multicultural concerns (Pope, 1993b). Rather, the literature is far more general in simply suggesting that multiculturalism is an appropriate approach. Multicultural dynamics appeared dramatically in higher education in the 1960s and 1970s as the civil rights movement and the Vietnam War became contentious and controversial issues on campus. Despite the prevalence of escalating conflict on many campuses, student affairs professionals had insufficient literature to guide their responses. During the 1980s and 1990s, there were published articles and books addressing multicultural issues and focusing on the importance of making college campuses more welcoming and multiculturally sensitive (Astin, 1992; Barr & Strong, 1988; Cheatham, 1991; Katz, 1989; Manning & Coleman-Boatwright, 1991; Ponterotto, Lewis, & Bullington, 1990; Reynolds & Pope, 1994; Woolbright, 1989; Wright, 1987). Recently, scholars have focused on the need to incorporate multicultural issues into the curriculum and training of the student affairs profession (Ebbers & Henry, 1990; Fried, 1995; McEwen & Roper, 1994a, 1994b; Pope, 1995; Pope & Reynolds, 1997; Pope, Reynolds, & Cheatham, 1997; Talbot, 1996a, 1996b; Talbot & Kocarek, 1997). Further, there have been efforts to infuse multiculturalism into the core theories and practices of student affairs (Evans, Forney, & Guido-DiBrito, 1998; Fried, 1995; Pope, 1995). Although there has been increased cognizance of the importance of multicultural issues in student affairs and higher education in general, it is unclear how much of this awareness has become integrated into the core values, beliefs, and practices of the profession. For example, two studies that explored the "great books" of student affairs observed that most books identified were written by White males and that few addressed multicultural concerns (Hamrick & Schuh, 1992, 1997).

Many scholars have argued that the student affairs profession needs to become more multiculturally sensitive and responsive (Barr & Strong, 1988; Cheatham, 1991; Howard-Hamilton, Richardson, & Shuford, 1998; Manning & Coleman-Boatwright, 1991; Pope, 1995). According to Talbot, "the student affairs profession will need to assume a leadership role in helping institutions bridge the gap between old skills and paradigms and the new tools necessary to effectively meet the needs of changing student populations" (1996b, p. 380). Despite these expectations, many student affairs practitioners have received minimal training in multicultural issues, and their work performance rarely has been evaluated using multicultural criteria (McEwen & Roper, 1994a, 1994b; Pope & Reynolds, 1997; Talbot, 1996a; Talbot & Kocarek, 1997). In student affairs it has become commonplace to view the knowledge and ability to respond to multicultural issues as a special skill cultivated by a few individuals rather than as a compulsory competency area for all professionals. Given that multicultural concerns and dynamics are occurring in almost every aspect of campus life, it is no longer defensible for student affairs professionals to rely solely on "multicultural experts." Instead, what is necessary is a reexamination of what constitutes basic competencies, knowledge, skills, attitudes, and values necessary for effective professional practice in student affairs.

Student Affairs Core Competencies

According to Pope and Reynolds, "the student affairs literature shows increasing attention to the core competencies, or general awareness, knowledge, and skills needed for efficacious and improved professional practice" (1997, p. 267). Scholars have suggested concrete competencies that are needed for student affairs practitioners (Barr, 1993b; Commission of Professional Development [COPA], 1988; Council for the Advancement of Standards [CAS], 1992, 1997, 1999; Creamer et al., 1992; Delworth & Hansen, 1989; Komives & Woodard, 1996; Miller & Winston, 1991). Moore (1985) focused her discussion of professional competencies on generic skills that could be found in any student affairs job description: interviewing, problem solving, management, instruction or training, conflict management, supervision, verbal and written communication, self-knowledge, and others. Barr (1993b) focused her list of essential competencies for middle and upper management program planning, outcome assessment and evaluation, budgeting and fiscal management, theory translation, conflict and crisis management, ethical and legal knowledge, as well as campus and community relationships. Some of the core competencies identified by Delworth and Hansen (1989) are assessment and evaluation, instruction, consultation, counseling and advising, program development, budgeting, and managing and using data and information resources. According to the preparation guidelines by the Council for the Advancement of Standards (CAS): "Preparation for practice in student affairs requires knowledge of the foundations of higher education and student affairs; knowledge of professional practice including student development theories, college student characteristics and effects of college on students, individual and group interventions, organization and administration of student affairs, and assessment, evaluation, and research; and supervised practice that includes demonstration of proficiency in appropriate educational skills and competencies" (1997, p. 1).

Creamer, Winston, and Miller (2001) identified specific skills and knowledge that student affairs administrators need in their roles as educators, managers, and leaders. Within the manager role, they specified competencies such as planning, assessment, budgeting, program assessment, and managing facilities. Influencing, collaboration, and self-knowledge were some of the competencies identified as part of the leader role. Finally, within the role as teacher they suggested skills such as lecturing, advising, coaching, and facilitating.

Komives and Woodard's list of essential competencies for student affairs (1996) was one of the few compilations to include multicultural issues as central to the development of student affairs professionals. Their competency list, viewed as those core skills that cut across student affairs roles, also included leadership; teaching and training; advising and counseling; program development and advising; and assessment, evaluation, and research. In 2003, Komives and Woodard updated their competency list suggesting that consultation, conflict resolution, community building, and professionalism be added.

Although various core competency lists exist, there appears to be a lack of consensus in the field regarding the core competencies for effective student affairs practice (Pope & Reynolds, 1997). Creamer et al. (1992) suggested there is a strong and compelling need for the student affairs profession to become more competency based than it is. Until there is agreement within the profession about what core areas of awareness, knowledge, and skills are essential, it is difficult to assure the profession—as well as important stakeholder groups such as students, parents, higher education administrators, and faculty members—that there is an understanding of what quality student affairs work entails.

Student affairs practitioners and scholars have nevertheless increasingly petitioned that any expectations of what entails quality practice include multicultural awareness, knowledge, and skills (Ebbers & Henry, 1990; King & Howard-Hamilton, 2001; McEwen & Roper, 1994a; Pope & Reynolds, 1997; Pope et al., 1997; Talbot, 1996b). In addition, the American College Personnel Association (ACPA) and the National Association of Student Personnel Administrators (NASPA), the two preeminent professional associations for student affairs professionals, have identified multicultural issues and skills as fundamental to the field (NASPA, 1987; Pope et al., 1997). Taking those suggestions one step further, Pope and Reynolds created a synthesized list of seven core student affairs competencies:

1. Administrative and management
2. Theory and translation
3. Helping and interpersonal
4. Ethical and legal
5. Teaching and training
6. Assessment and evaluation
7. Multicultural awareness, knowledge, and skills

Although each of the seven competencies is the subject of a chapter in this book, they warrant an introduction here.

The first core competency, *administrative and management,* constitutes those capabilities necessary to complete the tasks common to most student affairs administrative positions, such as fiscal management and budgeting, resource use and allocation, strategic planning, time management, delegation, and task supervision. *Theory and translation* entails thorough knowledge and understanding of the various theories necessary for effective student affairs practice, including student development, management, and organization development theories. In addition, this competency involves knowledge of and appropriate use of process models that prescribe the translation of theory to practice. *Helping and advising* involves the advising and counseling components of many student affairs positions, including communication skills, group dynamics, crisis intervention and conflict management, as well as campus and community relations. *Ethical and professional standards* includes knowledge of ethical standards and legal implications as well as the ability to make decisions and solve problems about complex ethical issues that are daily challenges for student affairs practitioners. *Training and teaching* consists of not only formal classroom style teaching but also the ability to design and present workshops, staff development and training, and offer consultation to individuals and groups on campus. *Research and assessment* requires that professionals have the ability to complete self-studies, program evaluations, and campus assessments (for example, quality-of-life assessments) and make meaning of the data collected. The final competency area, *multicultural awareness, knowledge, and skills,* entails the awareness of one's own assumptions, biases, and values; an understanding of the worldview of others; information about various cultural groups; and developing appropriate intervention strategies and techniques.

Multicultural competence is a distinctive category of awareness, knowledge, and skills essential for efficacious student affairs work; this category may assist student affairs practitioners in creating diverse and inclusive campuses. However, it is also vital that multicultural competencies be integrated into the other six core competencies. Although not *all* student affairs practitioners will become experts in multicultural issues (any more than they are expected to be assessment experts or authorities on budgeting), every student affairs professional must have a level of multicultural awareness, knowledge, and skills that allows them to competently work with diverse groups of students and colleagues.

The Dynamic Model of Student Affairs Competence (see Figure 1.1) is a visual representation of these crucial student affairs core competencies. The seven core competencies offer a parsimonious conceptualization of the requisite qualities and abilities for efficacious student affairs practice. Although all student affairs practitioners need some level of competence in these seven areas if they are to be effective in their work, some professionals naturally develop more proficiency in specific areas on the basis of work experiences and interests. Such differential strengths are acceptable so long as individuals can meet basic requirements for quality service. The level and depth of competence may vary with the individual and area of competence, but some standards need to be developed for minimal competence.

Figure 1.1. The Dynamic Model of Student Affairs Competence

Source: Adapted from Pope and Reynolds (1997), p. 269.

The Dynamic Model of Student Affairs Competence is not meant to be a measurement tool; however, the model can be used for professional self-assessment, goal setting, and possibly supervision and evaluation. Student affairs professionals or graduate students could use this model within a job or academic program as pretest and posttest, discussing their strengths and areas for growth when they began and how those areas change during the course of their employment or education. The open hub at the center of the model further illustrates the dynamic and fluid nature of the seven core competencies. Ideally, competence in one area may have an influence on other competencies as well. For example, understanding the literature on students of color further enhances knowledge of student development theory. Helping and advising skills are more fully enhanced if one has an understanding of how women and men communicate their emotions in different ways. Examining leadership from a multicultural perspective is a final example; leadership from this context requires a broader definition of what is meant by being a "successful" leader (Pope, 1995). Without careful consideration of an inclusive view of how to lead, it is easy to use the same techniques to motivate and involve everyone, which may have negative results. For example, individuals from some cultural groups are motivated by recognition and public support, while those from other cultural groups may be uncomfortable with individual attention and prefer that the team effort be acknowledged. Although each competency area is its own unique domain, the dynamic nature of student affairs work demands that individuals make connections across competency areas.

Multicultural Competence

Multicultural competence is not a new concept. The counseling psychology literature has been examining, cultivating, and expanding the profession's understanding of multicultural competence since the early 1980s. According to Pope and Reynolds, because of "intersecting histories and some overlapping professional goals," (1997, p. 267), initially using the multicultural competence models from counseling psychology and applying them in student affairs is an appropriate and meaningful starting place to explore multicultural competence.

Sue et al. (1982) first delineated the core multicultural competencies necessary for counseling, which included the tripartite model of multicultural competence (awareness, knowledge, and skills). Most multicultural training and competence models as well as instrument development in multicultural competence are based on this theoretical framework. According to Pope and Reynolds (1997), "counseling psychologists have continued to expand the depth of their understanding of the multicultural competencies necessary for effective psychological practice" (p. 267). Several revisions and expansions of the original Sue et al. (1982) model have occurred during the past twenty years, among them works by Sue, Arredondo, and McDavis (1992); Sue et al. (1998); and Sue (2001).

In addition to theoretical developments in multicultural competence in counseling psychology, there have been extensive applications in clinical practice, training, and research. During the past decade, professional psychology has worked to translate the theoretical conceptualizations of multicultural competence to concrete guidelines for effective practice. Several committees within the American Psychological Association (APA) have developed working guidelines to assist practitioners in translating the beliefs and assumptions regarding multicultural competence into actual skills and behaviors for work with specific populations (see APA, 1993, 2000). Such guidelines make it possible for professionals to be focused, inclusive, and systematic in their efforts to become more multiculturally competent.

Training programs, curriculum, and supervision implications have also been increasingly explored in the multicultural counseling literature. Enhancing professional performance and training the next generation of psychologists to be multiculturally competent are important steps in the process of advancing the ability of a profession to address the needs of all individuals. Many training and supervision models and approaches have been proposed; see, for example, Brown and Landrum-Brown (1995); McRae and Johnson (1991); Pope-Davis, Breaux, and Liu (1997); Porter (1995); Reynolds (1995a, 1997); Ridley, Espelage, and Rubinstein (1997); Sue (1991); and Vazquez (1997).

There has been growing interest in multicultural competence research and instrument development in the multicultural counseling literature. To date, four multicultural counseling competence assessment instruments have been developed and researched (D'Andrea, Daniels, & Heck, 1991; LaFromboise, Coleman, & Hernandez, 1991; Ponterotto et al., 1996; Ponterotto, Rieger, Barrett, & Sparks, 1994; Sodowsky, Taffe, Gutkin, & Wise, 1994). Although in varying phases of validation and research, these instruments are being used to assess individual multicultural competence as well as evaluate the potency of some educational or training interventions. Despite the unique aspects of the various instruments, Pope-Davis and Dings (1995) identified four key multicultural competencies present in most if not all of the measurements: multicultural awareness and beliefs, multicultural knowledge, multicultural counseling skills, and multicultural counseling relationships. The availability of these instruments offers several benefits to the counseling profession, among them greater depth and complexity in the understanding of multicultural competence, further research and assessment of multicultural competence, and additional development of training and educational tools to enhance multicultural competence.

The research and exploration of multicultural competence is more limited in student affairs than in the counseling psychology literature. Most writing has concentrated generally on multicultural issues, with less attention on multicultural competence. Typically, multicultural research has focused more on students than on student affairs professionals (Pope & Reynolds, 1997). To effectively integrate the concept of multicultural competence in student affairs literature and practice, student affairs practitioners and faculty members must examine multicultural issues in complex and comprehensive ways that will influence future research, education and training, and work practices.

Multicultural Competence in Student Affairs

According to Pope and Reynolds, "multicultural competence is a necessary prerequisite to effective, affirming, and ethical work in student affairs" (1997, p. 270). Using the tripartite model described in the counseling literature, multicultural competence may be defined as the awareness, knowledge, and skills needed to work with others who are culturally different from self in meaningful, relevant, and productive ways (see Pedersen, 1988; Sue et al., 1982; Sue et al., 1992; Sue, 2001). Although this definition accurately describes the current view of multicultural competence, the components described are necessary but not sufficient to be as inclusive as possible. Having the awareness, knowledge, and skills to address cultural issues with someone who is culturally different from one's self is critical. Having the awareness, knowledge, and skills to address cultural issues with someone who is culturally similar is just as crucial. When Whites work with other Whites around racial issues, or when women make consciousness-raising groups available to other women, there are multicultural attitudes, knowledge, and skills required in efficaciously addressing the issues and concerns of those individuals. The definition of multicultural competence must continue to change and embrace our growing understanding of the complexity of diversity. Moreover, the student affairs profession needs further clarification and discussion as to what constitutes the multicultural competencies necessary to effectively and ethically address multicultural issues (Pope & Reynolds, 1997). Although student affairs preparation programs are increasingly addressing multicultural issues in the curriculum (Talbot, 1996a), more specific and concrete multicultural competency criteria need to be determined. Initial efforts to develop assessment tools for measuring multicultural competence in student affairs have begun (see Pope & Mueller, 2000; Mueller & Pope, 2001); however, more research and exploration is needed.

In this chapter, multicultural competence is explored from two primary vantage points. First, various global multicultural competencies are briefly explored and applied to the range of work responsibilities and tasks in which most student affairs practitioners engage. Second, good-practice exemplars are highlighted to further emphasize the attitudes, knowledge, and skills that student affairs professionals need to develop to work effectively and ethically across cultural differences and with cultural similarities. More thorough understanding of the various multicultural attitudes, knowledge, and skills allows student affairs professionals to assess their own level of multicultural competence and to understand and consider the multicultural capabilities of individuals whom they are teaching or supervising.

The global conceptualization of multicultural awareness, knowledge, and skills is a useful place to start. Multicultural awareness constitutes those values, attitudes, and assumptions essential to working with students who are culturally different from a particular student affairs professional (Pedersen, 1988; Pope &

Reynolds, 1997). Self-awareness, or the ability to be aware of those values, attitudes, and assumptions, is a significant aspect of multicultural awareness. Without such self-evaluation, individuals may not realize that they hold inaccurate or inappropriate views of a particular culture in the form of stereotypes, biases, or culturally based assumptions. For multicultural development to continue, individuals must be able to challenge their misinformation and correct their erroneous assumptions and beliefs.

Multicultural knowledge consists of the content knowledge about various cultural groups that is typically not taught in many preparation programs. Historically, many theories and most research in student affairs were completed on White males, often from elite institutions. Despite long-standing beliefs of universality, it is difficult to confidently generalize the results from such studies to other individuals or cultural groups. To be multiculturally competent, student affairs professionals must gather information about the cultural groups with which they are working. In addition, they must learn about important cultural constructs such as racial identity and acculturation, and how these constructs influence the helping process. Individuals must gather more accurate and extensive information and be cautious with how they use such knowledge. If an individual's awareness and relationship to his cultural group is not explored, content knowledge by itself may perpetuate a cookbook or stereotypical approach to working with individuals who are culturally different from oneself.

Multicultural skills consist of those behaviors that allow us to effectively apply the multicultural awareness and knowledge we have internalized. Central to those skills is the ability to communicate across cultures and understand how culture influences the content as well as the verbal and nonverbal aspects of communication. Without a foundation of multicultural awareness and knowledge, it is difficult to make culturally sensitive and appropriate interventions.

Analyzing the student affairs profession and ourselves is fundamental to developing multicultural competence. However, it is vital that we accept this self-exploration and expansion of our hearts, minds, and skills as a long-term process without easy answers. The complexity of increasing multicultural sensitivity sometimes overwhelms individuals who are striving to do right. Lopez et al. (1989), in their developmental model of how individuals learn to become more culturally sensitive, suggested that for some individuals considering culture as a factor in the helping process may feel like a burden for which they are unprepared. Such an attitude is understandable when individuals begin the process of increasing their multicultural competence, but if we accept the developmental notion of challenge and support, then no challenge is too great so long as we have an appropriate amount of support. S. Sue and Zane (1987) insisted that obtaining cultural knowledge and learning culturally sensitive techniques is necessary and important but not enough. Their belief was that individuals should focus on the broader goals of credibility and gift giving. If in the process of helping students in a culturally consistent way we instill faith, trust, confidence, or hope, then we build credibility in the helping process. If we are able to build rapport or establish trusting relationships with students, then we are giving them the gifts of optimism and validation.

Over the decades, the construct of multicultural competence has continued to evolve at the same time as a richer and more complex understanding of what constitutes multicultural competence has developed. Recently, Sue (2001) offered a rich model—the Multiple Dimensions of Cultural Competence (MDCC)—which can be used to enhance our understanding and application of multicultural competence in a variety of settings, one of which is higher education. In his expansion of what is commonly known as multicultural competence, Sue emphasized the need to possess multicultural organization development skills so we can intervene and advocate within our institutions and the larger profession to develop new and more inclusive theories, practices, and organizational systems. According to Reynolds (2001b), "this is a profoundly important shift in the definition of multicultural competence which holds great promise in providing new ways of thinking about and achieving multicultural transformation" (p. 6). Traditionally, the focus of multicultural competence has been on the individual and her skill level rather than on the institution. Pope (1995) argued that individual or even group change is not enough to create multicultural campuses. Instead, she suggested that systemic change fundamentally altering the values and practices of an institution is vital to creating true or lasting multicultural change.

The growth and development of multicultural competence as a significant approach to addressing multicultural issues has been a positive and progressive advancement. Diverse conceptualizations, frameworks, and training models have yielded important knowledge and tools for professionals in counseling and student affairs. However, such rich information is not enough. Student affairs professionals need concrete and applied examples that illustrate how to implement the various multicultural competency models and translate ideas into action. Without such information, student affairs practitioners and faculty may be unsure which specific practices to incorporate into their multicultural change efforts. To that end, we offer some positive practice examples that we hope cultivate a more concrete and meaningful understanding of what it takes to address cultural issues effectively with students, staff, and faculty.

Exemplary Multicultural Practices in Student Affairs

Pope and Reynolds (1997) identified thirty-three characteristics of a multiculturally competent student affairs practitioner (see Table 1.1). This list is not exhaustive, yet it offers an important starting place for professionals to examine their level of multicultural awareness, knowledge, and skills. In the interest of increasing awareness of essential and concrete multicultural competencies for student affairs, eleven multicultural characteristics either gleaned or expanded from that initial list are highlighted here. These specific exemplary practices were taken from the consulting and teaching work of the authors. These examples are not meant to be viewed as the right way to do things; however, they are being shared as illustrations of attitudes, knowledge, and skills that may be successful in meeting the needs of diverse students, implementing multicultural interventions, or creating more multiculturally sensitive organizations and campuses. It is important to underscore the uniqueness of each campus environment as well as the complex overlay of individual and cultural similarities and differences that influence each individual's response to multicultural change efforts. There is no such thing as one size fits all; these exemplary practices are not meant to be cookbook offerings. Instead, they are meant to help student affairs professionals conceptualize and apply these notions of multicultural awareness, knowledge, and skills tangibly and realistically.

Table 1.1. Characteristics of a Multiculturally Competent Student Affairs Practitioner

Multicultural Awareness	*Multicultural Knowledge*	*Multicultural Skills*
A belief that differences are valuable and that learning about others who are culturally different is necessary and rewarding	Knowledge of diverse cultures and oppressed groups (i.e., history, traditions, values, customs, resources, issues)	Ability to identify and openly discuss cultural differences and issues
A willingness to take risks and see them as necessary and important for personal and professional growth	Information about how change occurs for individual values and behaviors	Ability to assess the impact of cultural differences on communication and effectively communicate across those differences
A personal commitment to justice, social change, and combating depression	Knowledge about the ways that cultural differences affect verbal and nonverbal communication	Capability to empathize and genuinely connect with individuals who are culturally different from themselves
A belief in the value and significance of their own cultural heritage and worldview as a starting place for understanding others who are culturally different	Knowledge about how gender, class, race, ethnicity, language, nationality, sexual orientation, age, religion or spirituality, and disability and ability affect individuals and their experiences	Ability to incorporate new learning and prior learning in new situations
A willingness to self-examine and, when necessary, challenge and change their own values, worldview, assumptions, and biases	Information about culturally appropriate resources and how to make referrals	Ability to gain the trust and respect of individuals who are culturally different from themselves

Multicultural Awareness	Multicultural Knowledge	Multicultural Skills
An openness to change, and belief that change is necessary and positive	Information about the nature of institutional oppression and power	Capability to accurately assess their own multicultural skills, comfort level, growth, and development
An acceptance of other worldviews and perspectives and a willingness to acknowledge that, as individuals, they do not have all the answers	Knowledge about identity development models and the acculturation process for members of oppressed groups and their impact on individuals, groups, intergroup relations, and society	Ability to differentiate among individual differences, cultural differences, and universal similarities
A belief that cultural differences do not have to interfere with effective communication or meaningful relationships	Knowledge about within-group differences and understanding of multiple identities and multiple oppressions	Ability to challenge and support individuals and systems around oppression issues in a manner that optimizes multicultural interventions
Awareness of their own cultural heritage and how it affects their worldview, values, and assumptions	Information and understanding of internalized oppression and its impact on identity and self-esteem	Ability to make individual, group, and institutional multicultural interventions
Awareness of their own behavior and its impact on others	Knowledge about institutional barriers that limit access to and success in higher education for members of oppressed groups	Ability to use cultural knowledge and sensitivity to make more culturally sensitive and appropriate interventions
Awareness of the interpersonal process that occurs within a multicultural dyad	Knowledge about systems theories and how systems change	

Source: Pope and Reynolds (1997). Used by permission.

Exemplary Multicultural AWARENESS

*A student affairs professional becomes aware that she has limited knowl-
edge and experience with a specific group that is culturally different from
her.* A multiculturally sensitive professional seeks out additional
training, pursues peer supervision with colleagues from his own
cultural group, and begins supplemental reading.

Being willing to evaluate our own strengths and weaknesses
with multicultural issues as well as with different populations is very
important. All of us have been exposed to misinformation and
have developed stereotypes on the basis of our life experiences,
teachings from our families and communities, and media influences. This is true whether we belong to a dominant group such
as Whites or are from a target group, perhaps Latino or Latina.
None of us is immune, and guilt and defensiveness often prevent
us from learning, growing, and developing more meaningful relationships with individuals who are culturally different from us.
Within a professional context, few if any of us have received adequate training to be prepared to address the myriad multicultural
concerns in higher education today. Therefore, those most willing
or able to take risks to admit what they don't know are most likely
to increase their multicultural sensitivity.

*A student affairs professional needs some awareness of his own cul-
tural heritage and how it affects his worldview, values, and assumptions.*
A multiculturally sensitive professional has spent time examining
how his life experiences, family background, and cultural influences affect how he relates to individuals who are culturally different from him.

Many of us have never taken the time to thoroughly explore
our value system; we may assume that what is normal for us is also
commonplace for others. This is especially true for individuals who
are members of a dominant group, such as men or heterosexuals.
Our family and cultural background profoundly affect our values
and worldview, and often we are not aware of the extent of this
influence until we take a step back to examine ourselves. Sometimes this awareness can be uncomfortable or painful, should we
observe that our values have become different from our families,

our friends, or the larger society. Whether we are a White person who begins to confront the racism in our family or an African American heterosexual person who challenges the homophobia within her community, such awareness can lead to difficult choices about how we want to live our lives.

A student affairs professional realizes that despite her longstanding personal commitment to multicultural issues and combating oppression, her life continues to center around relationships and activities with people who are mostly like her. Regardless of who she is, whether she is a Jewish woman, a White lesbian, or a woman of color, she recognizes that her friends are of a similar background and her social activities are often not inclusive of other cultural groups. As a multiculturally sensitive professional, she realizes that regardless of what she believes, she has never really changed her life.

It often takes a long time for this realization to occur because attitudinal changes are sometimes easier than behavioral changes. We work hard to challenge ourselves and our values, and we may even become a multicultural leader at work; yet when we look at our choices of who we socialize with, where we spend our money, what music we listen to, and where we live, we realize we lead fairly monocultural lives. It is sometimes difficult and challenging to live a fully multicultural life because it means putting ourselves into situations where we must constantly be aware of our values and worldview and how they affect others' perception of us, as well as how we form relationships with those who are culturally different from us or who have very different values. No one should feel the need to constantly be in the minority or among those who are different. Bernice Johnson Reagon (1983) suggested we all need time to be at home with others who are like us so it takes less energy to communicate and make sense of the world. This is why Tatum (1997) believes that we should not see student self-segregation as having a negative influence on community. Although we need to find more effective ways to encourage students to socialize in heterogeneous groups and build multicultural friendships, we do not need to take away important time with their own cultural group that allows them to build self-confidence and get support from others with common experiences and background.

Exemplary Multicultural KNOWLEDGE

A student affairs professional who is working in student activities with diverse student groups becomes aware of the lack of information she has about many cultural groups. She begins to feel it is affecting her advisement and her ability to form close and meaningful relationships with these students. A culturally knowledgeable professional seeks out information about diverse cultures through books, professional development, and, most important, personal relationships with individuals from different cultures.

The importance of cultural knowledge and information cannot be overemphasized. Because we have been underexposed to accurate and meaningful information about others (and even ourselves), we are really unable to fully understand others without acquiring additional knowledge. This educational process occurs most effectively when we gather our information from a variety of sources. Although crucially important, there is also some danger inherent in gathering information about groups, especially from books and other impersonal sources. Too often we use that information in a way that stereotypes individuals and ignores individuality. If we develop our understanding of diverse groups—bisexuals, Korean Americans, people with disabilities, Dominicans—through relationships with such individuals, we have more grounded and often more multidimensional understanding of the true diversity that occurs within any given cultural group. Simply put, we all must increase our contact with people who are culturally different from ourselves. Although many members of marginalized groups on campus, such as people of color or lesbian, gay, and bisexual (LGB) individuals, believe they already know "what White people are like" or how heterosexuals feel about them, it is just as likely that their perceptions are formed by stereotypes and assumptions and not necessarily applicable to any individual who is a member of that group. We need to understand and truly value the individuality of people.

At the same time, content information—knowledge about the history, traditions, values, customs, and issues of diverse groups—is important for individuals if they are to make meaning of who they are and how they view the world. It is important, for example, to understand that family ties and family proximity may be more important for a Latino student than a single, "once in a lifetime opportunity" to travel. It may be significant to know that many LGB individuals form an alternative—surrogate—family because their family of origin is not accepting of who they are. Such appreciation of the unique issues and realities of groups affects how we interpret their behavior and effectively meet their needs.

A student affairs professional begins to recognize that there are as many differences in values, life experiences, and identity among individuals of the same cultural group as between different cultural groups. He realizes that it is not membership in a cultural group that makes the difference but rather the meaning that cultural group has in a person's life. A culturally knowledgeable professional gathers information about identity development models; the process of acculturation; and how such processes affect an individual's identity, values, and relationships with others who are both similar and different. He also develops an appreciation of the multidimensionality of identity and how all individuals are influenced by membership and experiences in a variety of cultural groups.

Knowledge about the process of identity development allows us to understand the individual experiences and needs of a given student. If we know that a student of color grew up in a predominantly White area and her family viewed race as only one aspect of her identity, we can appreciate some of the challenges she might face in forming relationships with other students of color. This content knowledge about various acculturation models and identity development frameworks allows one to interpret students' behaviors meaningfully and accurately. It minimizes the stereotyping that often occurs when we focus only on differences between groups and not as well on the differences within groups. Viewing individuals multidimensionally is crucial to this process. Every person has many social identities that are influenced by race, gender, sexual orientation, and religion, to name a few identities. If we see individuals in terms of only one identity, we minimize the complexity of who they are. We may forget that people of color can be lesbian, gay, or bisexual, or that White women with disabilities have unique issues, concerns, and ways of viewing self that may be both similar and different from other White women. Comprehending such complexity is at the heart of what it means to be a culturally sensitive person and professional.

A student affairs professional, through her experience at an antiracism retreat on campus, begins to realize how little she knows about prejudice and oppression. She has limited understanding of how oppression manifests within institutions and how individuals from target groups internalize the negative messages about their group that affect their self-esteem and identity. A culturally knowledgeable professional educates herself about institutional and internalized oppression and tries to understand how oppression creates barriers on her own campus.

To fully understand multiculturalism, we need to understand prejudice, power, and oppression and how these systems work together to create barriers to access and success in higher education. Without such knowledge, we may become unwitting accomplices to frustration, discrimination, and even failure. For example, once we understand that limited access to money is only part of what affects the ability of a poor, first-generation college student to be successful in college, we have a better understanding of oppression. Sometimes even more powerful than money is access to understanding how college works and how one gains access to the unwritten rules for success in higher education. If we realize that many students of color internalize the negative and racist messages within society so much that they doubt their own ability to succeed, then we have a better understanding of oppression. Until we fully appreciate the true systemic nature of oppression, we are unable to combat its effects on us and the students we serve.

Exemplary Multicultural SKILLS

A student affairs professional realizes that he communicates differently with women than with men. He knows that he doesn't understand how members of other racial groups deal with their emotions. More important, he knows his lack of understanding of cross-cultural communication is affecting his relationships with individuals who are culturally different from him, yet he is unsure how else to act. A culturally skilled professional has the capability to assess how cultural differences influence communication and is able to genuinely connect and communicate with people who are culturally different.

Many of us do not realize the extent to which our family and cultural background, generation, socialization, and life experiences affect how we communicate with others. Our cultural values are imbedded in what we say and how we say it—in words and with our body. If we are not aware of those influences, we don't realize that not everyone views personal space in the same way, that eye contact means different things to different people, and that many individuals are not comfortable talking directly about certain topics. We need to learn how to read verbal and nonverbal cues and be able to differentiate when personality or cultural differences are affecting communication. We need to be able to talk openly and take the initiative in addressing cross-cultural communication issues. As the professional, whether we are advising undergraduate students or supervising graduate students or seasoned professionals, it is our responsibility, regardless of our own sense of vulnerability, to take the initiative rather than expect the individual who may feel vulnerable to take that risk.

A student affairs professional is uncomfortable when students and other professionals make stereotypical remarks or inappropriate jokes, yet she is not comfortable confronting their behavior. She wants to challenge the remarks but is worried about offending the other individuals or making the situation worse. A culturally skilled professional practices these skills in a supportive setting and then begins to take risks so as to optimize the success of the intervention.

It is rarely easy or comfortable to confront individuals about their culturally insensitive behavior, so it is important to learn how to make such an intervention. Unfortunately, there are not many laboratories outside of our personal and work relationships where we can practice doing so. Sometimes it is a matter of trial and error and not giving up even if it does not go well. It is important not to be judgmental or harsh in our feedback, and it is often effective to highlight how the behavior of others makes us feel. People may disagree with our perceptions of their behavior, but it is difficult for them to tell us that our feelings are inaccurate. These skills, no matter that they become more comfortable over time, are never easy. Dealing with multicultural issues is often messy and complicated, and once we accept this reality then we are less discouraged with the conflict and tension that can occur.

A student affairs professional must be able to accurately assess his own multicultural skills and comfort level in order to develop multicultural competence. If he has the awareness and the knowledge but doesn't know how to make culturally sensitive and appropriate interventions with individuals and in organizations, his ability to be a social change agent is compromised. A culturally skilled professional is comfortable talking about what he does and doesn't know and is willing to ask for feedback and assistance when dealing with a challenging issue. If he is unsure of what to do, he knows to consult or make an appropriate referral to another colleague, or possibly to a member of the individual's own cultural group when deemed appropriate.

If we expect to have all of the answers, we are setting ourselves up for disappointment and failure. There is no way that any of us can be prepared to effectively address all the multicultural issues and dynamics that occur on a college campus. The more we work together and support each other in this process on the personal and professional levels, the more powerful our interventions become. We need to be humble and accepting of our shortcomings, recognizing that we will inevitably make cultural errors in our interactions with those who are different from us. Making cultural assumptions, lacking important cultural knowledge, and making errors in our cross-cultural communication are unavoidable. The challenge then is not to become immobilized with these missteps but rather to rebound and learn for the future. It is just as important that we remain nonjudgmental about cultural errors and weaknesses of others. The more we do multicultural work, the more aware we become of how much we do not know and how this process is a lifelong endeavor. Ideally, this knowledge is not discouraging, and we are able to accept that multicultural competence is not a finite category of awareness, knowledge, and skill that we can obtain if we only work hard enough.

Multicultural competence is not about getting to a destination. We cannot develop ten multicultural programs (much less one) on our campus and expect that we have addressed most of the significant multicultural issues. Students and cultural issues are constantly changing, and professionals are continuously developing new awareness, knowledge, and skills about multicultural issues. If we make a long-term commitment to the process of multicultural change, within ourselves, our institutions, and our profession, then we are ensured of ongoing—although still not continuous—success.

Finally, if we want a campus to become multiculturally sensitive, a place where all individuals have the opportunity for success, it is important that we move our conceptualization of multicultural competence beyond an individual, or even a group, focus. Sue (2001) suggests we must be willing to make interventions that challenge our institutions and our profession. We must carry out social change that radically alters our assumptions and expectations about our students and our institutions. We must change how we evaluate the performance of practitioners and how we train future generations of student affairs professionals. We must rethink our knowledge base and develop new theories, models, and approaches that incorporate what we know about cultural diversity. Developing multicultural awareness, knowledge, and skills is not the only approach to creating a multiculturally sensitive and affirming campus. Multicultural competence offers important understanding and tools that undoubtedly contribute to efficacious practice in student affairs.

Summary

Multicultural competence is a compelling area of study that enables student affairs to enhance the theories, services, and programs offered to college students. The goal of multicultural competence is to create a more welcoming and affirming campus for all students by developing more relevant, meaningful, and culturally appropriate services. Student affairs professionals are well suited to this task because of their historical role of attending to the whole student and creating campus environments that enrich the personal and academic experiences of college students. Despite the philosophical connection between multiculturalism and the values of the student affairs profession, many student affairs practitioners and scholars are not effectively trained to address the complex and constantly evolving cultural dynamics on today's campuses.

By reexamining the core competencies of student affairs professionals and infusing the multicultural attitudes, knowledge, and skills that are needed to create a more multiculturally sensitive campus, both practitioners and scholars provide more ethical and effective programs and services. Multicultural awareness, knowledge, and skills are core competencies that all student affairs professionals need regardless of their job responsibilities and level of training.

This chapter suggests that multicultural competence is one of seven core competencies needed in student affairs; it seeks a thorough understanding of what particular awareness, knowledge, and skills are needed to work with others who are culturally different from oneself. Good-practice examples have been included so that student affairs professionals have a more concrete and practice-based understanding of what is meant by multicultural competence.

Chapter Two

Multicultural Competence in Theory and Translation

I have more than sixteen years of experience working as a vice president of student affairs at a major university and in the past several years, everything about my job and how I manage my staff has changed. My staff is much more diverse than it used to be and that diversity seems to create supervision and management issues that I am not always sure how to address. It seems that what I learned through practice, in professional development seminars, and way back as a doctoral student just isn't giving me what I need to do my job effectively. (White male vice president for student affairs)

Most of my professors have begun to incorporate multicultural issues into their courses, and I think that is really important. But I have concerns about how they are doing it. For example, we are reading about students of color and female students for my student development class but the readings are only supplemental. Our understanding of theory is still being based on the traditional standards like Perry, Chickering, and Kohlberg, and then we are told to also consider how it might be different for certain populations. Is this the best that they can do? (African American female graduate student in student affairs program)

I have been teaching in higher education programs for close to twenty years. In that time the literature has completely changed and the students today are demanding a wider range of readings and topics so they can feel prepared to deal with all students. They want to know how to deal with lesbian, gay, and bisexual students or international students and how the theories apply to those groups. I try to incorporate some diversity readings into all of my classes but they really can't expect me to become an expert on all of these different populations, can they? There is just too much to know—maybe they should rely on additional training at conferences and special seminars they receive once working in higher education to help them deal most effectively with diverse populations. (White female professor in a higher education program)

As in most professions, theory forms the foundation upon which much of student affairs practice and research is based. Ideally, theories should help inform why we choose particular practices, assessments, and interventions. Specifically within student affairs, theories help us communicate more effectively; understand how students learn and develop; identify more effective ways to supervise our staff and manage our departments; and help us design meaningful interventions, programs, services, and research endeavors. According to student affairs scholars, understanding theory and being able to apply it is an essential competency for student affairs practitioners (Barr, 1993b; Creamer, Winston, & Miller, 2001; Pope & Reynolds, 1997; Saunders & Cooper, 2001; Strange, 1987; Upcraft, 1993). Preferably, theory offers us a range of possible explanations to make sense of the behavior of individuals and groups on a college campus. Strange and King (1990) suggested that how individuals or groups behave on campus is often "observable, measurable, explainable, generalizable, and therefore to some extent, predictable" (p. 12). Using theory appropriately enables us to interpret and add meaning to what we observe or measure, and then effectively respond to those interpretations.

According to McEwen (1996), in her summary of the literature on the uses of theory, there are six significant ways in which theory assists student affairs educators: it describes, explains, predicts, generates, influences, and assesses. Most typically, theory is used to describe and explain the behavior of individuals, groups, or organizations. For theory to be useful, it must be understandable, consistent, comprehensive, explicit, and have some heuristic value (Walsh, 1973, as cited in Evans, Forney, & Guido-DiBrito, 1998). Some scholars believe it is appropriate use of theory that makes the difference between being a well-intentioned amateur and a professional (Strange, 1987; Strange & King, 1990).

Despite the value of theory and its importance in guiding practice, the student affairs profession, like many applied fields, struggles with integrating theory meaningfully and usefully into practice. Strange (1987) surmised that such difficulties might result from the tendency for student affairs and other applied professions to focus more on outcomes than explanations. Furthermore, individuals who desire to work in an applied field are often results oriented and may focus more on what they have done than on what they know, or on what they need to do rather than on what they have learned. Upcraft (1994) suggested that an appropriate response to the disconnect between theory and practice may be to engage theorists more directly in current campus issues and realities, and to reward practitioners who are able to apply theory effectively.

This chapter addresses what constitutes *theory and translation* competence in student affairs practice. A critique of theories used in student affairs is offered, and their limited attention to multicultural issues and application is explored. The impact of such omissions on professionals as well as students who receive services is discussed. Competence in theory and translation is redefined, and core multicultural awareness, knowledge, and skills that need to be infused into theory and translation are identified. Finally, good-practice exemplars are presented.

Theory and Translation in Student Affairs Work

The student affairs profession has borrowed and adapted theories from diverse academic fields: psychology, sociology, organization development and management, human development, philosophy, and ethics (Upcraft, 1993). However, some theories, such as college student development, are unique contributions that the student affairs profession has made to the educational community. Some of the theories used by student affairs have expanded and changed, and other new theories have been developed in the past twenty years to accommodate diverse populations and cultural considerations that were not included in the theories when first developed (see Baxter Magolda, 1992; Chickering & Reisser, 1993; Gilligan, 1982; Manning, 1994a; Pope, 1995). However, many student affairs scholars and practitioners still believe that the theories have not effectively incorporated multicultural issues and concerns (Evans et al., 1998; Manning, 1994a, 1994b; McEwen & Roper, 1994a; Pope, 1995).

The knowledge or theory base that any profession relies upon is crucial. This base undoubtedly shapes the philosophy, policies, interventions, and practices of practitioners and scholars alike. If this knowledge base is incomplete or distorted, either because voices are omitted or the theories fail to accommodate growth and changes that occur over time, then the profession's efforts are inherently weakened. Although student development theories may be the ones most often associated with the work of student affairs professionals, there are many other important theories that have shaped and influenced the field.

According to Winston, Creamer, and Miller (2001), student affairs professionals "need to be knowledgeable about theories of college student development, program design and implementation, organization development, assessment and evaluation, research design and implementation, interpersonal communication and facilitation, group dynamics, staffing practices, budget development, and resource allocation, as well as theories about how gender, sexual orientation, ethnicity, and cultural background affects students and their environments" (p. 32).

There are other theories that have been integrated into the student affairs profession to varying degrees, such as learning theory, environmental models, leadership theories, and involvement theory (Astin, 1984; Caple & Newton, 1991; Kolb, 1981; Strange, 1991; Upcraft, 1993).

In addition to these content models, there have been significant process models primarily addressing how to apply student development theory to practice (for instance, Knefelkamp, 1984; Rodgers, 1991; Rodgers & Widick, 1980). These process models present a guiding structure or framework by which practitioners can apply theories and make meaning. The models assist practitioners in a variety of ways, including helping to conceptualize and make sense of a student's point of view and using theories to plan training programs or outreach efforts. By grounding theories in practice, student affairs professionals can test their heuristic value and decide if the theories add to their educational and developmental interventions, thus leading to more thoughtful and professional practice (Rodgers, 1991).

Rodgers (1991) emphasized the importance of in-depth knowledge of theory as a prerequisite for true understanding and application. He developed a continuum for understanding theory that identified four levels of comprehension. The first level involves a vague understanding of a theory or construct. An individual may not really understand Perry's theory but has heard the terms *dualistic* and *relativistic* used to describe students' thinking. Or the person may recognize Chickering's or Gilligan's name but not really know the theories they developed. At this level, a student affairs professional does not have enough knowledge or understanding of theory to use it in practice. The second level of theory comprehension involves sufficient recognition or understanding to be able to briefly and superficially identify, describe, or define core constructs of a theory. For example, an individual at this level of comprehension might know and be able to make simple distinctions among organizational models in higher education, such as collegial, managerial, developmental, and negotiating models, but not know much more. This individual would have difficulty understanding and describing how these models, and the theories from which they originate, offer insight or allow us to interpret various aspects of college administration. This degree of theoretical understanding is inadequate for translating and applying theory to practice.

A third level of theory comprehension demonstrates a greater understanding and knowledge of specific theories and their core constructs than previously demonstrated. The comprehension is no longer superficial or vague, and the key constructs have meaning and relevance for the student affairs professional. An expanded description of this level might suggest that the person knows enough about the theory to explain it effectively to others. This level of comprehension is most likely sufficient for applying theory to practice, although the individual may have had little experience doing so.

The fourth and final level of theory comprehension moves beyond knowing the theory or construct, as in the third level, and instead requires an understanding of the deeper relationships among constructs and theories. The theories are known in enough detail that the professional understands the nuances involved. This more sophisticated knowledge allows the professional to understand how to create developmental or organizational change using the theory. This final level involves the professional staying current in new developments and applications of the theory. Effective student affairs professionals cannot stop learning about theory at the end of graduate school. The pursuit of theory must be a lifelong process that involves learning about new findings, measurements, and applications to maximize the move from theory to practice.

Given this continuum proposed by Rodgers (1991), it seems likely that new professionals, with limited work experience, are unlikely to have attained the final level of theory comprehension until they have had opportunities to apply theory and make meaning of it on the job. Likewise, seasoned professionals who have not actively worked with theory or taken the time to learn new theoretical developments in the field are also hindered in their efforts to use theory in practice.

Knowing theory and being able to apply it may be a necessary component of a competent professional; however, it is not sufficient. It is also important that one understand the limits of theory and the hazards of using it inappropriately. According to Evans et al. (1998), "appropriate use of theories requires that they be used tentatively rather than prescriptively and that the potential for individual variations is kept in mind" (p. 278). Theories are not meant to be used in a cookbook fashion any more than they are meant to classify or label students merely on the basis of descriptions of their behavior and attitudes (Kuh, Whitt, & Shedd, 1987).

In 1978, Parker identified three cautions for using theory; they remain relevant today. He emphasized that theories are meant to be descriptive rather than prescriptive. Student development theories, for example, can present information that describes how students have reasoned and behaved and allow us to make rational assumptions about their future needs. Theory cannot and does not tell us how students *should* think and act. So often, especially with linear developmental models, the underlying goal is to move the students along the continuum rather than understand or support where they are. A related concern expressed by Parker was the notion that educators may use theory to influence students' development and encourage their growth in specific directions. Parker argued that it was far more important for their growth and development that students be able to find their own way. Finally, although many theories are meant to describe and clarify universal notions of growth and development, it is important not to lose sight of the complex individual the theory is trying to describe. It is here that the need for mutually constructed theory and self-authorship, as described by Baxter Magolda (1992), becomes crucially important. An appreciation of the importance of students as knowers and as vital contributors to understanding their own growth and development is central to developing valid and meaningful theories.

Theories often illuminate evolving and complicated phenomena, and professionals must always strive to see an individual or organization from as many vantage points as possible to honor that complexity. This can be difficult whenever a theory seems to invite easy application. For example, it is often tempting for graduate students or new professionals, when they are first exposed to developmental theories like Chickering's or Baxter Magolda's, to use the theory to explain a student's behaviors and attitudes in a reductionistic or simplified fashion ("He's only a sophomore so he can't be working on developing purpose," or "All first-year students are Absolute Knowers"). However, every individual is multidimensional, and growth and development are rarely linear. As Fried (1995) stated, "reality is more complex than a single perspective explanation and . . . all observation is interpretive" (p. 29). Observation is always influenced by our own worldview or our interpretation of reality; this is especially apparent when considering how organizational dynamics or individual or group behaviors are affected by diverse values, cultural realities, and life experiences.

If these diverse values and cultural realities are not incorporated into a theory, the ability of practice to meet the needs of a diverse college campus is limited. Even though in the past twenty years many theories used in student affairs have attempted to move beyond their roots—which often did not initially incorporate cultural influences—much more research, theory development, and exploration remains to be done (Evans et al., 1998; Manning, 1994b; Pope, 1995; Rodgers, 1990; Wright, 1987). Most student and organization development theories used in student affairs today are based on research and practice with predominantly White, male, and privileged individuals and organizations. These early theories, based on universal assumptions about development, did little to address personal or cultural differences that might influence an individual's growth and development (gender, race, racial identity, ethnicity, sexual orientation, social class). An array of research studies have critiqued the applicability of these theories to diverse individuals; they have suggested that more inclusive theories be used in student affairs practice (see, for example, Gibson, 1995; Jiang, 2002; Jordan-Cox, 1987; McEwen, Kodama, Alvarez, Lee, & Liang, 2002; Pope, 1998, 2000; Taub & McEwen, 1991; Testa, 1994; Thomas, 2001; Utterback, 1992). Some theories have expanded in an effort to be more inclusive (Chickering & Reisser, 1993), and other new theories or models have been created or applied to student affairs in an attempt to be more inclusive in their explanations of individual and organizational development (for example, Baxter Magolda, 1992; Belenky, Clinchy, Goldberger, & Tarule, 1986; Gilligan, 1982; Josselson, 1987; Manning & Coleman-Boatwright, 1991; Pope, 1995), but little has been done that addresses the underlying assumptions and values of the core philosophies and theories of the student affairs profession.

Minnich (1990) and others have written about the necessity of exploring the underlying assumptions and worldviews that guide our behavior. She has argued that even if we are not immediately aware of all of our assumptions, they are no doubt still being applied to our everyday perceptions and interactions. These essential beliefs affect our daily interactions and beliefs about others. Although there are some universal human needs—namely food, water, shelter, and perhaps love—even with these basics, individuality and culture profoundly influence how the needs are met. We are constantly influenced by our subjective experiences and worldviews. Therefore, assumptions of universality limit our ability to make meaning of the attitudes, behaviors, and experiences of all students as well as create organizations and institutions that best meet their needs. Challenging a notion of universality inherent in a theory does not mean that the theory should be discarded or that it has particularly limited heuristic value. On the contrary, a theory typically offers important insights into understanding human behavior. However, caution is warranted when theories are applied without significant attention to the impact of individual and cultural realities.

Multicultural Competence in Theory and Translation

Given the limitations of current theory to address cultural realities and diverse experiences within higher education, it seems essential to redefine what competence in theory and translation means within student affairs. Specifically, what multicultural awareness, knowledge, and skills must be infused into theories to make them meaningful and appropriate for all students and student affairs professionals? For example, it is not enough to understand conflict resolution theories for working with students and student staff if one does not also have some understanding of cross-cultural communication differences. Therefore, if conflict between two roommates of different races continues to escalate, or if gender differences among a student orientation staff make it difficult for them to work together, then having additional awareness, knowledge, and skills to address these differences is paramount.

According to Speight, Myers, Cox, and Highlen (1991), redefinition requires finding a balance between understanding culture-specific knowledge and universality. To be meaningful, theories need to effectively balance an individual or organization's uniqueness with accounting for cultural differences and concerns. Theories need to be developed from both culturally distinct and universal points of view, thus lessening the tendency to conceptualize developmental change or organizational structures simplistically or in a reductionistic way.

Multicultural competence in theory and translation needs to involve more than simply applying current theories to underrepresented groups or developing new and unique theories for these groups. For example, if a theory has been developed using only White men as the research participants, it is not appropriate to assume that the theory, as currently developed, is also valid for White women and people of color. Nor is it enough to simply add women or people of color to the research participant pool and stir. If the original pool of research participants predetermines the underlying assumptions and beliefs of a theory, how can such theories ever hope to incorporate the diverse experiences of all students? Can a theory be truly inclusive if the sample on which it is based is not diverse? These essential questions need further exploration as ongoing efforts toward creating more multiculturally sensitive and inclusive theories persist.

In many ways, what is suggested here is not new. In 1978, Knefelkamp recommended a series of questions for scholars and practitioners to pose in the use of and evaluation of theory. The first question asked about the population on which the theory is based. This suggestion is not new; it is just not followed often enough.

Instead, we tend to invest so much time and energy just learning the theory that we fail to evaluate its usefulness in a variety of settings with diverse populations.

Importantly, the fact that a theory is based primarily on one population does *not* inherently make it a flawed theory. Nor does the fact that the theory is questioned and evaluated and perhaps even found wanting in some areas make it a flawed theory. It is simply a theory that may be more useful with the population upon which it is based.

The most influential theories within student affairs need in-depth exploration of their ability to incorporate and make meaning of the unique experiences of underrepresented groups as well as their ability to furnish necessary conceptualizations, tools, and strategies for working in a diverse setting. Do theories about program design, supervision, research and evaluation, group dynamics, budget development, college student development, learning, person-environment models, or leadership address the experiences of students of color; lesbian, gay, bisexual, and transgender students; or nontraditional students with differing developmental needs and issues? Do these theories, which are meant to be the basis for intervention and practice within student affairs, provide relevant and meaningful services for students or effective organizational structures and practices for a diverse workforce?

Using examples from student development and organization development theories, one can examine changes within these theories that have either been developed or should be incorporated in the near future. These examples show that theories can evolve and grow to better meet the diverse needs within higher education.

Chickering and Reisser (1993) illustrate how change can be made within student development theories to revise the initial theory that was developed almost forty years ago. In response to criticism of the relevance of the theory for diverse student groups, or whether the expected developmental path would be the same for all students, Chickering and Reisser made several important changes to their psychosocial theory, reordering, renaming, and emphasizing the centrality of particular vectors.

Similarly, Kodama, McEwen, Liang, and Lee (2002) have suggested that current psychosocial student development theory may not be appropriate for Asian American students; they have proposed a new model of psychosocial development for these students. Racial identity and external and cultural influences are integrated into the model they propose.

Another example involves the reconceptualization of organization development, instead using multicultural organization development (MCOD) theory as suggested by Pope (1995). Traditional organization development theories focus on planned, systemic change; however, their perspective and underlying values, goals, and practices have always been grounded in the dominant culture (Jackson & Holvino, 1988). MCOD theory was created to add a social justice perspective to the process of organizational development. Organization development theories and practices have been part of student affairs for quite a long time and have been unable to actively assist in the process of visioning and creating truly multicultural campuses (Pope, 1995). In the past ten years, several scholars and practitioners have suggested concrete tools and strategies related to MCOD to assist student affairs practitioners in their effort to create campuses that embrace diversity (for example, Grieger, 1996; Katz, 1989; Manning & Coleman-Boatwright, 1991; Pope, 1995; Stewart, 1991).

However, as important as these new or altered theories are, there remains room for improvement. For example, although the revisions offered by Chickering and Reisser are crucially important and did much to advance the applicability of the theory to a broader group of students, the experiences of Asian American and American Indians students are not fully incorporated into the revised theory (see Schuh, 1994).

Another caution with relying on these new or altered theories is that it is not enough to just change the theory. It is also essential to explore related variables and assess the degree to which they may influence the development processes the theory attempts to describe. For example, both race and racial identity have been found to have a significant influence on psychosocial development of students of color (see, for example, Alvarez, 2002; and Pope, 1998, 2000). Racial identity—one's sense of belonging to a particular group and the impact this sense of belonging has on one's thinking, perceptions, feelings, and behavior—is a powerful factor because it highlights the importance of within-group differences. For example, rather than just focusing on how lesbian, gay, bisexual, and transgendered students differ from heterosexual students or how international students differ from those born in the United

States, it is vital that differences within those groups be taken into consideration. There are no homogeneous groups that speak in one voice with only one perspective, and our theories and practice must honor this reality. It is important that there be additional research studying what other influences may affect how or when these various groups develop psychosocially or cognitively. Research that explores other influential variables is fundamental to understanding the experiences of all students, which will hopefully affect theory development and practice.

Researching or creating new theories for use in student affairs is clearly not the only way to develop multicultural competence in the area of theory and translation. In fact, most student affairs practitioners are not researching or creating new theories for use in student affairs, yet there are other important multicultural competencies to be developed in conceptualizing, translating, and applying these theories. Using the tripartite model of multicultural awareness, knowledge, and skills is a helpful and meaningful way to organize the various competencies that need to be incorporated into the multicultural practice of theory and translation in student affairs.

Multicultural Awareness

Arguably, multicultural awareness begins with a basic understanding of our own social identities in terms of race and ethnicity, gender, religion, sexual orientation, and class. Specifically, in relation to theory and theory translation one of the first aspects of multicultural awareness is simple acknowledgment and awareness that all theories are based on a particular view that may or may not incorporate the beliefs, values, or perspectives of all individuals. As stated previously, Minnich (1990) has suggested that our theories are shaped by silent and sometimes subtle points of view that are not shared by all individuals. If we can become aware of our assumptions and how and why we have them, we might then begin the process of decontextualizing particular theories and critiquing their use in specific environments with particular populations.

In terms of awareness, multicultural competence must also include the willingness to challenge one's point of view and address and remove any bias toward a particular group. We must be willing to acknowledge that our personal theories as well as the formal theories that we use are based on certain underlying assumptions about individuals, organizations, growth, and change. These assumptions affect our ability to conceptualize individuals; organizations; and underlying concerns, issues, and solutions. If we have certain assumptions, based on our understanding of psychosocial theory, about how and when typical college students deal with their sexuality, then we may be less attentive to how the experiences of LGB students who are coming out in college might differ. Likewise, if we adopt the view of some management literature that recommends public acknowledgment of good employee performance as a positive way to reinforce and support such performance, then we may not understand when individuals from particular cultures prefer and value more private acknowledgment and attention than a public display of appreciation. In fact, public acknowledgment might prove to be embarrassing or demoralizing for these individuals.

Multicultural Knowledge

Incorporating multicultural knowledge in theory and translation focuses on obtaining knowledge about the various theories and knowing enough about diverse cultures to effectively use or critique the appropriateness of the theories. This knowledge about culture can affect how one applies student development theories to our understanding of individuals or to the development of specific programs or interventions. Similarly, cultural knowledge can positively affect the application of organization development and other management-related theories and approaches.

Student affairs practitioners need to be familiar with the new and expanded theories that have attempted to incorporate multicultural information. Using Rodgers's model of theory comprehension (1991), practitioners must have as much in-depth knowledge of these new theories as they do the more established theories. Understanding how specific cultural constructs, concepts, and realities such as race, racial identity, acculturation, class, or homophobia affect how individuals and organizations operate in the world is essential to providing services that are culturally relevant and effective. Expanding one's knowledge about diverse groups is an essential aspect of this competency, whether this understanding comes from books and training or personal relationships and life experiences. Appreciating within-group differences is a crucial component of this competency and prevents the unfortunate habit of viewing individuals solely in the context of their group memberships.

Multicultural Skills

To apply multicultural awareness and knowledge to theory and translation, one needs the ability to critique theories and apply them to the practical experiences of a diverse student body and complex organizational structures; it is a crucial skill for any student affairs practitioner. As was described in Chapter 1 in Stanley Sue's description of global multicultural competencies (1998), a certain degree of cognitive complexity is required if one is to know when to see the cultural influences on individuals and organizations and when to step back and see the universal elements that affect all individuals.

Knowing how to deconstruct one's personal assumptions and core beliefs as well as the underlying beliefs of a theory being used is a fundamental skill that is rarely taught in graduate school. It is important to explore the core constructs used in the theory and examine how the essential values of the dominant culture influence those constructs. Fried (1995) has described, in length, how the dominant paradigm in the United States has shaped our vision and beliefs. She suggests other ways to view the world that are more dynamic and inclusive as well as how to apply them to teaching, training, and interpersonal relationships.

This deconstruction skill seems to have several important components. First, the ability to ask questions and examine how theories were constructed is an important step in the process. This questioning is most effective when it becomes second nature and occurs any time a new theory or practice is being learned. Second, stepping outside of ourselves and locating personal beliefs and perceptions is a skill that must be practiced and developed. We may never be able to totally disregard our own perceptions, but it is vital to become aware of how others might view and evaluate the same behaviors and beliefs. Once these skills become second nature, we can be more confident in our ability to understand, apply, and use theories in ways that are relevant and meaningful for all.

Exemplary Multicultural Competence in THEORY AND TRANSLATION

The specific exemplary practices highlighted here are not meant to be an inclusive or exhaustive list, but rather to suggest some important multicultural awareness, knowledge, and skills necessary for understanding and applying theory so as to benefit all students. Exploring these exemplary practices increases the opportunity to create a more complex, concrete, and meaningful understanding of multicultural competence.

Exemplary THEORY UNDERSTANDING AND TRANSLATION

A multiculturally sensitive professional, aware of the centrality of theory to effective practice, commits herself to deep study of theory. In addition, she consciously questions and evaluates not only the theory's applicability to all groups of students but also the broader cultural assumptions and norms upon which the theory has been assembled.

Valuing theory and applying it to the practical and dynamic work of student affairs is central to our success as a profession. Rather than just relying on theory learned in graduate school, it is important to spend time studying the evolution of theories. As professionals we need to advocate for application of theory in our work, including professional development workshops on our campuses. Focusing on theory in a vacuum or in a student affairs division that does not value theory is a difficult process; however, if we can institutionalize support for theory and its application, we have the opportunity to strengthen the work that we do.

Theory should never be viewed as a stagnant measuring tool by which we evaluate our performance and efforts. We need to learn enough about theories to wrestle with their underlying meaning and values. Applying them to a specific job on a particular campus is the only way to make theory relevant and meaningful. When theories do not seem to work or do not effectively explain student behavior or other phenomena on our campuses, it is important to question the theories and offer observations about what is missing.

We also need to know enough about the diverse populations on our campuses so that we have a sense of how theories may or may not apply to them. It is helpful to have extensive knowledge about cultural differences and the degree to which theories address cultural issues if we are going to use theories effectively across groups.

A multiculturally sensitive professional stays current with the student affairs literature and attempts to fill voids in his knowledge base. In addition, he sometimes finds it necessary to venture outside of the student affairs and counseling literature to expand his knowledge and understanding of groups that differ from him.

Working in higher education requires a certain commitment to professional development as institutions evolve and change and as generations of students grow and develop. What worked in the 1970s assuredly does not work today because our institutional structures are different, as are our students. To be effective, professionals have to extend their study of theories and their application. This means a commitment to lifelong learning. It may also involve participating in national, regional, or campuswide programs that can expand our knowledge base and skills. When in a leadership position, we should advocate for the professional development of our staff. The awareness, knowledge, and skills that are gained only strengthen campus efforts. Individuals who participate in conferences should be rewarded and given the chance to share what they have learned with colleagues and look for opportunities to apply what they learned on campus. A multiculturally sensitive professional is well read within the professional literature and beyond. Other professions (counseling psychology, the corporate world, elementary and secondary education) have studied multicultural issues and might have much to offer to student affairs in terms of theory and practice. Reading broadly and looking for alternative theories, strategies, and interventions strengthens our knowledge and skill base to more effectively address multi-cultural issues on campus.

A multiculturally sensitive professional sees the complexity of growth and change as an ongoing process rather than as a destination, whether for an individual or an organization.

Many theories offer meaningful yet incomplete views of human nature or organizational development and structure. A theory is meant to be more than a template that we use for comparison.

Effective professionals are able to see it as a general guideline instead of an absolute. Rather than use theory to stereotype or pigeonhole individuals or organizations, it is essential to individualize theories so that they have meaning for the individual person or context involved. It makes sense to have goals and values about what the ideal organization is or how students should grow and develop, but an effective practitioner understands that organizations and individuals grow at their own rate, and growth is often ongoing, uneven, and unpredictable. In fact, change and growth are usually messy, not something that can be easily controlled or managed. When multicultural issues are involved, this process can be much more complicated. Multiculturally sensitive professionals are able to value the process of growth and development by itself rather than focusing on the outcome to accommodate what a theory predicts should happen. There is value in simply understanding and appreciating the current developmental level of individuals or the culture of an organization. Genuine growth and meaningful change are more likely to occur if individuals and organizations are encouraged, supported, and valued where they are.

Summary

Arguably, the goal of using theory effectively is to create a campus environment that advances intellectual growth. To translate theory using various methods, models, and techniques is the work of the student affairs professional (Strange & King, 1990). Translating theory using these same resources but also adding culturally specific content and context is the work of the multiculturally sensitive student affairs professional.

This chapter has discussed the components that constitute theory and translation competence in student affairs practice. It has also offered a brief critique of theories used in student affairs and their limited attention to multicultural issues. The chapter suggests that the theories we use are neither all-knowing nor inherently flawed. Instead, we assert that every theory needs to be examined critically to ensure its appropriateness for a variety of individuals and organizations. Finally, the chapter has presented a number of good-practice examples.

Chapter Three

Multicultural Competence in Administration and Management

It is important that I find a way to increase the cultural sensitivity of my staff. From surveys conducted last year, I'd say most students of color feel that cultural diversity does not receive enough attention on campus. The president is concerned and so am I. She has charged me with finding a way to hold my staff accountable for their ability to reach out to underrepresented students and increase their satisfaction with the campus. My efforts in the past have not been successful and I am not sure of what to do. At some level, I wonder if cultural sensitivity training will make much difference. I've been around long enough to know that some White staff members work effectively with students of color but most don't know how to or don't want to learn. I don't want to waste my time or money providing diversity training that won't change their attitudes or behaviors. Yet I don't know what else to do. (African American male vice president for student affairs)

An irate parent called me during the second week of classes asking that I authorize a room change for his son. He does not like his son's roommate and feels he should be moved right away. When I asked what the difficulty was, the parent said that he didn't want his son living with that sort of person. When asked for more information, the father explained that his son's roommate is Black and he is worried about who or what his roommate will bring into the room. I explained to him that this was an issue between his son and his roommate and that I would investigate. When I spoke with the student, he reported having no problems with his roommate and did not think it was necessary to move. The father is being relentless and is threatening to withdraw his son from school. I am not sure what to do. (White female residence hall director)

One of the staff members I supervise has strong Christian values that I worry are affecting her work. She works with a wide variety of students, and in assessing her ability and experience in working with students who are lesbian, gay, or bisexual, I discovered that this was a point of concern. She said that she didn't think she would have any problem working with a student who was already LGBT but admitted it might be more difficult with someone who was in the process of coming out. She shared how it created a value conflict for her. I know she needs to be able to offer affirmative counseling to everyone but I don't know how to help her do that. Should I change her job description so that she does not have direct contact with students, mandate that she attend LGBT training, or what? I want to do the right thing but don't know what that is. (White male counseling center director)

The principle roles of student affairs work have always been educator, leader, and administrator (Creamer, Winston, & Miller, 2001). Having student affairs practitioners who are campus leaders, effective administrators, and capable educators is central to the success of any student affairs division. Although initially student affairs administrators were in charge of a relatively small division with interconnected services and programs, the range and type of functions, services, and responsibilities subsumed under student affairs have become increasingly diverse and complex (Stamatakos, 1991).

This broad range of functions can include (but is not limited to) housing, activities and student unions, judicial affairs, career development and placement, admissions, financial aid, counseling and health services, intercollegiate athletics and recreation, orientation, first-year programs, community service, peer education, student leadership programs, women's services, minority student services, services for students with disabilities, and international student services. Depending on institutional structure, some academic support services such as academic advising and tutoring may also be included within student affairs. According to Creamer, Winston, and Miller, "these traditional roles have been expanded in recent years to include more intentional efforts to shape the student learning environment and to make the campus a more inviting place for those who have been excluded from or ignored by higher education in the past, such as racial and ethnic minorities; nontraditional-aged students; gay, lesbian, bisexual, and transgender students; commuting students; students with disabilities; and women" (2001, p. 5).

In addition to the work functions used to categorize student affairs, the level and scope of the work are also quite varied. Student affairs practitioners may work in entry-level positions providing direct services to students, or they may work as midlevel supervisors or directors of multifaceted offices or units. They may also serve in executive-level positions where they are directly responsible for overseeing staff performance as well as substantial budgets (Creamer et al., 2001). Student affairs work is also performed at institutions of all sizes and types, from large research universities to small private colleges, from community colleges to elite liberal arts colleges, and from historically Black colleges or tribal colleges to predominantly White institutions.

The variety of tasks and activities in which the student affairs professional must demonstrate competence is broad, complex, and constantly expanding. On today's campus, student affairs administrators manage people, facilities, and budgets; create and influence policy that profoundly affects all aspects of an institution; develop innovative programs; respond to campus crises; and interface with academic affairs in meaningful ways. Student affairs practitioners have also assumed, or been assigned, the responsibility for "creating and sustaining multicultural communities on campus" (Creamer et al., 2001, p. 15).

While the agenda and expectations for student affairs and higher education continue to evolve and change, there is increasing acknowledgment and expectation that student affairs administrators need to develop specific skills to address multicultural issues and the changing student body on their campuses (Dixon, 2001; Pope, 1995; Ramirez, 1993; Talbot, 1996a). To effectively integrate these concerns into the work of student affairs, administrators must consider how diversity influences issues of leadership, planning, and teamwork (Ramirez, 1993).

The purpose of this chapter is to examine the administrative, management, and leadership tasks common to most student affairs positions and explore what multicultural competencies are essential in their implementation. The core assumptions and theories underlying administrative practice are reviewed, and an examination of what constitutes competency in the area of administration and management is offered. There is exploration of how this awareness, knowledge, and skill set have neglected to incorporate cultural realities and highlighting of how in historical terms the underlying administrative theories and practices of student affairs have excluded multicultural issues and knowledge. The multicultural competencies that need to be infused into administration and management practices to provide more meaningful and culturally relevant services are identified, and strategies for developing such awareness, knowledge, and skills are discussed. Finally, good-practice exemplars of how to effectively incorporate cultural realities into our understanding of effective administrative theory and practice will be presented.

Administration and Management in Student Affairs

Historically speaking, the student affairs literature has emphasized specific skills and knowledge bases that were necessary for administrative and management competence. Anthologies such as those edited by Barr (1993b), Miller and Winston (1991), and Komives and Woodard (1996) offer chapters that focus on specific management-related competencies. Among the knowledge areas receiving attention are human and student development theories, organizational theory (including organization development and management theory), leadership theories, environmental theories, and translating theory to practice. Skill and practice-oriented areas explored in the literature include budgeting and fiscal management, supervision and evaluation, managing physical facilities, program development and implementation, selecting and training competent staff, political dimensions of decision making, the role of the middle manager, technology and information systems, and strategic planning.

Miller and Winston (1991) classified student affairs activities into four separate yet overlapping categories: organizational maintenance, staff, management, and educational. The first three are most intimately connected with the administrative and management tasks within student affairs. According to Miller and Winston, organizational maintenance functions concentrate on those activities and skills that must be executed to keep the organization working effectively, such as facility management and institutional policies and procedures. If these tasks are not completed effectively, the integrity and competence of a student affairs division and unit will be questioned. Staffing functions are those activities that involve selecting, training, supervising, and evaluating professional, support, and paraprofessional staff members. Knowledge and skill in leadership and motivation as well as interpersonal skills are prerequisites for competence with staffing. Finally, management functions involve those activities and skills, such as fiscal planning and policy as well as program development, that help administrators implement the institutional missions and goals.

According to Barr (1993b), "the administration of student affairs programs, services, and activities has grown increasingly complex" (p. xiii). Others, such as Miller and Winston, suggest that "although management techniques are extremely important to effective administration of student affairs programs, techniques alone are not enough to accomplish the myriad of required tasks" (1991, p. xiv). There are many challenges facing student affairs administrators that require the development of new perspectives and abilities, among them rapid development of technology; diminishing financial resources; emphasis on accountability, liability, and assessment; privatization of services and programs; community service and leadership; and increasing specialization of services (Sandeen, 1993).

With changing roles and responsibilities, it is difficult to develop a static list of tasks and responsibilities for all student affairs administrators. Sandeen suggested using professional standards such as those developed by the American College Personnel Association (ACPA, 1993), the National Association of Student Personnel Administrators (NASPA, 1993), and the Council for the Advancement of Standards or CAS (Miller, 2001) as a basis for practice rather than relying on uniform administrative structures, tasks, and responsibilities that may not meet the individual needs of a given institution.

Blimling and Whitt (1999) also recommended moving beyond traditional frameworks and skills used to conceptualize student affairs and rely instead on a student-centered approach that emphasizes principles developed from the most effective practices within student affairs. According to Blimling and Whitt, focusing on best practices creates less emphasis on developing a unified mission for student affairs, and it concentrates more attention on finding common ground among divergent opinions. The best-practice principles thus developed are also flexible, dynamic, and easily applied across institutions.

Barr (1993b) highlighted some core themes that student affairs administrators can use to enhance their administrative effectiveness. Barr emphasized the importance of prioritizing staff development, offering effective supervision, and implementing an effective staff selection and training program. This first theme highlights the importance of attracting and retaining skilled staff members as a foundational ability necessary for all student affairs administrators. Having an effective staff requires investing time, energy, and resources as an ongoing commitment. Another theme suggested making a commitment to diversity necessary for success as an administrator. This underscores the importance of understanding the changing demographics and dynamics within higher education and how they affect student affairs practice. Barr also highlighted the importance of enhancing one's management skills to offer more effective and meaningful programs and services. The type, range, and usefulness of these skills must continuously grow to meet the ever-changing needs, concerns, and dynamics in student affairs. In addition to developing effective management skills, student affairs administrators need to develop more effectiveness in addressing conflict and crises and in managing how student affairs staff members respond to these significant events. The possible crises and critical events seem almost endless: a fire in a residence hall, a racial conflict between students, a student suicide, gang-related violence on campus, and so on. Student affairs administrators need a process in place and adequate staff training to be prepared for any critical event. Another theme includes understanding how legal issues and governmental influences affecting student affairs require that we often consult with outside legal experts in planning and responding to various campus issues.

In addition to the development of some of these essential skills and diverse knowledge base, Barr (1993b) highlighted the importance of student affairs administrators' understanding and valuing the mission, goals, and structure of their institution so they can contribute to such key campus tasks as strategic planning and policy development. Part of this process requires making a commitment to the assessment and evaluation process of student needs and program effectiveness. This assessment process allows us to allocate human and financial resources, immediately and in the long run, to those programs and services that most effectively meet student needs.

There are three final themes suggested by Barr (1993b). She emphasized the importance of developing meaningful and collaborative relationships across campus and with significant off-campus constituent groups. Working to establish good relationships with academic affairs is especially crucial to success. Community involvement is an essential component to creating a synergistic, educational, and dynamic campus environment. Finally, Barr suggested that being involved professionally and actively reading the student affairs literature is an indispensable aspect of our professional development and is necessary to increase awareness and knowledge of significant issues as well as develop new skills.

Reisser and Roper (1999) also identified significant themes that student affairs administrators need to address if they are to provide efficacious and useful service: "the need to understand organizational culture, the necessity for organizations to have an elevating goal or compelling vision, the requirement of good channels of communication, the importance of planning and taking action, the willingness to take risks, an understood sense of urgency, competent employees, and commitment to personal and organizational growth" (p. 118).

The student affairs literature has addressed administrative and management issues extensively and provided theory and practice-oriented strategies for both new and seasoned professionals. Although some recent writings have addressed multicultural issues or dynamics, there are limited resources that incorporate multiculturalism in a comprehensive and integrative manner. Typically, multicultural implications are addressed in an additive or superficial way that does not help practitioners integrate multicultural issues into specific competencies required to be effective managers and administrators.

In terms of knowledge base, as with student development theories, the theories most commonly used within administration and management (organization development, leadership, management theories) do not adequately address multicultural issues. For example, although organization development theory addresses relevant issues such as organizational change and strategic planning that could be used to create multicultural change within higher education, the theory has not incorporated those issues. According to Pope (1993b), organization development theory is based on the current organizational values, goals, and culture practices, which perpetuate the status quo and do not directly or adequately incorporate multicultural practices. Although traditional organizational theories have failed in these efforts, some new models or frameworks for addressing multicultural issues at the organizational level within student affairs have been introduced within the past ten years (see Dixon, 2001; Grieger, 1996; Manning & Coleman-Boatwright, 1991; Pope, 1993b, 1995).

Administrative and management practices and skills also have fallen short of incorporating multicultural issues and concerns. Although it is commonly acknowledged that cultural issues need to be addressed within student affairs administration (CAS, 1992; Dixon, 2001; McEwen & Roper, 1994a; Pope, 1995; Pope & Reynolds, 1997), practitioners need more specific suggestions and ideas to effectively infuse multicultural strategies and skills. Cultural issues are relevant and need to be addressed within every core area or function within administrative practice (budgeting, program and strategic planning, staffing and supervision, and the like). As an illustration, in the United States the dominant White culture values and rewards assertion and independence as effective leadership traits, while some other cultures reward and emphasize cooperation and consensus as the hallmarks of effective leadership. It is important to consider what values and assumptions underlie our practices. Within the staffing and supervision area, for instance, how one recruits, trains, and supervises individuals from different cultural groups may vary. How cultural issues are integrated into programming efforts also has to be considered. Is cultural programming focused on specific months and populations—Lesbian, Gay, Bisexual, and Transgender Pride Week; Black History Month—or is it focused on more global areas such as cross-cultural communication?

If multicultural awareness, knowledge, and skills are not incorporated into administrative and management competence, student affairs administrators are forced to use incomplete theories to explain multicultural dynamics on campus; offer generic interventions to address multicultural concerns; or create additive, and often fragmented, approaches to tackling multicultural issues. As Pope (1993b) and Grieger (1996) have suggested, such sporadic, uncoordinated, incomplete efforts are woefully inadequate and do little to create a multiculturally sensitive and inclusive campus environment.

Multicultural Competence in Administration and Management

Given the difficulty that higher education has experienced in effectively addressing and incorporating multicultural issues, multicultural scholars have suggested the need for new approaches, ideas, and tools. According to Pope, "paradigmatic shifts are essential for student affairs practitioners to create genuine and lasting multicultural campus environments" (1995, p. 233). To create a campus that fully embraces cultural diversity in people, values, and ideas, new frameworks or models highlighting the steps and processes necessary for such a change are needed. Jackson and Hardiman (1994) and others (Grieger, 1996; Katz, 1989; Pope, 1995) have suggested using systemically designed organizational and cultural change efforts to create multicultural environments. Student affairs administrators who have responsibilities for creating, managing, and evolving various programs, services, and systems on campus are ideally suited to conceptualize, design, and implement this type of systemic and systematic change process.

According to Cox, "managing diversity is crucial to the accomplishment of organizational goals and therefore should be of paramount concern to managers" (1993, p. 11). He further states that the goal is to design and implement organizational structures and practices that accentuate the advantages and minimize any disadvantages of cultural diversity. Ideally, creating a multicultural campus environment encourages the success of all individuals on campus and removes any barriers that inhibit the development of any individual, idea, goal, or plan. As stated by Pope (1995), "making intentional change to guide the transformation of campus environments and integrate the value and beliefs of multiculturalism is a complex undertaking" (p. 236).

In an attempt to acknowledge that complexity and guide systemic change effort, it is essential to use the theory, tools, and strategies of organizational change frameworks. Initially, organization development experts believed that planned change theories and strategies could be used to fully address and redress organizational inequity and assist in the development of multicultural organizations. However, the organization development interventions were too focused on training efforts and did little to change organizational power and culture (Chesler, 1994). In addition, traditional organization development theories and practices are too rooted in the perspectives of the dominant culture and have been unable to incorporate multiple cultural worldviews.

Multicultural Organization Development (MCOD)

In an effort to move beyond those limitations, multicultural organization development (MCOD) emerged as a tool in the late 1980s and early 1990s for creating more multiculturally sensitive organizations (see Cross, Katz, Miller, & Seashore, 1994; Jackson & Holvino, 1988). MCOD is a systematic planned change effort using behavioral science knowledge and technologies for improving organizational effectiveness (Pope, 1995). MCOD theory states that a multicultural organization is a healthy organization because it "reflects the contributions and interests of diverse cultural and social groups in its mission, operations, and . . . service delivery; acts on a commitment to eradicate social oppression in all forms within the organization; includes the members of diverse cultural and social groups as full participants, especially in decisions that shape the organization; and follows through on broad external social responsibilities, including support of efforts to eliminate all forms of social oppression and to educate others in multicultural perspectives" (Jackson & Hardiman, 1981, p. 1).

Multicultural organization development supports the transformation of organizations into socially just and socially diverse systems through questioning and assessing underlying beliefs, everyday practices, and core values (Pope, 1995). Socially just and socially diverse systems are organizations that value social diversity in their membership and strive to eliminate social injustice or oppression within their organizational practices, systems, and methods (Jackson & Hardiman, 1994). Pope and others (Grieger, 1996; Grieger & Toliver, 2001; Sue, 1995) have encouraged the use of MCOD in higher education and counseling settings as a structured method for creating multicultural change.

Within the MCOD field, several models or frameworks have been developed that offer concrete strategies, steps, and tools for conceptualizing a multicultural organization and implementing a systematic change effort. Jackson and Hardiman (1994) developed a process for long-term systemic organizational change with four components. The first involves creating a multicultural internal change team that is responsible for guiding all aspects of the transformational effort. A support-building phase is the second crucial component in creating a multicultural organization. During this phase, the organization's readiness level for individual and organizational change and development is assessed, and, if necessary, interventions are designed to increase awareness and openness to multicultural change within the organization. The third component or leadership development phase focuses on the awareness, involvement, and ability of the senior leadership within the organization to lead a multicultural change effort. Finally, it is essential that every organization create a self-renewing process for multicultural systems change.

Within this process, Jackson and Hardiman propose four steps:

1. Establishing a diverse and thorough MCOD assessment plan.
2. Developing an MCOD intervention plan based on information gathered through the assessment phase.
3. Implementing an MCOD implementation plan that is integrated into all organizational subsystems.
4. Using an evaluation process that assesses the value and effectiveness of the MCOD plan and makes changes as appropriate. This MCOD model is intended to be a never-ending process with an emphasis on making constant improvements and changes that are far-reaching and transformational.

Two other MCOD models, one by Pope (1995) and the other by Grieger (1996), have been proposed and applied to the student affairs profession. These models were developed to assist student affairs administrators in developing and assessing the multicultural and diversity strategies on campus.

Multicultural Change Intervention Matrix (MCIM)

Pope designed the Multicultural Change Intervention Matrix (MCIM) for use in conceptualizing and planning multicultural interventions in student affairs. The 3 x 2 matrix (Table 3.1) was developed as a schematic illustration of MCOD principles as applied to student affairs and higher education. The MCIM has two major dimensions. The first focuses on the possible targets of any multicultural intervention (individual, group, or institution). The second identifies two levels or types of intervention: first-order and second-order change.

Table 3.1. Multicultural Change Intervention Matrix (MCIM)

Target of Change	Type of Change	
	First-Order Change	*Second-Order Change*
Individual	A. Awareness	B. Paradigm shift
Group	C. Membership	D. Restructuring
Institutional	E. Programmatic	F. Systemic

Source: Copyright © 1992 by Raechele L. Pope.

Lyddon (1990) examined first-order and second-order change as initially differentiated by Watzlawick, Weakland, and Fisch (1974) in their discussion of family systems. The latter work described first-order change as one within the system that does not create change in the structure of the system. Second-order change is anything that fundamentally alters the structure of a system.

Lyddon offered a further explanation of first-order and second-order change originally conceptualized by Watzlawick et al. (1974). This explanation uses fundamental mathematical concepts to distinguish between the two types of change. In arithmetic, a set of numbers may be combined in various ways using the same mathematical operation, without changing the numbers or makeup of the set. For example, $(3 + 2) + 6 = 11$ and $2 + (3 + 6) = 11$ are the numbers three, two, and six added differently yet resulting in the same answer. Lyddon believes, in such a case, "a myriad of changes in the internal state of a group (that is, changes among its members) makes no difference in its definition as a group. This type of change maintains the coherence of a system and is referred to as first-order change" (p. 122). However, if the mathematical operation is changed from addition to multiplication, as with $(3 \times 2) + 6 = 12$, then a different outcome results. According to Lyddon, this change depicts a transformation in the definition of the group and is second-order change. Second-order change, then, is a paradigm shift. It is a radical transformation in how the group is viewed and defined.

Another way of illustrating the radical transformation necessary for second-order change is through the use of one of the most familiar Gestalt psychology perception figures. The figure is perceived as either an old woman with a large nose or a young woman with fine features wearing a hat with a feather. To be able to see both images in the figure, one must concentrate and make a conscious effort to view the figure differently from one's initial perception. This effort is similar to the paradigm shift needed to create second-order change in organizations, groups, or individuals.

As shown in Table 3.1, the MCIM offers six ways to conceptualize and structure multicultural change efforts. By increasing understanding of the range of targets and goals that may be used, one can more easily expand the types of activities, strategies, and tools. Through exploration of the six cells of the MCIM, more multicultural interventions can be considered.

Cell A change efforts (first-order change, individual) typically involve education at the awareness, knowledge, or skill level. This type of educational effort is often content focused, as with information about various racial, religious, or other cultural groups. Possible examples are cultural communication workshops, programs on the economic and social conditions of a particular cultural group, or an antiracism presentation.

A cell B change effort (second-order change, individual) is primarily aimed at the cognitive restructuring level, suggesting a worldview or paradigm shift. Such a worldview shift requires more intensive, interactive, or experiential emphasis in the program design. These interventions are often more process oriented and challenge an individual's underlying assumptions. An example might be a prolonged and extensive consciousness-raising workshop that is individually focused and experientially oriented (that is, an individual is challenged to examine belief and thought systems and to be introspective and self-challenging).

A cell C change effort (first-order change, group) is a change in the composition of a group in which members of underrepresented groups are added, but there is no change in the goals or norms of the group. Cell C focuses on diversity in terms of numbers, without examining the interpersonal and structural dynamics of a group. An example might be the traditional recruitment efforts that increase the number of people of color or White women on a staff without altering the environment or examining and modifying the unit or divisional mission.

Cell D change efforts (second-order change, group) might involve total restructuring of a group with a new mission, goals, and members. This type of transformation examines group makeup, values, and goals prior to changing the group. Any new members must be involved in this self-examination and planning process. An example is hosting a retreat for a specific unit or department to reexamine and reformulate its philosophy, values, and goals, including the multicultural goals and objectives. Rather than adding a few multicultural goals, this approach demands a reexamination of the entire mission and purpose of the unit and allows multicultural issues to be integrated into the unit's central mission.

A cell E change effort (first-order change, institutional) might involve a programmatic intervention aimed at the institution or division that addresses multicultural issues but does not alter the underlying values and structure of the institution. Creating a new position within student affairs to direct a cultural center or developing an ongoing multicultural training program are two examples of a change effort that may not alter the institutional dynamics, values, or priorities. Another example might be adding a multicultural section to a student affairs mission statement without changing the evaluation or budgetary criteria, which typically does not create institutional or divisional change.

A cell F change effort (second-order change, institutional) requires more direct examination of underlying institutional values, goals, and evaluations that then are linked to multicultural values and efforts. An example might be requiring goal-directed multicultural initiatives within all student affairs units that directly link the outcome of those initiatives to budget allocations or basing hiring, salary, evaluation, and promotion decisions on individual multicultural competencies.

The six cells of the MCIM are separate and unique; however, their relationship with each other is fluid and dynamic. For example, awareness is an important part of creating a paradigm shift within an individual. Or programmatic efforts may be a necessary precursor to developing systemic change. The dotted lines between the various cells are meant to portray this interconnection and encourage the use of all six levels and targets of multicultural intervention. The relationships between the various cells have yet to be studied; research examining the philosophical assumptions of the MCIM must be undertaken. Because the MCIM is still a new model, there is much research to be completed. Although the dualistic nature of our society might encourage readers to assume that second-order change is "better" than first-order change because it creates long-term and structural transformation, it is vital that each type of intervention be seen as a valuable and necessary part of the multicultural change process.

According to Pope (1993b), most multicultural interventions within student affairs have focused on first-order individual change that never alters the values, goals, or activities of student affairs. To create a multicultural organization, change efforts must be focused on all three targets (individual, group, and institutional) and on both levels (first-order and second-order change; Pope, 1995). The MCIM creates opportunities for an inclusive strategic plan that is fully integrated into all levels of the student affairs division and that increases the opportunity for true systemic change. Pope identified three significant uses of the MCIM for student affairs: (1) assessment, (2) strategic planning, and (3) curricular transformation.

Assessment

One of the strengths of the MCIM is that it can be used for assessment. The instrumentation for the MCIM is still in its early stages of development, but the MCIM is well suited for codifying and understanding the range of multicultural interventions implemented in student affairs and higher education (Pope, 1993b). For example, Pope conducted a national study to identify, examine, and assess the number, level, and type of multiracial change interventions currently used on individual campuses. The MCIM afforded the framework for discerning the type of interventions used nationally. Similarly, the MCIM can be used to assess the multicultural interventions employed on an individual campus, a student affairs division, or a single department or unit of a campus. Because the MCIM is such a versatile model, it can be used effectively with quantitative, qualitative, and case study research designs or assessment projects. The assessments can assist practitioners in setting goals and identifying the type and level of intervention required to ensure that comprehensive incorporation of diverse cultures, values, norms, and ideas is developed.

Strategic Planning

The MCIM also has value in the area of strategic planning. Developing a strategic plan offers an institution vital evaluative information. It can answer questions concerning what the institution is doing, why it does so, who does it, and how well and how efficiently it is being done. "Furthermore, a [strategic] plan will help to determine if the institution is fulfilling its stated mission" (Ern, 1993, p. 442). Strategic planning is an essential tool in creating a multicultural campus. Campus leaders who strive to develop a multicultural campus and who include these goals in their institutional mission statement and yet do not include these issues in the strategic planning process are likely to be unsuccessful and ineffective in their efforts. In essence, creating multicultural campus environments requires systemic and systematic change. The MCIM can be used to conceptualize the multicultural change efforts currently being used, set goals and priorities, and design future change efforts. For example, as one component of a strategic plan, a student affairs division could: review its current goals and functional responsibilities, evaluate its internal and external responsibilities, create future-oriented goals, identify finance and resource needs, and integrate multicultural aspects into each of these four areas. The MCIM can be used to ensure that these efforts are focused on second-order change and targeted at the divisional level. Strategic multicultural change at this level could, for instance, directly link budget allocations, performance evaluations, and staffing decisions to current and longer-range goals and functional responsibilities.

Curricular Transformation
A third use of the MCIM is in the area of curricular transformation. Those attempting to infuse multicultural issues into a specific academic program or department, a college division, or the entire academic unit of a campus can use the MCIM as a tool. Student affairs professionals can use it to integrate multiculturalism into student affairs preparation programs and other courses they may teach (for example, resident assistant courses or first-year experience courses). In addition, student affairs professionals can make a significant and unique contribution to academic affairs by sharing expertise and tools for multicultural curricular transformation through the use of the MCIM. It not only can assist faculty in determining what type of outcome they want for their individual course or program, but it may also offer a conceptual framework to assist faculty in deciding how to achieve their goals. This model offers a useful framework for assessing the type and level of multicultural education in the classroom. Initially the MCIM might be used to assess the current level of infusion of multicultural issues into

the overall curriculum; for example, does the institution require multicultural courses? Are these courses focused on awareness or content knowledge? In addition, one could assess the type of courses offered within a particular program or department. Once this assessment has taken place, another example of how to use MCIM to transform the curriculum could involve designing individual courses to either attempt to address both first-order and second-order change perspectives or primarily focus on the type of learning that might occur in any of the six cells of the model. Chapter Seven explores multicultural curricular transformation in greater depth.

Multicultural Organization Development Checklist

On the basis of the work of Pope (1993b), Grieger (1996) also offered a tool, the Multicultural Organization Development Checklist (MODC), to assist student affairs administrators in their efforts to create multicultural student affairs programs, offices, and divisions. Eleven distinct categories were proposed within the MODC to guide student affairs administrators in assessing their multicultural efforts as well as in developing new multicultural interventions and diversity plans. Those categories are mission statement, leadership and advocacy, policies, recruitment and retention, expectations for multicultural competency, multicultural competency training, scholarly activities, student activities and services, internship and field placement, physical environment, and assessment. Grieger views the MODC as a structured guide to assist student affairs divisions in assessing their multicultural change efforts. She suggests introducing the checklist within the context of professional development for all staff and involve staff members in discussing how to implement the checklist in the most empowering and constructive manner.

Although the development of MCOD tools and related multicultural change frameworks is still in the formative stage, there are growing opportunities for student affairs administrators to structure multicultural change efforts. Reisser and Roper (1999) emphasized the positive value of risk taking for student affairs administrators. In their view, "responsible leaders will challenge staff to move beyond the limitations of the status quo" (p. 121).

Multicultural change at the organizational level will not occur on its own; it requires "expertise, focused reflection, commitment, specific competencies and purposeful action" (Pope, 1995, p. 235).

Multicultural Organization Development (MCOD) Template

Since MCOD tools have not been created or fully adapted for higher education, it is essential that MCOD experts develop ways to assess and intervene within the college environment. Focusing on the institutional level is paramount, but it is important to emphasize that a significant aspect of an organizational intervention must focus on how to address multicultural issues residing in the diverse levels, units, and tasks within student affairs. Reynolds, Pope, and Wells (2002), adapting the MODC of Grieger (1996), created the Student Affairs MCOD Template (Table 3.2). To create a more strategic diversity plan, the template can be used by student affairs departments, departmental subunits (for example, an individual residence hall of a Department of Residential Life), or the entire student affairs division. The template suggests how a student affairs division or department on a particular campus might integrate multicultural values and expectations into all aspects of an organization, from the mission statement to the evaluation process. This template identifies ten specific, key targets for multicultural intervention (mission statement, policy review, multicultural competency expectations and training, and others). It also highlights the purpose or importance of those key areas. Finally, it identifies specific components to be included within a diversity plan. For example, in the key area "multicultural competency expectations and training," components identified as a starting point for a diversity plan are to offer regular and ongoing diversity training, make available effective multicultural supervision for professional and student staff, specify how multicultural tasks and responsibilities are part of overall job expectations (for both graduate students and professional staff), and evaluate and reward performance on the basis of the successful completion of multicultural goals. Student affairs professionals looking for assistance in structuring their multicultural interventions are encouraged to view this template as a useful tool.

Table 3.2. Student Affairs MCOD (Multicultural Organization Development) Template

MCOD Category	Purpose	Specific Components
1. Comprehensive definition of the term *multicultural*	In the interest of serving students, an inclusive and broad definition of *multicultural* should be chosen. Encouraging discussion of definitional issues is essential so there is agreement among staff members as to where diversity initiatives might be focused.	• Use an inclusive definition of *diversity* • Identify the student groups who have historically been underserved or underrepresented in higher education (e.g., people of color; students with disabilities; nontraditional students; female students; religious minorities; international students; first-generation college students; and lesbian, gay, bisexual, and transgender students)
2. Mission statement	A student affairs department or division mission statement identifies its values and priorities and ideally identifies diversity issues as central to the department or division mission.	• Explicit use of words such as *multicultural* or *diversity* must be an essential part of the mission statement • Incorporate the mission statement into all department publications and advertisements such as brochures and Websites

MCOD Category	Purpose	Specific Components
3. Leadership and advocacy	Multicultural change efforts in higher education are most successful when they involve the commitment of the top leadership within a college. However, if such top leadership is not available, individuals may take responsibility within their own sphere of influence and attempt to create change.	• Set short-term and long-term diversity goals for each year • Give additional rewards and support to those staff members who fully participate in the multicultural vision of the student affairs department/division • Seek out additional multicultural training to assist efforts toward creating a multicultural department/division • Document how supervisors will assist their supervisees in the development of multicultural competencies
4. Policy review	Multicultural organization development focuses on all significant subsystems of an organization, such as mission, policies and procedures, training, and evaluation. Reviewing the current policies, procedures, and forms is one way to ensure that diversity issues are included in all aspects of an organization.	• Conduct a full review of departmental policies and procedures to assess their impact on diverse populations and make changes as appropriate

(continues)

Table 3.2. (continued)

MCOD Category	Purpose	Specific Components
5. Recruitment and retention of a diverse staff	To have a truly multicultural department/division, it is essential that the staff be culturally diverse. Without a diversity of voices, life experiences, and cultural backgrounds, staff may be limited in their ability to meet the needs of some students. In addition to recruiting a diverse staff, addressing interpersonal and structural dynamics within the environment helps to create a welcoming and nurturing environment for all staff members.	• Develop and follow proactive diversity recruitment strategies that identify where advertisements will be sent and how a diverse candidate pool will be developed • Include multicultural awareness, competence, knowledge, and skills as an integral part of the job description • Evaluate all job candidates on those criteria • Use ongoing supervision to explore retention-related issues
6. Multicultural competency expectations and training	Multiculturally competent attitudes, knowledge, and skills are fast becoming the standard within student affairs by which staff members may be evaluated. It is no longer acceptable to have a multicultural expert on staff to meet the needs of specific student groups. Training or retraining staff members in multicultural issues helps them feel more equipped to meet the needs of all students. Mentoring graduate students and encouraging the	• Create opportunities for staff to attend local, state, or national conferences or workshops that address diversity issues • Offer diversity training every year • Provide effective multicultural supervision for all professional and student staff members • Specify how multicultural tasks and responsibilities are part of graduate students' overall job expectations

MCOD Category	Purpose	Specific Components
	development of their multicultural awareness, knowledge, and skills is essential for effective supervision.	• Assign diversity goals to each staff member and base annual evaluation on how they contribute to the multicultural vision of the department/division
7. Scholarly activities	It is the responsibility of all professionals to contribute to the field of multiculturalism through professional writing or presentations that reflect on their experiences. Such work instills more commitment to the process, creates a positive image for the department/division, and provides opportunities for staff members to receive feedback and support from colleagues across the country.	• Encourage, support, and reward staff members who pursue any multicultural scholarly activities (writing for publication or presenting at professional conferences)
8. Departmental/ division programs and services	Incorporating multicultural content and sensitivity into all programs and services, from advertisement to implementation, makes for accessible and meaningful activities. It is also helpful to identify underserved student groups and develop ways to meet their needs more effectively, including the development of new and creative programs and services.	• Review all programs, activities, forms, and services for multicultural content and values • Develop plans for more thorough and deliberate infusion of diversity material in workshop agendas and materials • Create at least one new and innovative program each year to contribute to the multicultural change efforts on campus

(continues)

Table 3.2. (continued)

MCOD Category	Purpose	Specific Components
9. Physical environment	The physical environment sends an important message about what it values. It is important to create an affirming and caring environment where individuals of diverse backgrounds feel valued. Creating a setting that has music, artwork, and other visual images that are representative of diverse cultures not only makes those individuals feel welcome, it also educates and expands the awareness of others. Staff members need to be conscious and thoughtful in how they approach this issue; ongoing dialogue is central to creating an inclusive and accepting environment.	• Review individual offices and public space to ensure they are void of offensive or insensitive materials • Ensure that all offices and programs are accessible and welcoming to students with disabilities • Display culturally inclusive artwork, music, and magazines in public spaces to create a welcoming environment • Discuss how to respond to insensitive or offensive verbal or nonverbal conduct in any programs or services

MCOD Category	Purpose	Specific Components
10. Assessment	To create a multicultural department/division, an assessment of the multicultural strengths and weaknesses is necessary. By knowing who it is serving and how satisfied they are with the service, a department/division is better able to develop effective programs and services. Once an accurate evaluation has been completed, it is easier to set goals and plan strategically. Self-evaluation is not enough. It is vital to gather information about the perceptions, attitudes, and experiences of the students, staff, and faculty who use the services for a more accurate picture of the type of changes needed. The goal of assessment is ultimately to create some accountability for the multicultural change efforts.	• Create an evaluation system that assesses the effectiveness of its services and outreach efforts to all students • Assess student satisfaction with the multicultural sensitivity of the service or outreach effort as well as the multicultural competence of the staff • Gather information about the demographic background of students who use any program or services • Set yearly goals to either increase the percentage of students from under-represented groups who use their office or improve the students' overall level of satisfaction with those services

Source: Adapted from Reynolds and Pope (2003).

Although MCOD interventions at the organizational level are most effective for creating genuinely multicultural campuses, student affairs educators without such broad position responsibilities should not feel powerless to create change at the levels for which they are accountable. MCOD principles and strategies can just as easily be employed in smaller, more narrowly focused units as well. MCOD has a greater chance of broader effect as part of a campuswide effort, but a single unit, such as the Division of Student Affairs or the Department of Campus Activities, or even a subunit such as a single residence hall in a large residence hall system, can create lasting multicultural benefits for the people involved with that unit. The key is to focus on the areas for which one has both responsibility and authority. For example, an individual residence hall director (RD) on a large campus may be responsible for a single hall housing four hundred students. The RD may supervise one graduate assistant and sixteen resident assistants and develop a close working relationship with the six-person executive council of the building's residence hall government. It is within this element that the RD has both responsibility and authority. The MCOD strategies that the RD could use focus on this particular residence hall and the students who live, work, and study there. She could use the MCIM to assess the environment (the residence hall) and develop a strategic plan to address multicultural issues. She could also adapt the checklist offered by Grieger (1996) for use in her hall and use it to develop appropriate multicultural interventions. Or she could use the MCOD Template as the basis for her individual residence hall interventions.

Learning and incorporating the broader knowledge base of MCOD and other systemic and systematic interventions is necessary in creating a multicultural campus. The need also exists for student affairs educators to learn and integrate specific skill sets to become more effective administrators, managers, and leaders. Rogers (1996) offers a foundational set of behaviors and beliefs for effective campus leadership that expand the role, function, and relationship of leadership and also make visible the dominant worldview that pervades the traditional leadership paradigm. Here is her list :

- Understanding, valuing, and nurturing the group process
- Collaborating and engaging in creative conflict

- Creating environments based on trust and empowerment
- Encouraging diverse voices
- Knowing yourself and changing yourself first
- Creating and articulating a shared vision
- Understanding and using political processes
- Developing a multiperspective view

Rogers's suggestions are quite progressive in that they require a totally new way of viewing leaders and new methods of practicing leadership. Each of the behaviors and beliefs that Rogers proposes, when overlaid and infused with unambiguous consideration for the multicultural context of our campuses, students, faculty, and staff, undoubtedly improves multicultural competence in administration and management.

Exemplary Multicultural Competence in ADMINISTRATION AND MANAGEMENT

The particular exemplary practices described here are not intended to be an inclusive or exhaustive list but rather to suggest some important multicultural awareness, knowledge, and skills necessary for infusing multicultural issues into administration and management tasks, functions, and responsibilities within student affairs. By exploring these exemplary practices, one sets as the goal to create a more complex, concrete, and meaningful understanding of multicultural competence.

A student affairs professional may be committed to multicultural issues and individually provide effective services for underrepresented students but realize that he has no idea how to influence the attitudes, expectations, and behaviors of others in his own office. A multiculturally sensitive professional knows how to move beyond his or her own individual awareness and skills and strive to create change in organizational structures and practices.

As stated previously, it is not enough just to intervene on the individual level to create openness toward multicultural issues. There must also be an effort to create institutional or organizational change where multicultural issues are embedded in the job expectations, training requirements, and policies and practices of a specific program or office. Through the use of systemic and systematic interventions, multicultural values and norms can become less dependent on individuals to champion them and instead become a mainstream part of the organization. Developing the skills to intervene on the organizational level so that we can create multicultural change requires reading more about multicultural organization development and other related change efforts. It also requires finding allies within our organization who are committed to these values and will work together to create change. There are models that can be used to create meaningful multicultural organizational change and help individuals deal with institutional barriers.

A student affairs professional has worked hard at being an effective supervisor and has consistently received excellent evaluations from the graduate assistants she supervises from the student affairs preparation program on campus. After receiving negative feedback from two graduate students of color that she supervised, she is questioning her ability to effectively supervise students of color. A multiculturally competent professional works hard at building effective relationships with all of her supervisees and is willing to directly address their cultural differences and their potential impact on their working relationship.

Staff and student supervision is arguably one of the most important responsibilities of the student affairs professional. The definitive test of effective supervision may be one's ability to recognize and reward areas of strength, identify and co-construct plans for strengthening areas requiring improvement, develop and motivate employees and students, and at the same time maintain a commitment to achieving institutional or departmental goals. Supervision is both an important administrative responsibility and a helping skill that requires a supervisor to have the ability to work effectively with individuals who are culturally different from him. If supervision does not meet their needs, supervisees from underrepresented groups are likely to get their supervision needs met from their peers or not at all. Biases, stereotypes, and cultural differences affect management and supervision; unwritten rules influence our perceptions of performance and can affect the success or degree of success of those whom we supervise. The reality is that on any given campus there are always numerous cultures operating simultaneously (campus culture, racial and ethnic cultures, the culture of gender, student cultures, faculty culture). Each culture has its own attitudes and beliefs about what is important and what the requirements are for success. Cultural values define how a campus does its work; how faculty, students, and staff are to behave; and how they are to be rewarded. In some places on campus, the rules are explicit and obvious to any viewer. Other rules are far subtler and not as easily detected by an observer. Problems often develop on campus if the rules are clear only to those with intimate familiarity with the dominant culture. Supervisors may not share the rules because they assume that everyone knows them: classroom etiquette, language standards, hours of work and punctuality, how questions are asked or disagreement is expressed, dress code or hairstyles, expectations of written work (reports and memo formatting), relationships between faculty and students as well as supervisors and supervisees, how performance is recognized or contribution is credited, and office decor. To make the campus equitable and fair, supervisors have a responsibility to ensure that all of those whom they supervise have knowledge of these unwritten rules.

Another crucial component of effective supervision is the degree to which issues of culture are directly addressed within the supervisory relationship. Cultural issues that influence the supervisee, whether in the relationship with their students or with their supervisors, need to be explored within the supervisory relationship. The literature on multicultural supervision within counseling psychology further emphasizes that because of the power differential between supervisor and supervisee it is important for supervisors to initiate such conversations and let their supervisees know that cultural issues are a legitimate and important topic for supervision. Research by Mueller and Pope (2001) discovered that in those supervisory relationships where cultural issues were discussed, student affairs practitioners had a higher level of multicultural competence.

A student affairs practitioner is aware of the importance of understanding how cultural differences affect groups but is unsure how to address conflict between cultural groups on campus. A multiculturally competent professional works diligently to assess the true source of group conflict rather than assume that culture has nothing to do with the situation, or always assume that cultural differences are the problem.

One of the challenges of using culture as a lens for viewing and understanding the world is finding a balance in interpreting the cultural, universal, or individual influences on human behavior and relationships (Speight, Myers, Cox, & Highlen, 1991). In any given human interaction there exist universal similarities, such as emotional reactions or interpersonal needs; individual differences in personality and life experiences; and cultural differences in language, worldview, values, and communication style. There is often a tendency to let unchecked assumptions determine our assessment of a given interaction or interpersonal conflict. Too often we overinterpret or underinterpret the influence of universality, individual, or cultural differences. As student affairs educators in individual supervision, group advisement, or a classroom setting, it is our responsibility to gather the necessary information and clarify our assumptions before ascribing an interpretation to the behaviors we observe.

For example, an assistant director of a health center is responsible for training and supervising a twenty-person peer educator program. He expressed concern to two of the peer educators about their attendance patterns for group meetings on the basis of his perception of their behavior. He indicated that their late arrival and uneven attendance was disruptive to the group. The confronted students argued that their attendance was no different from that of any other peer educator; they were able to furnish sufficient examples to support their claim. This assistant director listened carefully to the students and in the end concurred with their assessment. He began to wonder whether his initial interpretation was influenced by the fact that the two students he confronted were the only peer educators of color.

Such behavior does not automatically presume intentional bias; rather, it may indicate unconscious stereotyping. To resolve this type of situation, a practitioner would need to address and resolve the cause of his misperception. One possible cause might be that in fact there was no attendance problem, but his perception existed because there were so few students of color working as peer educators. As such, the absences (or lateness) of the students of color were highlighted, giving the false impression that the students of color were often absent. Another possible interpretation might be that there is a difference in cultural values regarding the importance of attendance or arriving on time for a meeting. This type of discrepancy must be directly addressed and resolved.

Ongoing cross-cultural miscommunication could also cause an attendance problem. If, for example, a student was feeling ignored, slighted, embarrassed, or devalued at the meetings and based these feelings on perceived cultural insensitivity, absence could result. Finally, of course, it is always possible there really is an attendance problem that must be immediately addressed and rectified.

Summary

Administration and leadership, as key responsibilities for any student affairs professional, require complex, continuously changing, and flexible skills if one is to be a successful and effective administrator. Acquiring multicultural awareness, knowledge, and skills as an administrator is one of the current challenges within student affairs.

Given the lack of concrete strategies and tools available for incorporating multicultural issues, multicultural scholars have suggested the need for new approaches and ideas to create multicultural campus environments. One such model, multicultural organization development (MCOD), has been introduced into the student affairs profession as a means for organizing multicultural change efforts (Pope, 1993b). MCOD emphasizes the need for systemic and systematic change at all levels of an organization; several models for implementing an MCOD plan have been developed. Without a strategic plan, multicultural change efforts are likely to be uncoordinated, uneven, and unsuccessful.

Chapter Four

Multicultural Competence in Helping and Advising

I have been working in the multicultural affairs office on my campus for over ten years and have a good working relationship with many of my students. They are often hanging out in my office and talking with me about their lives. One Latino student in particular, Carlos, has spent a lot of time in my office although he doesn't disclose many details about his life. I have never thought much of it but one of my colleagues thinks he is gay and is trying to find the courage to tell me. That is definitely not my perception so I don't know what to do. Do I bring up the topic or wait for him to initiate? If it is true, how come I missed it? (African American female staff member in a multicultural affairs office)

I am a new student affairs professional working in the career counseling office at a major research university. Our office serves all students and lately I've noticed that working with some international students is very challenging. Some of them have very narrow goals about what they want to do, which often seems influenced by their family. They are determined to maintain those choices even if their skills and interests do not match. Other international students may want to make different choices, but they are completely conflicted about challenging the wishes of their family. I really don't know how to support them yet honor the realities of their family and culture. (White male counselor in a career counseling office)

I have worked in residence life for several years and enjoy being a hall director. I recently began a new position and am working with the resident assistant staff hired by my predecessor. One new resident assistant on my staff is bright, personable, and has a lot of enthusiasm. He also has cerebral palsy, which affects his mobility and communication. Although I like him and believe that he will probably be an excellent RA, I find myself a little uncomfortable when we interact. I am always aware of his disability and worry about how some of the residents will perceive and interact with him. I wonder if he has similar concerns, yet it feels disrespectful to raise the issue with him. I don't want him to think I don't believe in him. I've just had so little experience working with people with disabilities. (White female hall director)

Helping, advising, and counseling skills are essential tools for student affairs practitioners, whether they work in a counseling-oriented position such as career counseling or a leadership position such as in student life (Reynolds, 1995b). Since helping students is central to the history, goals, and responsibilities of student affairs work, developing related awareness, knowledge, and skills is an important aspect of the training and development of student affairs professionals. When describing core competencies needed for student affairs practitioners, many scholars include skills related to interpersonal communication and helping (Barr, 1993b; CAS, 1999; Komives & Woodard, 1996; Pope & Reynolds, 1997). Some of the basic helping and advising knowledge and skills needed to work effectively with students, staff, and faculty are microcounseling skills (active listening, empathy, reflection, nonverbal skills, paraphrasing), group skills (group dynamics, group process and leadership skills), conflict and crisis management, problem solving, confrontation, relationship building, consultation, mentoring, and supervision (Reynolds, 1995b).

Helping, counseling, and interpersonal skills assist in creating productive and meaningful relationships with students, staff, and faculty on campus. Although most student affairs professionals are not counselors and may not possess the skills, experience, or desire necessary to offer therapy to students, they often provide support and regularly help students with important life decisions. Whether student affairs professionals are prepared to be counselors or not, they still need to know how to respond to the real emotional and personal needs and concerns of students. Student affairs professionals are often visible on campus and may offer such fundamental support that students approach them with specific questions, problems, and concerns of a very personal, and sometimes quite serious, nature. In this type of situation, knowing how to provide support for a student in distress and refer the student to appropriate resources on campus is an example of a core counseling skill that every practitioner needs.

These basic helping skills are also foundational to the development of many other essential competencies within student affairs: teaching and training, leadership development, program development, assessment, and the array of individual and organizational interventions that student affairs practitioners implement daily. Addressing the interpersonal issues that often occur within training sessions, knowing how to challenge and support student leaders in their personal development, and empathically responding to students in distress are just a few examples of tasks that student affairs professionals regularly engage in that require a significant level of understanding and skill in working with others.

The purpose of this chapter is to examine the multicultural awareness, knowledge, and skills necessary for student affairs practitioners to be effective and ethical in their helping, counseling, and advising roles. This chapter addresses the core assumptions and underlying beliefs that have an impact on the helping, counseling, and advising that are central to student affairs. A definition of competency in helping and advising is also offered. Student affairs professionals need helping and interpersonal skills that are relevant and useful for working with students and colleagues (individuals or groups) who have been historically underserved and underrepresented in higher education. Examples of not addressing multicultural issues or assumptions in interpersonal and helping interactions are shared. There is also a brief critique of how helping and counseling have historically excluded multicultural issues and knowledge; the impact of these omissions on student affairs is discussed. Finally, multicultural competence in helping and interpersonal skills is redefined, and strategies for developing such awareness, knowledge, and skills are explored.

Helping and Advising in Student Affairs

Helping interactions and skills are foundational to student affairs work. Although most student affairs professionals are not counselors, all have the opportunity to work with students or colleagues in a way that can assist or support their growth and development. Whether a student affairs professional provides therapy or not, it is still possible to be therapeutic in her or his efforts or interventions. A therapeutic climate is one in which self-exploration and growth is encouraged and a positive and affirming relationship is developed. Sanford (1967), Blocher (1978), and others have explored a key principle of therapeutic helping within a student affairs context in their discussions of the importance of balancing the amount of challenge and support in our interactions with students. If given too much support, students may be tempted to quit trying or possibly take advantage of such support. If challenged too much, students may feel overwhelmed and worried about their ability to succeed, and they may not try their best. A proper balance of challenge and support ensures that students are challenged to do their best, yet feel supported enough to make mistakes. According to Evans, Forney, and Guido-DiBrito, "the range of optimal dissonance for any particular person varies, depending on the quality of the challenge and support that the environment provides as well as the characteristics of the individual" (1998, p. 26). Rodgers (1991) conceptualized this challenge and support balance as a person-environment interaction that is central to learning and development. Such balanced and developmental interventions are possible in every student affairs area, whether it be judicial affairs, student government advisement, residence hall programming, career counseling and placement, or another fundamental area of student affairs work.

Counseling theories and interventions, as typically described in the counseling literature, have more of a clinical focus than may be useful or meaningful in typical interactions with students. However, all helping interactions, regardless of the theory in which they are based, share certain assumptions about individuals and helping. These assumptions are grounded in counseling ethics and beliefs about how individuals change and grow.

One of the central assumptions about helping stems from the ethical command of "do no harm," which means that counselors or helpers must assist others in a way that does not allow harm to continue or create further harm (either psychological or physical). To do no harm, counselors or helpers need to understand the difficulties and issues that clients experience and then assist clients in discovering new and more effective ways to address their concerns. When necessary or appropriate, helpers must know their limits in helping others and consult or refer as the situation requires.

In addition to the ethical mandate to do no harm, several other core beliefs or assumptions are acknowledged across the diverse theoretical perspectives and worldviews within counseling. These core beliefs are also relevant to any helping relationship found within the student affairs profession. First, empathy, or "seeing the world through another's eyes, hearing as they might hear, and feeling and experiencing their internal world" (Ivey, D'Andrea, Ivey, & Simek-Morgan, 2002, p. 28), is essential to building an effective helping relationship. Good communication skills, such as active listening, empathy, attending behaviors, and asking open-ended questions, build the foundation for helpful interactions. In addition, the helping relationship itself is one of the primary tools for assisting others with their problems or concerns. Building a collaborative relationship where there is trust and respect heightens the opportunity for successful interactions and interventions. According to Okun (1997), developing trust is fundamental to the creation of a successful and meaningful working relationship. Creating a significant interpersonal connection is a core aspect of helping competence, whether a student affairs professional is helping a student through a personal crisis or assisting a student in making an important academic or career decision.

Helping competence involves the attitudes, knowledge, and skills essential to working with and helping others with their concerns, issues, and problems, individually or in a group. These competencies include, but are not limited to, communication and microcounseling skills, conflict and crisis management, problem solving, empathy and positive regard, self-awareness, ethical integrity, knowledge of related theories (such as those in student development), and building effective relationships. Historically, the counseling and helping profession was not prepared to meet the needs of a diverse clientele, and the assumption of universality or the need to treat all people the same was a prevalent belief among most helpers (Pedersen, 1987; Sue & Sue, 1999). Such universality was also present in counseling theories and practices, and it was believed that if the dignity of human beings were embraced and their individual concerns and issues were addressed, then there would be no need for cultural distinctions. There are still some within the counseling profession who believe that universality and attention to individual differences is far more effective and important than attention to multicultural counseling and competence (Patterson, 1996). The presumption of universality or "one theory fits all" has also been an issue within the student affairs profession as concerns over the relevance and meaningfulness of certain student development theories and constructs have been expressed in the past two decades (Evans, Forney, & Guido-DiBrito, 1998; Fried, 1995; Pope & Reynolds, 1997).

Scholars increasingly believe that if theory and practice do not incorporate cultural differences, the important worldviews, values, and realities of many individuals are minimized, ignored, or viewed as irrelevant. Since individuals from diverse cultural, religious, class, and gender background and life experiences may view the world distinctively and act in varying ways, theory and practice must make meaning of those differences and approach those individuals in unique and meaningful ways. Understanding the diverse experiences of others can create insight, empathy, and openness to others who are culturally different. Without such multicultural awareness and knowledge, helpers may make negative assumptions, draw inappropriate conclusions, and ultimately base their interventions on faulty assumptions or negative beliefs. If in their interactions, for example, student affairs practitioners assume all students are heterosexual, they may alienate LGBT students or make them less likely to seek out practitioners for assistance. If they have limited understanding of the role of family in the lives of many Latinos, the centrality of faith among many African Americans, or the significance of community for many Native American students, student affairs practitioners will be ill prepared to address the needs of students of color. Multicultural competence in a helping context is essential to affirming, effective, and ethical work in student affairs (Reynolds, 1995b). To become multiculturally competent, student affairs professionals must learn about the specific multicultural counseling or helping awareness, knowledge, and skills necessary to do their job.

Multicultural Counseling Competence

Multicultural counseling competence—the ability to provide effective, relevant, and meaningful counseling services to clients from diverse backgrounds—did not become a mainstream construct until the 1990s (Sue & Sue, 1999). Some groups, such as people of color, have historically been underserved or had a higher attrition rate within counseling (Jackson, 1995; Sue et al., 1982; Sue & Sue, 1999). Within higher education, similar concerns have been expressed about the ability of student affairs professionals to effectively meet the needs of such diverse student groups as students of color or lesbian, gay, and bisexual students (Cheatham, 1991; Evans & Wall, 1991; Katz, 1989; Woolbright, 1989; Wright, 1987). Significant progress has been made in the multicultural training and education of counselors and student affairs practitioners in the past ten years, but many continue to have limited experience and ability to work effectively with others who are culturally different from them across any number of variables (race, ethnicity, social class, sexual orientation, religion, nationality).

Multicultural competence has become a significant force in the field of counseling (Sue, Bingham, Porche-Burke, & Vasquez, 1999). However, according to Reynolds and Pope (2003), despite its increasing relevance there continues to be no unifying definition or theory of multicultural competence. Sue (2001) offered a conceptual framework to clarify, integrate, and enhance our understanding of multicultural competence. The construct of multicultural counseling competence has evolved and changed significantly since first introduced as a tripartite model of awareness, knowledge, and skills by Sue and colleagues (1982). The earliest writings built the case for multicultural competence and urged the helping profession to move from having a few multicultural experts to making all professionals competent to work with all clients. Research studies, models, and assessment tools focused on multicultural counseling competence have been developed to further enrich this essential area of study. There has been growing emphasis on the definition or specification of what constitutes multicultural counseling competence.

Several multicultural scholars have expressed concern over the traditional definitions of multicultural counseling and have argued for redefinition of this key construct. S. Sue and Zane (1987) suggested that counselors focus less on culture-specific knowledge or techniques and more on developing meaningful relationships through building credibility, relieving symptoms, and instilling hope. Their belief was that forming effective relationships is as essential and powerful as having culture-specific information and creates an openness that is necessary for change to occur. Speight, Myers, Cox, and Highlen (1991) called for a reconceptualization of the definition of multicultural counseling by emphasizing self-knowledge, worldview, and other core concepts rather than overemphasizing either culturally distinct or universal conceptualizations of human behavior.

S. Sue (1998) also suggested a more unifying and global conceptualization for multicultural competence. Sue believed that it was important to identify the general counseling skills necessary in building cultural sensitivity and competence. He suggested several characteristics that included both general and culture-specific counseling skills. One characteristic, scientific-mindedness, is the ability to form a hypothesis and educated opinions rather than merely relying on assumptions about clients. This skill requires access to information, openness to new ideas, and creativity, which are essential in developing a meaningful and relevant understanding of clients' concerns and worldview. Dynamic sizing is another factor, which Sue defined as "knowing when to generalize and be inclusive and when to individualize and be exclusive" (p. 446). Such flexibility is essential in preventing stereotyping, which can occur any time helpers are trying to determine what group characteristics or concerns might apply to a given individual. Speight and colleagues (1991) explored the need to expand our thinking beyond dichotomous or either-or reasoning. Reynolds (2001b) further suggested that this complex and contextual reasoning was essential for determining the degree to which individual and cultural factors were influencing people and their interactions.

Expanding, revising, and redefining our understanding of multicultural competence have been the keys to its evolution as a core construct within the counseling literature (Reynolds & Pope, 2003). In one of the most recent reconceptualizations of multicultural competence, Sue (2001) offered an expansion of multicultural competence in his Multidimensional Model of Cultural Competence

(MDCC). His dynamic model suggested some important ways to expand and enhance our definition of multicultural competence and how to create multicultural change in individuals, organizations, institutions, and society (Reynolds, 2001b). Specifically, Sue recommended that cultural competence move beyond individual awareness, knowledge, and skills and incorporate the helping professions, institutions, and society by challenging the underlying values, policies, and structures of those systems. Sue suggested that advocacy needed to be a central component of multicultural competency: "Multicultural counseling competence must be about social justice—providing equal access and opportunity, being inclusive, and removing individual and systemic barriers" (2001, p. 16). In his conceptualization, individuals are not multiculturally competent unless they invest in changing institutional structures, professional core values and practices, and societal assumptions and systems. In other words, unless we attempt to make society and social institutions less biased and more affirming, we are not fully contributing to the well-being of those we are attempting to serve. Recently, Vera and Speight (2003) not only emphasized the necessity of including a commitment to social justice within multicultural competence but also offered a social justice agenda and explored how to incorporate this perspective into research, teaching, and practice.

Scholars of multicultural counseling increasingly argue that it is not enough for practitioners to simply expand their counseling skills so they can better meet the needs of others who are culturally different from them (Grieger & Toliver, 2001; Lee, 1998; Parham, 1999; Sue, 2001). These competencies need to include developing the skills to advocate within our institutions and the profession to develop new and more inclusive theories, practices, and organizational systems (Reynolds & Pope, 2003). Our efforts to become multiculturally competent as professionals need to extend to assisting our institutions in becoming more multiculturally sensitive and incorporating multicultural values at all levels of the institution. This conceptualization fits well with the work on multicultural organization development and institutional change in higher education by Pope (1993a, 1993b) and others (Grieger, 1996; Grieger & Toliver, 2001; Katz, 1989; Manning & Coleman-Boatwright, 1991).

Multicultural Competence in Helping and Advising

According to Reynolds and Pope (2003), "exploring and understanding the dynamic and growing multicultural competence literature is an important first step when applying these philosophies, models, and strategies" (p. 369). Through comprehending the diverse and complex definitions and conceptualizations of multicultural competence, specifically in a helping relationship, student affairs professionals are better equipped to apply their understanding to actual situations and challenges where multicultural awareness, knowledge, and skills are needed.

Although multicultural scholars have specified many multicultural counseling competencies and suggested how to apply and implement these skills (Arredondo et al., 1996; Hansen, Pepitone-Arreola-Rockwell, & Greene, 2000; Sue, Arredondo, & McDavis, 1992; Sue et al., 1998), there have been few efforts to integrate these multicultural helping skills into a student affairs context. Reynolds (1995b, 1999) proposed six specific multicultural competencies for those in helping roles within education. Reynolds and Pope (2003) expanded this list of specific multicultural competencies to include advocacy skills as well as use of multicultural organization development tools and theories as a necessary helping skill. As discussed previously regarding work on the expansion of multicultural competence by Sue (2001) and others, multicultural organization development, advocacy, and activism may be the skills and tasks that student affairs professionals need to address core barriers to multiculturalism on their campuses (Reynolds & Pope, 2003). If these barriers inhibit the ability of students to grow and develop, it would seem that student affairs professionals have an ethical responsibility to assist in the multicultural transformation of their campus.

These are the seven multicultural competencies suggested by Reynolds and Pope:

1. Acquiring appreciation, knowledge, and understanding of cultural groups, especially those individuals and communities that have been historically underserved or underrepresented
2. Increasing content knowledge about important culturally related terms and concepts such as racial identity, acculturation, or worldview

3. Enhancing awareness of one's own biases and cultural assumptions, and assessing one's own multicultural skills and comfort level
4. Developing the ability to use that knowledge and self-awareness to make more culturally sensitive and appropriate interventions
5. Developing an awareness of the interpersonal dynamics that may occur within a multicultural dyad
6. Deconstructing the cultural assumptions underlying the counseling process
7. Applying advocacy skills to assist in the development of a more multiculturally sensitive and affirming campus

These seven multicultural competencies are essential to effective, ethical, appropriate, and meaningful working relationships with students, staff, and faculty in higher education. To more fully understand these competencies, each is explored here and applied to diverse student affairs settings, roles, and responsibilities. A complex and dynamic understanding of multicultural helping and counseling is developed through application of these seven competencies within student affairs.

Self-Awareness

Being aware of one's own biases, assumptions, worldview, and areas of discomfort is a necessary step in developing culturally sensitive and affirming helping skills. Our experiences shape our impressions and expectations of others; it is almost impossible to avoid being exposed to stereotypes about various cultural groups. The important task is to acknowledge any biased information we have learned and strive to unlearn it. This commitment requires putting ourselves in unfamiliar and uncomfortable situations so we can learn firsthand about our biases, misinformation, and comfort zones.

Learning how to assess our own multicultural skills and comfort level is an important foundation for self-awareness. Many who work in the helping professions assume they are able to work effectively with everyone, but this may not reflect the reality of their abilities and knowledge. Unless we are willing to ask the difficult questions about the individuals or groups we know the least about or find the most challenging, we will never develop the essential skills and awareness to be effective in our work. In addition to examining our interactions with others, it is helpful to ask others for feedback about our multicultural helping skills. According to Reynolds (1995b), "this honest self-reflection and appraisal will allow counselors and advisors to seek out the training or supervision they need to become more multiculturally sensitive" (p. 165). An example of the type of self-questioning that must occur is for helpers and counselors to ask themselves how multicultural their own life is. In other words, how diverse are their friends, neighborhood, and activities? Are most of their friends and social activities centered in the cultural frameworks they know best, or do they regularly expose themselves to individuals and cultures that are new and unfamiliar?

If a career counselor is working with a student who has a significant learning disability and wants to major in premed, and the counselor attempts to steer her away from that field (even if it is meant to protect the student from a demanding curriculum), the bias may negatively affect their working relationship as well as the student's future dreams and plans. If the director of student activities who is working with student groups assumes that students are heterosexual unless they happened to belong to the Lesbian, Gay, Bisexual, and Transgender Association, she or he misses opportunities to assist in the growth and identity development of many LGBT students who are part of other student groups and are not yet comfortable being openly lesbian, gay, bisexual, or transgendered.

Knowledge and Understanding of Cultural Groups

Specific information about the history, traditions, beliefs, resources, strengths, and issues of various cultural groups is a necessary prerequisite to understanding their concerns, meeting their needs, and forming effective relationships. Having some awareness increases a helper's ability to have empathy for the experiences, feelings, and concerns of these diverse cultural groups. If specific information is lacking, it is easy to assume that individuals from other cultural groups have beliefs, experiences, and culture that are similar. Likewise, unless there is adequate understanding of group differences as well as the individual variations that occur within a given cultural group, it is tempting to presume universality among group members and stereotype them by treating them all alike. Having some general knowledge about cultural differences and a firm commitment to be careful in applying information about a cultural group to a specific individual is a critical step in building an effective relationship with someone who may be culturally different. For example, understanding how some Native Americans incorporate indigenous religious practices into their daily lives may assist one in helping a Native American student use those resources to address her concerns.

An important aspect of assisting individuals from various cultural groups is learning about their experiences in higher education and at their campus in particular. By knowing the history of various cultural groups within the educational system, it is possible to gain insight about their approach and expectations of their college experience. For example, because historically African Americans were segregated into a separate, and sometimes inferior, higher education system, their efforts have often focused on attaining equal access within higher education. Conversely, primary schools were used to forcibly assimilate Native Americans into the White culture and take them away from their families and their native culture; surely this has affected their trust and desire to engage in higher education. Understanding history and experience of this sort may clarify and enhance the complexity of our worldview as well as our perceptions of the various cultural groups.

Using another illustration, if a Native American student at a predominantly White college who is being honored for her academic achievement tells her EOP advisor about her difficulty in being able to attend the campuswide ceremony, the advisor needs to know enough about Native American culture to understand what cultural influences may be affecting the student. If she knows that many Native American cultures focus primarily on the community rather than the individual, thus making public acknowledgment of individual achievement somewhat uncomfortable for some Native Americans, the advisor is better able to understand the student's struggle and offer appropriate and meaningful support. Without the necessary knowledge to conceptualize students' issues in a culturally inclusive and affirming manner, helpers may not be able to effectively assist students.

Knowledge About Cultural Concepts

There are some important cultural concepts that influence how individuals view themselves and interact with others. Knowing about acculturation and identity development is as important as understanding the cultural group differences that may occur. Research has shown that membership in a particular cultural group is not as significant as how individuals feel about their own cultural group and what cultural beliefs and practices they have internalized. These concepts are particularly helpful in understanding within-group differences that affect how individuals feel about themselves and relate to members of their own cultural group.

Imagine a residence hall director who is trying to build community within a residence hall that has a significant students of color population. He may notice there is ongoing tension and sometimes conflict between the African American students from the city and the African American students who grew up in other parts of the state. If he is surprised by this difference and unsure how to address the tension, it may be that he lacks knowledge about how their life experiences have affected their view of their race and identity. If a staff member in the Office for Students with Disabilities is having difficulty relating to some students with disabilities because their view of living with a disability is different from hers, she may need to further examine the identity development literature and be open to exploring her own identity and its influence on her identity and relationships with others. Knowledge of these key cultural concepts is essential to comprehending the complexity of culture and its effect on the helping relationships.

Culturally Responsive Interventions

Being exposed to cultural knowledge and developing self-awareness is a necessary but insufficient approach to developing multicultural competence in helping and counseling others. Learning how to use that knowledge and awareness to be more responsive in one's interventions and efforts is just as necessary. This means having enough self-awareness to know when miscommunication is occurring or when one's assumptions are interfering with the counseling or helping process. A central component in helping across cultures is the ability to assess and adapt one's intervention as it is occurring so that problems can be addressed along the way. This may require seeking outside consultation or peer supervision to assist in helping students deal with their personal issues. Sometimes using a cultural broker or individual from a student's community who can help mediate a cultural or family system is necessary to resolve an ongoing issue.

For example, if a Latina first-year student who is on full scholarship from another state is not doing well academically and struggling with feeling homesick and fitting in with other students, she may need additional community support and resources. In addition to assisting her academically, it may be crucial to talk with her about her family and how she is coping with the long distance. Rather than assuming that she is experiencing the typical developmental process of individuation and becoming independent, it is vital to realize that her reality as a Latina student may be different and require alternative approaches or interventions. Or consider how to design a leadership training workshop for the residence hall association in a hall housing many international students, without an understanding that students from different cultures may view government or leadership quite differently from how students from the United States do. If a helper or advisor does not comprehend the complexity of those diverse experiences and expectations and how they may affect student leadership, it will be difficult for her to be an effective advisor and create a meaningful and productive training program. Rather than using leadership training designs from other campuses, it might be helpful to find alternative resources that address cultural issues or create a new training model that can explore unique campus issues.

Dynamics of a Multicultural Dyad

To be an effective helper, it is important to develop an awareness of the significance of the interpersonal process and dynamics that occur when working with someone who is culturally different from us. As stated by Reynolds (1995b), "cultural differences can have a profound effect on the communication and relationship development process"

(p. 165). It means moving beyond the content of the interaction (what is being said) to the process or interpersonal dynamic that is occurring. An essential interpersonal and helping skill is the ability to track and assess the communication process to ensure that individuals are being understood and that they comprehend what others are saying. This means being able to read nonverbal cues and believing that what is not being said is as important as what is spoken.

If student affairs professionals do not appreciate how students from cultures or countries other than their own may communicate differently—how they deal with physical space, eye contact, social greetings, and the like—they may misinterpret the students' behaviors or make assumptions about how the students are interpreting their communication or relationship. Being able to read tension or discomfort, or assess whether complying with specific expectations is genuine or forced, can be helpful in working with others who are culturally different. Building effective relationships is highly influenced by the credibility process described by S. Sue and Zane (1987). Credibility is developed when the helper demonstrates cultural knowledge and sensitivity and doesn't appear to view or treat everyone the same.

The key to building affirming relationships with others who are culturally different from us is being able to look for similarities and differences simultaneously. According to Reynolds: "Multiculturalism is about understanding ourselves and others who are different from us. To me, multiculturalism is, at its core, about people and relationships. And all relationships are about discovering our commonalities, our cultural differences, and our personal uniquenesses. Balancing those three aspects of all human interactions is often confusing, frustrating, and scary" (2001a, p. 111).

Cultural Assumptions Underlying the Helping Process

There are cultural assumptions imbedded in all that we do, from what we view as normal to how we speak and relate to others. So often we assume that we believe and see the world just as others do, until we enter a situation or relationship where cultural differences become apparent. We bring our worldview or paradigm into every interaction without reflecting on the hidden and influential assumptions that shape so much of what we think and do (Fried, 1995; Katz, 1985; Minnich, 1990).

Likewise, in the counseling and helping process there are many values and beliefs that shape the questions we ask, how we view the people we are trying to help, and which viable solutions can help them address their concerns. Historically, the values of counseling or helping as traditionally defined are based on the White middle-class culture. According to Reynolds (1999), "deconstructing those underlying and often hidden values is vital before one can make counseling more accessible and relevant to some people of color and other individuals who may not subscribe to White middle-class values" (p. 222). For example, the process of helping implies a formal relationship that abides by certain rules, such as where helping can occur and what type of contact the helping should include. In a typical helping relationship, individuals meet within an office during a set time, the relationship is not meant to be mutually beneficial, and the helper is supposed to be an expert who is somewhat detached from the people he is trying to help. This model of helping may be quite unfamiliar to individuals from cultures or family systems that encourage support primarily or only from family, friends, and community or religious leaders.

Taking time to examine the underlying beliefs of the helping relationship is essential in being able to effectively help all individuals. This means exploring what we do as well as how and why we do it that way. Rather than assume how we have defined our helping role is comfortable for every student, it is more important to assess and evaluate our helping efforts and be willing to redesign our interactions and relationships. Rather than only having formal office hours as a residence hall director, it might be more effective to spend time in the public spaces of the residence hall or in the dining hall with students. Instead of assuming all students go through a similar individuation process that helps them separate from their family and become adults, it is vital to get to know each individual and see what effect life experiences and cultural background have had on that person. Understanding the unique worldviews of students and being clear about how the helping process makes certain assumptions about growth and change is important because the awareness creates opportunity for better relationships.

Advocacy Skills

Advocacy and activism on the individual and organizational levels are crucial skills that student affairs professionals need if they are to contribute to or initiate a multicultural change process on campus (Reynolds & Pope, 2003). It is not enough to help individual students deal with their concerns or to address barriers to multiculturalism individually. Redefining multicultural competence to include advocacy reinforces the notion that multicultural issues are everyone's responsibility rather than the job requirement of a few individuals. Although helping typically focuses on a one-to-one relationship, if the campus system creates barriers (internal or external) that interfere with students' ability to succeed, then it seems appropriate to advocate for change within the system. This type of advocacy entails working openly with various campus offices and constituency groups to build a more culturally sensitive and affirming environment.

Creating effective collaboration means rethinking one's tasks and responsibilities and learning how to work cooperatively with other offices and staff members on campus. Rather than addressing only individual student concerns, it might be helpful to consult with other professionals and ask if they notice other students having similar concerns. For example, if the director of student activities notices that Muslim and Jewish students seem to be lacking a voice on campus, she might want to reach out to other student affairs offices on campus and come up with a strategy for addressing the concern. If students of color who live in a residence hall complain that there are no meaningful student activities on the weekend, then maybe staff members need to advocate on their behalf across campus to ensure that their voices are being heard.

The seven multicultural competencies highlighted in this chapter do more than yield insight into how to work more effectively with students who are culturally different; they offer a new paradigm for forming meaningful, responsive, and effective relationships with students. Assessing and understanding how cultural similarities and differences affect all helping relationships is the key to multicultural competence. It is important to acknowledge there is no such thing as "generic" helping or counseling skills, and there are cultural issues (race, social class, gender, age, sexual orientation) that influence every helping relationship.

Developing multicultural competence is a developmental process that is ongoing and challenging. According to Reynolds (1995b): "Like any other competency or skill, developing multicultural sensitivity and skills requires intentional effort and practice. Developing critical consciousness or self-awareness through praxis (action and reflection) is necessary for counselors and advisors to change themselves and the world around them" (p. 167). Applied examples of what type of multicultural competency is necessary for student affairs professionals offer opportunities for practitioners to assess their own practices and try new strategies and approaches when working in helping relationships with students.

Exemplary Multicultural Competence in HELPING AND ADVISING

The specific exemplary practices discussed here are not meant to be an inclusive or exhaustive list; rather, they suggest some important multicultural awareness, knowledge, and skills necessary for helping students. By exploring these exemplary practices, there is increased opportunity to create a more complex, concrete, and meaningful understanding of multicultural competence.

A student affairs professional begins to realize that some of her miscommunications with students and colleagues are being influenced by cultural differences. A multiculturally sensitive professional learns more about how communication style and points of view may be influenced by cultural upbringing and life experiences.

Unless we understand how specifically culture influences communication, we may be unable to effectively communicate with others who are culturally different from us. So much of what we say, how we say it, and the meaning we take from others' communication is influenced by our culture and upbringing. We may develop assumptions and stereotypes about communication that cause us to misinterpret others' words or intentions. We need to understand that nonverbal communication—eye contact, touch, voice, gestures, physical space from others—is influenced by cultural beliefs and patterns. Verbal components such as formality of language or how directly or indirectly a person communicates are important because they affect how people present themselves and are perceived by others. Receiving additional training, reading appropriate books, and observing how others interact are all ways to address these issues and improve the effectiveness of our communication.

A student affairs professional recognizes that most of his relationships are with people who are culturally similar and that he sometimes feels uncomfortable forming relationships with others who are different from him. A multiculturally sensitive professional actively seeks out these relationships and learns how to build genuine and meaningful relationships with others who are culturally different by taking risks and being willing to make mistakes.

There is nothing like practice to enhance our communication skills, especially when there are opportunities for feedback and learning. Relationships require people to take risks, communicate outside their comfort zone, and find areas of commonality with people who seem quite different. Through those experiences, we can learn how to read the cues of others and deal more openly and effectively with cross-cultural conflict. Withholding judgment and not making assumptions are two central keys to forming positive working relationships with those who are culturally different.

A student affairs professional recognizes that she needs more experience working with and advising diverse student groups. These opportunities are often challenging, but they give her the opportunity to extend her group skills and learn how to work more effectively with student groups whose culture and life experiences may be entirely unlike hers.

Knowing how culture affects group dynamics and communication is essential for any student affairs professional. Whether working with student organizations, paraprofessional staffs, or professional staff groups, the professional should recognize that cultural differences can have an impact on how a group deals with conflict and emotion or works together. It is important to have knowledge about group differences and how they might affect communication, conflict, and other group processes. As was addressed previously, some cultural groups are more open and expressive with their ideas and emotions than others that may be more reserved or quiet. It is also important not to automatically assume that cultural differences within a group are the source of any conflict or concerns. One of the most challenging aspects of advising or supervising groups is being able to discern the true source of interpersonal problems within a group and develop an appropriate strategy to build cohesion and effective communication. Offering effective training to student groups that addresses group dynamics and cultural issues is essential to building meaningful collaboration. Such training can yield common experiences and language that can be used throughout the year to strengthen the group.

A student affairs professional is worried that her lack of experience in dealing with various cultural groups affects her ability to deal with them in intense situations such as personal crisis or interpersonal conflict. She fears she is less able to effectively discern what is going on and is unsure how to deal with the emotion in a genuinely supportive manner. A multiculturally sensitive professional learns how to address the emotions of others even when expressed in a way that is different from her preferred mode of expression.

Communicating in intense situations is challenging even for the seasoned professional because it is difficult to know how to address others' emotions effectively and helpfully. Expanding our understanding of how other cultural groups deal with conflict, death and loss, shame, and other complicated emotions and beliefs is essential to meeting the needs of students. Even knowing that not all cultural groups and individuals within them deal with such situations in the same way is a good first step. It is difficult for many individuals, from a variety of cultural groups, to reach out to others they do not know well when they are in crisis. For others, there are cultural beliefs about the inappropriateness of sharing one's problems and conflicts with individuals outside the family or culture. Being sensitive enough to read social and communication cues and not assume that what is presented is necessarily the full story helps the professional be better equipped to support students in need.

A student affairs professional understands that his supervisory relationships vary with the type of people involved. He is concerned that he acts differently with those supervisees who are culturally different from him. A multiculturally sensitive professional learns how to apply what he knows about building effective cross-cultural relationships in a supervisory context.

Supervision and mentoring are extremely important and powerful tools that offer colleagues and graduate students the chance to learn about multicultural competence. These skills might be viewed as part of administrative and management competencies; however, they also are centered in communication and helping skills. Effective multicultural supervision and mentoring can offer the professional concrete opportunities to more fully explore and experience multicultural issues. These relationships can potentially play a significant role in integrating multicultural issues into an individual's personal and professional identities (Reynolds, forthcoming). Through examination of actual work experiences and concerns, professionals can learn effective ways of addressing multicultural issues meaningfully and productively that extend what they learn in graduate programs, workshops, or other professional education. By mentoring and supervising others on multicultural issues, we are forced to extend our ability to teach others and build our own confidence and competence.

Summary

Creating an effective repertoire of culturally sensitive helping, advising, and counseling skills is a necessary component of becoming a multiculturally competent professional. These helping skills are used daily and create the foundation for many other competencies. Developing helping skills that can be used effectively across cultures requires that student affairs professionals be committed to exploring and understanding themselves and others. Seeking out additional training and diverse work experiences is vital to building the knowledge base and on-the-job training that creates open-minded, self-reflective, and flexible helpers in student affairs.

Culture affects so much of who we are, how we view the world, and how we relate to others that it is difficult to imagine how it is not centrally tied into all helping interactions. Understanding how culture affects the helping process and how to be sensitive to cultural differences in interpersonal interactions is a competency best developed through training and work experience. This chapter has described the types of specific awareness, knowledge, and skills that are necessary to integrate multiculturalism into the helping and advising competency; it has offered effective practice examples so professionals will have a more applied understanding of helping and advising multicultural competencies.

Chapter Five

Multicultural Competence in Assessment and Research

We've had a Safe Zone program on our campus for three years now, and we need to assess its effectiveness in order to apply for funding to continue the program. I know that the overall goal of the assessment is to measure its effectiveness; I'm just not sure who to ask and what to ask. I've shared a few sample items with some of the students from our campus LGBT group, and they seemed perplexed at best and offended at worst by some of the questions I drafted. I know how important this program has been to visibility and generating support, and I want to see it continue successfully. This assessment project is key to that success, but I don't know if I'm going about it correctly. (Residence hall director, Safe Zone member, and heterosexual ally to the LGBT community)

Over the past ten years, we've had a dramatic increase in the number of Asian American students on our campus. We've noticed, however, that like the other students of color they rarely make use of our office. When we conducted a study last year, we developed a questionnaire designed especially to measure their career needs, and only had a return rate of 7 percent. We plan to do this again this year, and maybe we'll include some incentive with the mailing, but I'll be so disappointed if our participation rate is as low as it was last year. (White staff member of a campus exploration center)

I've been on this campus for three years now, and each year I become more and more aware of how inaccessible our entire campus is. This becomes especially obvious to me when we have students with disabilities participating in summer orientation. At the end of last summer, I was determined to do something about this. Another year has gone by, and I still haven't done anything. I believe a good place to start would be to find out more from the students themselves how they experience this campus and how they believe the campus can be more accessible. Should I write a survey? Conduct a focus group? I just don't know where and how to start. And I'm a little uncomfortable approaching any of the students to get their advice on where to begin. (White male assistant director of new student orientation)

It has already been established that the changing demographics on college campuses require student affairs practitioners to be prepared to work in a multicultural environment (Ebbers & Henry, 1990; Pope & Reynolds, 1997). The core of this preparation is developing an understanding of the diversity of students as well as how to design programs and policies that respond to that diversity (Brown, 1991; McEwen & Roper, 1994b; Talbot, 1992). Research and assessment are critical to this understanding and knowledge. McEwen and Roper (1994a) suggest that it is the ethical responsibility of those who prepare student affairs practitioners to include the study of research and evaluation emphasizing culturally sensitive research techniques and instrument designs. Once in the profession, and as consumers of research, student affairs practitioners are well positioned to guide research that answers difficult questions about the diversity of college students, how they experience the campus, and how campuses can foster learning and student development (Stage, 1992b). Specifically, Upcraft and Schuh (1996) argue that issues of access and equity raise a number of important questions best answered and understood by competent assessment.

The purpose of this chapter is to discuss how multicultural awareness, knowledge, and skills can be infused into student affairs assessment and research. Definitions, as well as the distinctions and commonalities among the practices of assessment and research, are offered. Since these practices share many fundamental techniques, infusing multicultural sensitivity into those techniques is discussed, particularly self-awareness and assumptions of the research, defining a population, issues related to selecting measures, and data collection considerations. This chapter also addresses the benefit of using qualitative methodologies in multicultural research.

Assessment and Research in Student Affairs

Within the student affairs profession, a great deal of assessment and research is occurring. Much of this research is being done by faculty in student affairs preparation programs. Some of it is by students in the form of master's theses and doctoral dissertations; other research is being conducted by professionals in student affairs research offices as well as by individuals within specific student affairs departments (Malaney, 1999). Perhaps because of the range of people engaged in these activities, there is a lack of consensus about the distinctions among research, assessment, and evaluation. It is beneficial, then, for any discussion on assessment, evaluation, and research to first define each term in relation to the others.

Upcraft and Schuh (1996) present useful and functional definitions for each of these terms. *Assessment* in higher education involves the collection, analysis, and interpretation of data used to describe the effectiveness of an institution or an individual department or division within a given institution. Upcraft and Schuh's definition of assessment does not include measuring an individual student or client for the purposes of counseling or individual treatment. Instead, assessment in student affairs considers the students, clients, or any constituency in the aggregate. Practitioners interested in individual client assessment that considers multicultural issues are urged to explore the counseling psychology literature (see, for example, Dana, 2000; Ibrahim & Kahn, 1987; Suzuki & Kugler, 1995; Suzuki, Ponterotto, & Meller, 2000).

Assessment is used largely for the purposes of determining effectiveness; *evaluation* is the application of assessment data to improve the effectiveness of an institution, department, division, program, or intervention (Upcraft & Schuh, 1996). Evaluation may occur as a program is developing so as to monitor and improve it, or at the conclusion of a program to judge its overall quality or worth (Madaus, Scriven, & Stufflebeam, 1983). In either case, evaluation is designed for the practical purpose of decision making, either during or after implementation of a program or policy.

Upcraft and Schuh (1996) also discuss the definition of *research* in relation to assessment, referring to the work of Erwin (1991), who proposed two differences between assessment and research: (1) assessment is used to guide practice, while research is used to guide theory; and (2) assessment is often focused on individual campuses, while research can have implications for student affairs and higher education on a larger scale. Consequently, research may be viewed as the collection and interpretation of data for the purpose of developing, testing, or enhancing theory for the eventual objective of informing practice.

Another useful conceptualization of educational research, assessment, and evaluation is offered by Gay and Airasian (2000). These authors suggest that all of these activities can be viewed on a continuum, from basic research to evaluation research. The methods of data collection and interpretation along the continuum do not necessarily distinguish the forms of research from one another; instead, the key differences lie in the purpose, applicability, and generalizability of the forms of research. On one end of the continuum lies basic research, which seeks to develop new theories or refine existing ones. It is concerned with understanding *why* something is happening. Its applicability is limited, but generalizability is broad. Further along the continuum, applied research concerns itself with testing theory for veracity in addressing educational problems. It considers the *what* of educational problems. What works best in a given situation? This type of research tends to be applicable to educational problems, but since it is usually done on a specific campus generalizability is limited. Evaluation research, argue Gay and Airasian, is at the far end of the continuum, since it is the most practical and applicable, and the least generalizable, form of research. Evaluation research, in this conceptualization, parallels Upcraft and Schuh's notion (1996) that evaluation is use of data to enhance the effectiveness of a specific educational practice to determine whether it should be altered or continued.

In sum, research informs theory, while assessment (and the related activity of evaluation) guides practice. There are distinctions among these activities, but they do lie on a continuum, pursuing similar objectives and sharing comparable approaches. With this in mind, we regard research and assessment as discrete yet overlapping terms and treat them as such in this chapter.

Multicultural Competence in Assessment and Research

This examination of assessment and research in student affairs considers the range of research activities in light of five areas that have been identified (McEwen & Roper, 1994a; Wilkinson & McNeil, 1996) as requisite for becoming a multiculturally competent researcher:

1. Awareness of assumptions that influence the research process
2. Issues in defining the populations of interest
3. Appropriateness of measurement instruments
4. Data collection techniques
5. Alternate research approaches

Some of these issues may be relevant to specific types of research and assessment or dependent upon the varying degrees of the role that cultural diversity plays in the research process. Regardless, all need to be considered in becoming a culturally competent student affairs researcher.

Awareness and Knowledge Issues

One of the first issues that should be considered when approaching a research or assessment project is awareness of one's own assumptions and worldview, since they may have implications for the entire research process. *Conscientizacão,* or deeper consciousness, a term introduced by Freire (1970), permits reflection and integration of personal and professional knowledge that affects one's reality. This idea may be useful to professionals in understanding how their assumptions may affect their work. Pedersen (1988) referred to lack of this awareness as *cultural encapsulation,* a term introduced by Wrenn in 1962, whereby reality is defined through a lens of one's own assumptions and stereotypes. Pedersen suggested that a number of assumptions produce cultural encapsulation, which ultimately leads to ineffective relationships in helping professions.

Wilkinson and McNeil (1996) extended the assumptions proposed by Pedersen (1988) to the research process because of their relevance for multicultural research. The first assumption is related to the definition of normal behavior. If a researcher does not examine her assumptions about what is normal behavior (or normal attitudes or normal needs), she may interpret as pathological or deficient anything deviating from that normalcy. Suppose a researcher who assumes that the normal cognitive process is linear and "rational" is studying a group that stresses "multidimensional" thinking, where feelings and intuitions are used to analyze data; the researcher may regard the participants' thinking as "scattered" and deficient. Similarly, the belief that all constructs are universally understood—the second assumption—has implications for research. When the researcher measures a construct, such as "leadership," and assumes that this is understood as the researcher understands it, the validity of the results is questionable. The third assumption occurs when researchers maintain they are culturally aware and do not seek to learn more or challenge their existing assumptions. In this case, it is essential that the researcher measure, understand, and interpret behavior from the perspective of the population being studied rather than from his own cultural perspective.

In addition to being aware of one's assumptions, Wilkinson and McNeil (1996) also suggest that researchers should be knowledgeable about cultural variables that may affect the research process: (1) collectivism versus individualism (Pedersen, 1988), (2) communication style, and (3) time orientation. Cultures that have been identified as using a collectivistic perspective emphasize the welfare of the group, cooperation and conformity, and interdependence. Cultures identified as collectivistic include Latino, Asian, and Native American (Axelson, 1985; Marin & Marin, 1991; McAdoo, 1993). On the other hand, cultures that are more individualistic emphasize independence, pursuit of personal objectives, and competition. Katz (1989) described White culture in this way. The implication this variable has for research, as identified by Wilkinson and McNeil (1996), is that individuals from collectivistic cultures may prefer a more personal contact from the researcher; provide more socially acceptable responses to questions; attempt to avoid conflict (by hesitating to offer an alternative point of view in a focus group, for example); and view the researcher as an authority figure, again with a tendency to furnish responses they believe the researcher desires. It is important to bear in mind that this discussion, which focuses on tendencies and characteristics of particular groups, is not meant to stereotype any particular group. Cultural differences between groups do exist, but there is also variation among individuals within a given cultural group.

With regard to communication style, Wilkinson and McNeil (1996) suggest that this variable may also be influenced by the values of an individualistic or collectivistic culture. The communication style among individualistic cultures is characterized as direct, open, frank, and even confrontational. Assertive expression of thought and feeling is emphasized in individualistic cultures. Among collectivistic cultures, just the opposite is the case; the preferred style of communication is nonverbal and indirect. In addition, communication that may lead to confrontation is avoided. Also avoided are topics considered taboo by that culture (such as sex or death) until trust is established. Differences in these communication styles may require the researcher to consider methodologies that capitalize on these communication styles (or avoid an approach that may hinder data collection). For example, if a researcher is interested in understanding the sexual mores in a group of students, she may need to take into account the differences in self-disclosure among the racially diverse students in the group. Or a survey instrument may yield a high response rate from some students (that is, White students), but Asian American students may "require the use of personal contact with an interviewer who can inspire trust and be alert and responsive to nonverbal cues" (Wilkinson & McNeil, 1996, p. 196).

Finally, time orientation may have an influence on a researcher's timeline for a project or appointments for individual interviews. Speigel (1982) notes that time orientation may differ with the cultural group. Future-oriented cultures (for example, White culture) often favor punctuality, planning, and time broken down into organized blocks and schedules. Katz (1989) suggests that for many White people, time is viewed as a commodity that is saved or spent. Other cultural groups that are more present oriented are less concerned about punctuality and organize their use of time according to the needs at the moment, not by a schedule. Because of these differences, researchers should be aware of their own time orientation and the need to be flexible depending on who their subjects are. It would be erroneous for a future-oriented researcher to assume that present-oriented participants are uninterested or reluctant to participate simply because they did not show up on time or at all. These participants may simply be responding to something else important at the time, or they may not give the same cultural importance to punctuality.

Defining the Population

In research where race and ethnicity are variables, it becomes essential for the multiculturally competent researcher to develop approaches for appropriately identifying different cultural groups (Wilkinson & McNeil, 1996). Illovsky (1994) argues that research categories (race, ethnicity, African American, Latino, minority, White, gay, lesbian, poor, rich, and so on) too often inadequately define and describe the diversity of the population being studied, resulting in less meaningful conclusions or limited generalization of the findings. Compounding this, according to Illovsky, are problems associated with researchers who do not account for differences within racial and ethnic groups with regard to other demographic variables as well as acculturation or identity development stages. For example, it may not be enough to study frequency of use of, and satisfaction with, career counseling centers, using race alone as a variable. Sometimes differences exist within various racial groups with regard to help-seeking attitudes and behaviors, and those differences may be mediated by acculturation. The degree to which, for instance, first-generation Asian American students seek out, accept, and adhere to both White societal values while retaining their ethnic identity (that is, acculturation) may account for significant differences within this particular racial group.

A good place to begin this discussion is to define and distinguish race, nationality, ethnicity, and culture from one another. However, it is worth noting that there is a great degree of social and political complexity involved in this discussion (Carter, 1995; Ponterotto & Pederson, 1993) as well as considerable disagreement on terminology among social scientists. Still, what we offer in this chapter is an integrated conceptualization of each of these terms, a definition of each upon which there is general agreement.

Race, as a term, is probably the most hotly debated of the three. In its original use, race referred to biological or physical characteristics (skin color, nasal index and lip form, texture of body hair) found in common among a group of humans with shared genetic heritage (Simpson & Yinger, 1985; Johnson, 1990). This led to identification of three basic racial groups: Caucasoid, Mongoloid, and Negroid (Atkinson, Morten, & Sue, 1989). Ponterotto and Pedersen (1993) and Carter (1995) offer a thorough discussion by scholars on the evolution of the term; they agree that race has both social and political meaning that is based, in part, on biological or physical characteristics. A widely agreed-upon classification of racial groups used in psychological and multicultural research is White American, African American, Asian American/Pacific Islander, and Native American. Hispanics and people of Latin descent or origin are not, by standard definition, a racial group and may belong to any of these four groups (Ponterotto & Pedersen, 1993).

Both *nationality* and *ethnicity* often refer to country of origin or a geographically defined group, but ethnicity extends that definition to include a group's social and cultural heritage as well as, in some cases, its religious identity (Carter, 1995). Examples of various ethnic groups are Irish, Haitian, African American, Polish, Chinese, and Italian. Ponterotto and Casas (1991) suggest that Jews are, by definition, an ethnic group since they share a common social and religious heritage.

Culture differs from race and ethnicity in that it is a term that can describe the diversity within certain ethnic groups or nationalities. Unlike race, which has biological (albeit arguably flawed) and sociopolitical underpinnings, or ethnicity and nationality, which refer to geographic, religious, and social heritage, culture refers to specific behaviors, skills, attitudes, and language that are learned and then transmitted to the next generation, usually within a specific physical environment (Carter, 1995). Culture is thus not limited to racial or ethnic groups but can also include groups defined by sexual orientation, geographic location, socioeconomic status, and so on (Ponterotto & Pedersen, 1993; Pope, 1993b; Reynolds & Pope, 1994).

Wilkinson and McNeil (1996), Illovsky (1994), and Marin (1984) offer a thorough discussion on the implications of racial categories in multicultural research and the dilemmas posed for researchers. From this discussion, two main concerns arise. First, there may be disagreement among social scientists on the labels used, which can limit the meaning and the generalizability of findings or the ability to conduct meta-analysis of multiple studies. Second, participants of studies may take exception to being categorized into a particular group with which they do not identify, creating resentment that can influence their willingness to participate or affect how they respond to questions.

Illovsky (1994) argues that the issue of racial and ethnic categorization in research must be addressed and resolved at the national and professional levels. In the meantime, both he and Wilkinson and McNeil (1996) make several recommendations. One suggestion is to define which variable is of interest (such as race, ethnicity, or culture) and then make sure to differentiate or account for any confounding factors. If, for example, race is the variable of interest, the researcher should account for the diversity of ethnicities and cultures within a race or the varying degrees to which acculturation may influence one's self-identity. When investigating the psychosocial development of Latino American students, a researcher may find that by asking the participants to identify their ethnicity (Puerto Rican, Mexican, Cuban, and so on) and by measuring acculturation, a useful context can be created for reporting the findings as well as for accurately reporting the limitations of the investigator's generalizations.

Researchers who are using various terms in their research design or in their demographic assessment instruments may benefit by acquainting themselves with the group(s) they plan to study. It may be the case that some groups, given their culture or geographic location, have a preference for a certain term over another. A researcher may learn, for example, that in one area of the country, the population being studied prefers the term *Latino* to *Hispanic American*. In this case, she or he should consider using the former term. Finally, Marin and Marin (1991) recommend that researchers consider asking the participants to write down their race or ethnicity rather than check it off from a prescribed list. This may allow the researcher to more accurately describe the group and set a context for the generalizability of the findings.

As for writing results and reports of research and assessment projects, the *Publication Manual of the American Psychological Association* (2001) offers extensive guidelines on avoiding bias in language with respect to racial groups. The manual suggests that the writer comply with the two key principles of specificity and sensitivity. These principles reflect the suggestions already noted here. First, writers are better served to err on the side of being more specific, not less, when describing the population being studied. For example, rather than write "Asian Americans" it may be helpful (and more accurate) to refer to their country of origin by writing "Chinese Americans." Second, writers should consult with their participants on preferred terms and should avoid language that may be considered pejorative, such as "Oriental." Some additional

APA guidelines with regard to labels are that they should be capitalized (for example, Black or White) and that multiword labels should not use a hyphen (for example, Asian American). Finally, the APA manual guidelines suggest that racial identifications (or any social identification) should be used only when relevant and "should not be mentioned gratuitously" (p. 63). Writers are urged to refer to the *Publication Manual of the American Psychological Association* (fifth edition) for more specific details on reducing bias in manuscripts and reports with respect to race, gender, sexual orientation, ability, and age.

Instrumentation

Tests and survey instruments of people and environments are commonly used in student affairs research and assessment; they have great utility in theory development and practical applications for increased understanding. However, they can be ineffective, inappropriate, and even harmful if there is a lack of careful consideration in development or selection as well as administration of these measurements (Walsh & Betz, 1995). In this section, we explore some of the significant issues and considerations in selecting and using measurements that are multiculturally sensitive.

Much of what has been written about multiculturalism and measurement can be found in the counseling psychology literature. Only recently has there been attention to the utility of theory-based instruments with respect to multiculturalism, and in particular to students of color (for example, Pope, 1998). With regard to measurement instruments themselves, two primary concerns are raised consistently: (1) cultural bias inherent in the development of the instrument (Drummond, 2000; Padilla, 2000; Walsh & Betz, 1995), and (2) "nonequivalence of research instruments" (Wilkinson & McNeil, 1996), in which instruments are used that may not be written in the primary language of the research participants.

Walsh and Betz (1995) suggested that an instrument can be biased in three possible ways: content, internal consistency, or validity. The most commonly discussed type is content bias, wherein the items contained in the instrument are more familiar to and better understood by one cultural group than another. In some cases, content bias can give one cultural group an unfair advantage over another, particularly if the assessment is used for decision making (Padilla, 2000). The second form of bias lies in the internal consistency (reliability) of the items within a given measure. Walsh and Betz (1995) warn that if the internal consistency is shown to be different across racial groups, then the test is measuring something different across those groups. Finally, validity can be another manifestation of cultural bias in assessment instruments. Here, an instrument may demonstrate that it reasonably predicts a score on a criterion measure for one racial group but not for another group. As asserted by Walsh and Betz, it should not be assumed that a measure of scholastic aptitude similarly predicts academic performance (GPA is an example) for White students and African American students. In instances where a measure does not predict well for one group, Walsh and Betz argue that it should not be used with that group for the intended purpose (such as scholarship or admissions decisions).

These three forms of test bias are a manifestation of assumptions of normalcy, discussed by Pedersen (1988), wherein the developers of an instrument assume the construct(s) they are attempting to measure are understood and valued universally. For example, if a scale measuring autonomy and independence is used, it would not be surprising for the scoring procedures to imply that a high score on autonomy means the individual is "normal" or healthy and mature. In some cultures, however, interdependence is more highly valued than independence, and individuals from this culture—mature and healthy as they are—might score low on this instrument and be viewed as deficient.

Given the importance of this issue, several suggestions for researchers are warranted (Walsh & Betz, 1995). First, researchers should investigate the development of an instrument of interest, including the standardization samples and how (and if possible, by whom) the items were generated. It is also important to examine studies of the instrument's reliability and validity across groups to identify any of the psychometric properties that may be questionable. Second, the researcher should consult with experts on the construct they wish to study (and the measurement of it) or members of the group of interest to determine the cultural relevance of the construct and any language that is potentially offensive to a particular group. A pilot study of the instrument with a multiracial sample may also yield some useful information about the test's potential cultural bias. Finally, the researcher should find out how cultures understand the constructs being studied so that the researchers avoid making assumptions about those cultural groups once they begin making interpretations of their findings.

Still, as Walsh and Betz (1995) contend, to simply discard a test that may contain a cultural bias is as imprudent as not responding at all to the concerns raised about that cultural bias. An assessment instrument that demonstrates appropriate psychometric properties (reliability, validity, factor structure) may still be considered for use given its wide utility even while acknowledging its limitations. They suggest that augmenting the data with other forms of assessment further enhancing our understanding of the range of cultural differences can compensate for the weaknesses of a given assessment instrument. On the other hand, Walsh and Betz insist that the decision whether to use a particular instrument should not be based solely on the instrument's psychometric performance. An instrument may have high psychometric quality, but it remains the responsibility of the researcher to use professional judgment in deciding the appropriateness of a test for a particular group or for its intended purpose. Suzuki and Kugler echo this caution when they state: "The responsibility for selecting, administering, and interpreting test results in a culturally sensitive manner remains with the clinician. Although some would fault the tests as being 'biased,' when used appropriately these instruments yield important objective information that can be used in planning effective treatment and educational planning. When used inappropriately, the results can be tragic" (1995, p. 513). An even more resolute stance is taken by others who argue that instruments that are biased and favor one cultural group over another should not be used, particularly when evaluating differences between groups (Padilla, 2000).

In addition to cultural bias, a more explicit way in which an instrument may not be suitable for use in research is if it is to be used with individuals for whom English is not a primary language (Wilkinson & McNeil, 1996). As noted earlier, this is referred to as "equivalence of research instruments." A seemingly simple solution to this predicament—translating the instrument to another language—entails a rather complex set of procedures (Wilkinson

& McNeil, 1996). The process involves skilled translators, correlations, and reliability measures as well as interviews with members of the cultural groups being studied to identify any translation problems in the interpretation of the data. Needless to say, the process is quite demanding, does not guarantee cultural equivalence, and cannot be thoroughly described here. Any researcher interested in obtaining information through cross-cultural measurement is urged to become familiar with the "serial translation approach" developed by Herrera, DelCampo, and Ames (1993).

Data Collection

Researchers should bear in mind the cultural variables discussed previously (collectivism versus individualism, communication style, time orientation) when developing procedures for data collection (Wilkinson & McNeil, 1996). Awareness of these variables may strengthen the data collection process in a way that does not offend participants and ultimately yields a higher return rate. With these variables in mind, Wilkinson and McNeil make four suggestions for collecting data: (1) consider the benefits of using a more personal approach in data collection, (2) use research assistants who are culturally similar to the population being studied, (3) use the native language of research participants, and (4) be familiar with the culture of the research subjects. Each of these four suggestions is described in greater detail here.

In many instances, research and assessment conducted in student affairs involves surveys and other paper-and-pencil measures. For purposes of efficiency, mailings are typically conducted to invite participation. This impersonal approach may not appeal to individuals from collectivistic cultures. They often prefer personal contact and are more likely to participate if they know the researcher and are personally invited. Collectivism is one of three key factors identified by Marin and Marin (1991) that underscore the benefits of the personal approach to data collection. Two other factors are time orientation and experience as research participants. Time orientation of the potential subjects may also play a role in data collection. Individuals from cultures that are present oriented may not respond as immediately to requests for research participation, and as time elapses they may not end up as a participant. Finally, some potential subjects, given their cultural group, may have had little experience as research participants and might lack understanding of the research process, or those with experience may have had negative experiences that preclude their participation.

For each of these factors, personal contact can mediate any of the difficulties associated with data collection in cross-cultural research. Using a research team or assistants in the data collection process can augment personal contact. Although personal contact can take time and may present challenges associated with multiple data collectors (for example, consistency collecting data and ensuring interrater reliability), the benefits with respect to greater and more diverse participation are not to be discounted (Wilkinson & McNeil, 1996).

Employing assistants in the data collection process can be helpful, but it may be even more useful to have assistants from the same racial or cultural background as the participants. If research assistants share the same background as the participants, there may be greater likelihood of initial trust and rapport. This is especially true when the research topic is uncomfortable to the participants or is considered taboo in their culture (sex, death, family issues, and so on) or when the participants are apprehensive or doubtful about the entire research process (Wilkinson & McNeil, 1996).

Wilkinson and McNeil (1996) also encourage researchers to "speak the language of the subject." This implies speaking the same primary language as well as knowing the nonverbal language of the culture. Some cultures emphasize nonverbal cues as well as intuition. Much can be lost in the communication involved in obtaining data if the researcher relies solely on verbal communication. Furthermore, the researcher (or research assistant) should know and understand the nuances in dialect and meaning assigned to words. Speaking the same language as the participants also involves understanding how socioeconomic status may affect the level of education of the participant and require particular vocabulary to ensure clarity and understanding.

Finally, as discussed earlier in this chapter, it is important for the researcher to know the culture of the subjects being studied. In the data collection process, this can enhance communication and reduce misunderstandings that lead to noncompliance. For example, as Wilkinson and McNeil (1996) and Marin and Marin (1991) discuss, compensation for participation can vary in its effect depending on the culture. The researcher should consult with the population of interest to determine the appropriateness and type of compensation to use. This knowledge may help the researcher get the most out of the compensation without offending the participants. Researchers might, for instance, have sufficient knowledge about a particular culture to learn that compensation in the form of money is less desirable (that is, it may be regarded as a bribe), whereas compensation in the form of community service (such as providing workshops) may be more beneficial to the group.

Alternative Research Approaches

Up to this point, much of the discussion in multicultural competence in research and assessment has, for the most part, presumed that the data are largely being collected through a survey or some other type of paper-and-pencil instrumentation. In short, it is quantitative. It would be imprudent not to consider the many ways research and assessment can be done that are not quantitative and that, by virtue of their design, may be entirely appropriate and effective when conducting multicultural research.

There has been a great deal of discussion about the benefits of conducting qualitative research when trying to learn about and understand, with breadth and depth, students and the environments in which they learn (Caple, 1991; Stage, 1992b; Manning, 1999; Stage & Russell, 1992; Magolda, 1999; Jones, Arminio, Broido, & Torres, 2002). With regard to multicultural issues, Fried (1995) and Attinasi and Nora (1992) argue that quantitative approaches to understanding this issue on campus have limitations. Fried (1995) suggests that much of the research in student affairs is governed by scientific and empirical methods, which rely on statistical techniques widely used in other behavioral sciences. When discussing the scientific paradigm with regard to the challenges of diversity, Fried argues, "We have reached the limits of the scientific paradigm as a frame of reference for understanding and coping with this complexity" (p. 35). Similarly, Attinasi and Nora suggest that structured survey instruments, when used to study college students, reveal their inadequacy with respect to accounting for cultural and subcultural diversity and distinctiveness among students.

In a broader discussion, Stage and Russell (1992) propose a set of assumptions that they contend underlie some researchers' reliance on standardized instruments as legitimate research tools. Among these assumptions are that (1) everything that is important to know can be obtained through surveys and standardized instruments; (2) the individuals who decide on the content of standardized measurement know precisely what is valid and worthwhile to know; (3) the use of questionnaires, along with appropriate sampling techniques, ensures a representative sample; and (4) the students who complete standardized measurements are equal in their ability to understand and respond to the items. Given some of the assumptions discussed previously in this chapter that researchers need to be aware of (for example, normality and universal understanding), the shortcomings of relying solely on standardized measurements, as outlined by Stage and Russell, become apparent.

This is not to suggest that quantitative measures are not useful; however, there are significant limitations in their use. Attinasi and Nora (1992) suggest that, in studying student-related diversity issues (retention, academic progress, psychosocial development, and so forth), one should make use of qualitative techniques such as ethnographic inquiries, which can be useful in establishing frameworks for understanding phenomena that can, in turn, be verified quantitatively. Likewise, quantitative research methodologies (such as cause-and-effect relationships) would be strengthened and illuminated by using qualitative research methodologies: "This argues for researching student outcomes and assessing student progress with a variety of methods" (p. 19).

Ponterotto (2002) specifies some of the unique strengths of qualitative methods in conducting multicultural research. First, when researchers enter the world of the participants, their worldview is suspended, allowing them to understand and experience the worldview of the participants. The researcher becomes a learner as opposed to an expert, thereby distributing the power and decreasing the possibility of marginalizing the research participants. Second, when the research participants are allowed to describe their experiences in their own words rather than be categorized into preestablished constructs and scales, they may gain new insights and are "further empowered as citizens" (p. 398). Finally, the researcher may benefit personally and professionally from close and sometimes intense interaction with the participants. As a result, researchers may become more conscious of their own biases, assumptions, and privileges. In sum, Ponterotto argues that the relationship between researcher and participant in qualitative design can yield a high degree of consciousness as well as empowerment, which can facilitate action on both parts to address oppression.

Stage and Russell (1992) observed that concerns about what may be missed if there is sole reliance on quantitative approaches have long been discussed (see Caple & Voss, 1983; Durst & Schaeffer, 1987; Parker, 1977). Stage and Russell introduced the concept of "method triangulation" to student affairs researchers and assessment professionals more than a decade ago. Although the concept is also identified by other terms, method triangulation refers to the use of "multiple methods in the study of a single phenomenon" (p. 487). Underlying this definition is the belief that qualitative and quantitative methodologies are complementary rather than adversarial and that the strengths of one approach can compensate for the deficiencies of the other in studying a phenomenon. For example, as pointed out by Stage and Russell, if a researcher studies students' attitudes toward cultural pluralism, she or he can administer an attitude survey, conduct focus groups, record attendance and participation at campus diversity programs, and track the number of bias-related incidents on campus. Even in instances where data from the multiple approaches contradict one another, interpretations of such contradictions can lead to a deeper and richer understanding of the phenomenon being studied.

Qualitative research design readily lends itself to collectivistic cultures in that it takes a more personal approach to understanding a given phenomenon. Participants of a study are referred to as "informants" rather than subjects, to connote their interactive role with the researchers. Many of the qualitative research techniques were developed by anthropologists and others who were among the first researchers engaged in cross-cultural research (Attinasi & Nora, 1992). Still, the reader should not assume that qualitative research methodologies are inherently "multicultural." In fact, many of the ideas discussed earlier in this chapter, although they were applied to quantitative approaches, are useful in qualitative research and assessment methodologies. For example, the qualitative researcher needs to be self-aware and knowledgeable about the individuals being studied. The qualitative researcher may also benefit by consulting with members of the culture or group being studied in planning the research or assessment as well as in interpreting the findings.

Exemplary Multicultural RESEARCH AND ASSESSMENT PRACTICES in Student Affairs

As noted in previous chapters, the specific exemplary practices that follow are not intended to be an all-inclusive list so much as they are to highlight some important multicultural awareness, knowledge, and skills necessary in conducting assessment and research in student affairs. By exploring these exemplary practices, one has an opportunity to create a more complex, concrete, and meaningful understanding of multicultural competence.

A student affairs professional realizes that previous residence hall quality-of-life surveys have yielded disproportionately low responses among students of color. A multiculturally skilled researcher examines the research design and the survey instrument itself to identify how the data collection can be more inclusive and representative.

Whenever an assessment or research project is planned, we need to examine our assumptions as we conceptualize the study. What constructs do we wish to study? Are they universally understood? Is there a bias in the construction of the instrument? Members of a residential community may have differing views on "quality of life" according to their culture and life experiences, and they may detect a biased perspective of what defines quality of life and conclude that the survey does not address their understanding of the concept. Demographic labels used in a survey may also cause some individuals to feel resentful and thereby inhibit their desire to complete the entire survey. Finally, we need to understand that members of collectivistic cultures may have a preference for personal contact in inviting their participation in research. Feelings of resentment, lack of understanding, and impersonal approaches may result in some students being uninterested in participating in data collection procedures. The findings of the study may, as a result, lack reliability and validity.

A student affairs researcher wishes to replicate a study on issues of body image and psychosocial development among White college women, this time using Asian American students. A multiculturally sensitive researcher reexamines her assumptions about the universality of body image as a women's issue. She concludes that perhaps, as currently discussed in the literature, body image is a relevant issue primarily for White, heterosexual American women; she looks more closely at the literature to understand how women of color perceive body image. Also, a multiculturally sensitive researcher understands the culture she is studying to better understand how to establish rapport, trust, and open communication so she can obtain the data she needs to make her interpretations.

It is important for the multiculturally competent researcher to know and understand the culture he wishes to study, not only in terms of the construct being studied but also regarding communication styles and issues that may be highly sensitive. We often assume that what might work for one culture is a parallel and appropriate methodology for another. But greater awareness and understanding of differing cultures may lead to methodologies that result in the volume of reliable and useful data needed to analyze and make interpretations.

A student affairs professional has gathered data through the staff and records of the University Advocate office on the incidence of harassment toward Muslim students. A multiculturally sensitive professional acknowledges that there is additional and important data available that can paint an even richer and more complex picture of this phenomenon. She conducts interviews and focus groups with the Muslim students who have been the direct and indirect targets of harassment. She is able to use all of these data in evaluating the institution's outreach efforts to Muslim students.

As student affairs professionals, we have a great appreciation for data to guide and measure our interventions. Still, we typically rely on surveys, document analysis, and anecdotal reports from our colleagues to gain perspective on a campus phenomenon and tend to overlook the actual *experience* of the students as an important and useful source of data. As multiculturally sensitive professionals, we must remember that students may be reluctant to report their experiences through the sometimes formal and impersonal procedures we have established. We may have to make deliberate and thoughtful outreach efforts to better understand their experience on campus. As Magolda (1999) reminds us, there is much to be learned if we take the time to allow students to "tell us their stories" (p. 13). It gives students, as Ponterotto (2002) acknowledges, a sense of empowerment since "storytelling" allows them the opportunity to tell us what they want us to know (Magolda, 1999).

A student affairs professional studying the campus climate for gay and lesbian students is confused by the number of students who write on the demographic portion of her survey that they are "queer." A multiculturally sensitive researcher recognizes the political and identity development connotations of the term and includes it as one of the demographic categories in her survey.

Defining the population to be studied is an important aspect of our research and assessment efforts. It allows us to be clear about the demographics of the population we are studying, which can have a profound effect on the generalizability of our findings. If we have limited categories for participants to identify, they may feel resentful, which can affect their willingness to participate or the way in which they respond to the questions or items in the data collection process. Rather than potentially limiting categories to terms we are familiar with, it is advisable for researchers to familiarize themselves with the very groups they wish to study and to learn how they may self-identify. We may learn, in this process, how geographic location or identity development become key variables in defining a population.

Summary

Research and assessment skills are the keys to better understanding our students and the environments within which they learn and grow. Given the growing diversity of college students, the environments they shape, and the complexity of the issues that can arise, it is necessary for researchers to enhance their research ability with heightened multicultural awareness, knowledge, and skills. If multicultural competence is infused into research and assessment practices, the findings and conclusions can be more valid, reliable, and useful, particularly when what is studied involves diverse students or issues related to diversity and creation of a multicultural campus.

This chapter has discussed the role of research, assessment, and evaluation in student affairs and the common purposes and similar approaches of each activity. The emphasis in this chapter has been on infusing multicultural awareness, knowledge, and skills into these similar approaches. Specifically, this chapter has highlighted how knowledge about other cultures and awareness of one's own assumptions and expectations can enhance cultural sensitivity of the researcher. This chapter has also identified how multicultural competence can influence a number of research activities: defining the population, selecting and administering instrumentation, identifying procedures in collecting data, and conceptualizing alternative research approaches. In sum, this chapter has discussed suggestions for researchers and assessment professionals who seek to be more culturally sensitive and for their findings to be more valid and reliable.

Chapter Six

Multicultural Competence in Ethics and Professional Standards

There was a racial incident in my residence hall building between a White woman and several African American men. My resident advisor staff is very racially diverse and they have very strong feelings about the incident and the students involved. Their job requires that they be available to all students. Some of the RAs of color feel torn between their responsibilities and personal feelings and are struggling to make good decisions. I try to provide a safe space for them to express their feelings away from the residents but sometimes I think I am sending them mixed messages by encouraging them to say how they feel when they are with me and then worrying whether they are being neutral enough on the job. (White male hall director in a first-year residence hall)

As the director of student life, I try to encourage the efforts of student groups to earn money to support their activities that are not funded by student government. I work at an urban community college with many first-generation college students and a high percentage of students of color. Lately I've been worried about the number of student groups that are working with credit card companies and getting money for each student they sign up for a credit card. So many students are being burdened by credit card debt in addition to their large student loans, and I worry about my role in supporting this practice. Should I discourage student groups from engaging in this type of fundraising because it may be exploitive, or do I let students work it out on their own? (Latina female director of student life)

As an untenured faculty member in a student affairs preparation program, I have been working hard to meet the expectations of my colleagues. Although I love teaching and building relationships with students, I don't always feel supported by my peers for investing so much time with them. Lately I've been listening to the concerns of several gay and lesbian students who are feeling invisible and are not sure the program or profession is for them. No one knows that I am gay, and I am afraid to come out and share who I am for fear of how my colleagues will judge me. Yet I feel as if I am letting the gay and lesbian students down by not being true to myself. I just don't know what to do. (African American male faculty member)

Addressing ethical issues and making decisions about challenging ethical dilemmas has always been at the heart of the work of student affairs professionals (Brown, 1985; Kitchener, 1985). According to Canon (1996), "it is the student affairs providers, more than any other constituent group in higher education, who attend to the human needs of students, respond to concerns about individual differences, and remind the campus community of the principles of justice and personal dignity to which it aspires" (p. 107). The student affairs profession has extensive opportunities and great potential to influence student values and the values of the campus because of their proximity to the daily lives of students (Brown, 1985).

The foundational beliefs and theories within student affairs embrace all aspects of a student's development—intellectual, social, emotional, spiritual, physical, academic, vocational, financial, and moral (Blimling, 1998). Through the rubric of student development, which emphasizes the whole student, student affairs practitioners have endless opportunities to observe and interact with students while they eat, work, play, and live. The student affairs profession has always emphasized "a commitment to student learning, an appreciation of individual differences, and an emphasis on education for effective citizenship, personal responsibility, and high standards for ethics and values" (p. 70). These goals and values of student affairs have always blended well with the expectations within higher education to develop "responsible and ethical citizens as well as trained professionals and competent thinkers" (Brown, 1985, p. 68).

The task of addressing ethical concerns in higher education has only become more delicate, complex, and demanding as campuses have grown and changed (Fried, 1997; Rickard, 1993). Moore and Hamilton (1993) suggested that environmental changes in the diversity of students, the shifting vision of the campus as community, and the monocultural and linear nature of the theories underlying the student affairs profession require an attitudinal shift in how the student affairs profession addresses ethical issues and their underlying values. According to Brown (1985), "higher education is in great need of a new way of thinking and acting on ethical principles" (p. 78). Some ethics scholars have called for a paradigm shift in how we conceptualize and respond to ethical issues in higher education (Brown, 1985; Canon, 1996; Fried, 1997; Fried, 2003; Moore & Hamilton, 1993; Sundberg & Fried, 1997).

Incorporating cultural realities and nuances into our understanding of the diverse values that students, staff, administrators, and faculty bring to campus is an essential aspect of this new ethical paradigm. Expanding our appreciation of what constitutes an ethical dilemma and developing alternative ways to resolve such conflicts will assist our efforts to meet the needs of a diverse campus. Multicultural issues are not separate from ethical issues on a campus college. Indeed, Pope and Reynolds (1997) have suggested that developing multicultural awareness, knowledge, and skills is an ethical imperative for the student affairs profession. In other words, not only must we develop multicultural competence to be ethical and effective practitioners, we must also incorporate our understanding of multicultural issues and values into our conceptualization of ethics and how we respond to ethical concerns on campus.

The purpose of this chapter is to examine the multicultural awareness, knowledge, and skills that are necessary for student affairs practitioners to be effective and ethical professionals. This chapter addresses the core assumptions, values, and underlying beliefs that make up the ethical principles and professional standards. How we define competency in ethical decision making is explored. Student affairs professionals need meaningful and effective ethical models for understanding the complex and sometimes contradictory challenges present in higher education today; the potential outcomes when multicultural points of view and diverse cultures are not incorporated within our ethical decision making are explored. There is also a brief critique of how ethics have not incorporated multicultural issues and influences and how those omissions have affected the student affairs profession. Multicultural competence within ethics is explored, and strategies for developing such awareness, knowledge, and skills are identified. Finally, good-practice exemplars or illustrations of how to effectively incorporate multicultural realities within our conceptualization of ethical dilemmas and implementation of strategies for addressing such concerns are highlighted.

Discussion of ethics, professional standards, and ethical decision making is often accompanied by exploration of legal issues and implications. Such connections are helpful and necessary, but it seems important to focus primarily on the ethical issues in student affairs in this chapter because of their connection to the underlying values and assumptions of the field. Clearly, ethical and effective student affairs practitioners must consider the legal implications and consequences of their decisions, policies, and practices; however, legal issues seem to constitute the frame for our work, while ethical considerations bring substance or meaning to what we do. According to Gehring (2001), "student affairs practitioners need not be lawyers to be effective in their roles, but they must have a basic understanding of the legal parameters affecting their work" (p. 108).

Legal concerns are central to a number of areas of responsibility within student affairs: admissions, disability services, judicial, housing, and counseling, to name just a few. Issues of inclusion, nondiscrimination, and affirmative action, which have significant legal implications for higher education, appear to have become permanent topics in campus conversations. Awareness and knowledge of the law and its constraints, as well as the rights of all community members, are essential in developing and implementing effective and meaningful policies, interpreting such policies to concerned individuals and groups, and building trust in the campus leadership (Gehring, 2001). For the purposes of this chapter and book, legal considerations are addressed and incorporated as appropriate; however, there are many more thorough and specific references that explore the legal implications of multicultural inclusion in higher education (see Bills & Hall, 1994; Howard-Hamilton, Phelps, & Torres, 1998).

Ethics and Professional Standards in Student Affairs

Every profession creates standards by which they evaluate the effectiveness and ethical nature of their work. It is important to understand the fundamental values and beliefs of the profession and their influence on professional practices.

Underlying Values of the Student Affairs Profession

Using some of the foundational documents of the student affairs profession, Young (1993) identified three essential values of the field: human dignity, equality, and community. Within those core values, Young also described some instrumental values: freedom, altruism, and truth were viewed as part of human dignity, while justice was seen as an aspect of community. Young further stated that the character and expression of our values as a profession have evolved over time owing to many internal and external factors, including campus diversity.

McWhertor and Guthrie (1998) emphasized the need to articulate and develop an understanding of the core values or ethic of the profession. They viewed this professional ethic as the implicit values that underlie the decisions, behaviors, and practices of the profession. These core (yet often hidden) values influence how we address and resolve ethical situations and dilemmas every day. These values, according to McWhertor and Guthrie, occur in four contexts, which shape the development of an individual's ethic: personal, institutional, professional, and legal.

Personal values, which are often overlooked within the literature, are shaped by our individual characteristics and experiences—such things as family, religion, geographic location and travel opportunities, demographic background, academic performance—and the meaning that those events and relationships have for us. Although these values are often minimized, it is important to acknowledge that we all bring personal values and beliefs, influenced by our life experiences, to our work environment.

Institutional values incorporate the mission, structures, politics, and legacies that shape the expectations and practices of the campus. This context is often downplayed, despite the tremendous influence the culture and values of our institution have on our thoughts and behaviors. Consider the example of a student affairs professional working at a Catholic university, who is told that whenever he does safer-sex educational workshops on campus he is required to have a priest accompany him and share the teachings of the Catholic Church. The unique values and practices of this particular institution have a profound impact on the individuals who work there and bring their own personal values and expectations about what constitutes ethical practice.

Professional values, which receive the most attention in the literature, constitute the fundamental values that professionals are expected to embrace and implement as part of their daily practice. It is assumed that these professional values are incorporated into our personal belief system and used as the foundation for our work. Relying on these core values allows us to influence the campus culture and create a welcoming environment for meaningful and ethical practice.

Finally, we must consider the legal implications of our underlying ethics or values. For example, if a college counselor is worried about the safety or well-being of a student and decides to break confidentiality so as to inform her residence hall director and parents, there are legal implications for the decision. Luckily, according to Canon (1996), ethical principles and legal considerations do not typically suggest contradictory action. However, when legal issues are involved, it is vital that we be thorough in our decision-making process and consult with appropriate campus personnel.

According to McWhertor and Guthrie (1998), an individual's ethic or underlying values, shaped by these four contexts, are constantly being expressed within all aspects of her or his life. These values are dynamic and ever-changing as one grows and develops. It is out of this dynamic and contextual process that core ethical principles have been developed for the student affairs profession.

There are several lists of underlying values or ethical principles articulated within the profession—such as those of Clement (1993), McWhertor and Guthrie (1998), and Rickard (1993)—but Kitchener (1985) is most frequently cited for her five principles of student affairs work: respecting autonomy, doing no harm, benefiting others, being just, and being faithful. This list has significant heuristic value in its ability to honor both the simplicity and the complexity of ethical principles. These principles serve as the basis for ethical standards within the student affairs profession that have been codified into professional standards (ACPA, 1993; NASPA, 1999).

Professional Ethics

The ethical codes of the ACPA address issues of professional responsibility and competence, student learning and development, responsibility to the institution, and responsibility to society. The NASPA ethical code focuses more on administrative principles that are connected to ethical standards in such areas as institutional mission and goals, management of institutional resources, conflict of interest, equal opportunity, and promotion of responsible student behavior. Both professional codes call for respect for diversity as central to their ethical principles or values.

According to Winston and Dagley (1985), ethical codes serve several purposes:

- To be used as guidelines for ethical decision making
- To clarify the responsibilities of practitioners
- To protect individual practitioners and the profession
- To be used as a performance appraisal tool
- To affirm the public and its needs and concerns
- To be used as a teaching tool

Ideally, codes "shift some of the responsibility for ethical decision-making from the individual practitioner to the larger group or, more specifically, to the profession" (Winston & Dagley, 1985, p. 50). Therefore, the profession needs to be willing to openly acknowledge its core values, beliefs, and principles, which should be translated into common practices and goals. This professional responsibility is especially important for student affairs in terms of incorporating multicultural issues and values at the center of our values, theories, and practices (Pope, Reynolds, & Cheatham, 1997).

Despite wide use of Kitchener's core principles, Upcraft and Poole (1991) presented a significant critique of the usefulness of these principles within the student affairs context. Since Kitchener's principles (1985) were influenced by the biomedical and counseling fields, Upcraft and Poole believed they were not fully appropriate for the student affairs profession. Their belief is that within student affairs, ethical decision making is an administrative task and skill that must balance needs and obligations that are sometimes contradictory, such as the rights of the individual versus the needs of the community. Their analysis of Kitchener's work led to the development of a two-dimensional framework that they believe can assist in resolving ethical dilemmas.

In addition to the critique of Upcraft and Poole (1991), there has been some discussion of whether ethical principles or professional standards should be used as the basis for ethical decision making. According to Canon (1993), ethical principles afford flexibility that can be used to adapt to diverse contexts and circumstances, whereas ethical codes or standards are based more in legalistic and professional expectations. On the other hand, ethical principles can also be abstract, vague, and not always helpful when applied to concrete problems and dilemmas (Canon, 1996).

Although at first glance Kitchener's principles—such as "do no harm" and "respect autonomy"—may appear to be fairly universal and neutral, some scholars believe they are also subjective and culture-bound. Fried (1997) highlighted how "ethical systems that guide human behavior are always based in fundamental assumptions about reality" (p. 7). Fried specifically noted the influence of Christianity, scientific empiricism, and positivist philosophy in the development of student affairs professional ethical principles and belief systems.

Cultural Implications of Professional Ethics

The subjective nature of ethical principles is grounded in the multiple and diverse ethical belief systems that individuals bring to every interaction and ethical dilemma (Fried, 1997). As an illustration, the principle to do no harm assumes that there can be universal agreement regarding what is harmful. This assumption may not always hold true. It is often the case in circumstances involving individuals from diverse cultural perspectives that their differing points of view affect how they see the situation (Kochman, 1981). For example, in a conflict between an African American and a White staff member in which the former feels that the latter is being culturally insensitive, there may be different perspectives on what is happening. According to Kochman, White individuals are often more focused on their intent, which is typically to do no harm, while the African American individuals are often more conscious of and sensitive to the effects of the conflict. In other words, from the African American's perspective, it doesn't matter whether the White staff member intends to be culturally insensitive or harmful; the hurt is still real. So, in this situation, whose definition of harm should be considered?

Using the other example of autonomy, it is important to acknowledge that the principle of respecting autonomy is steeped in the core values of the United States that emphasize individuality and freedom (Fried, 2003). These values are positive and affirming; however, they may not have as much meaning for students who are raised in cultures that emphasize collective and family responsibility. Imagine a student affairs practitioner worried about one of her student leaders who visits home frequently and prioritizes the needs of her parents and siblings over her own. Although there may be merit to the concerns that such choices jeopardize her academic potential and individual development, the professional must also consider how the student's Latina heritage is affecting her choices. Without consideration of the cultural centrality of family, challenging the student's choices may also minimize the strength she gathers from her family and the responsibility she feels toward them.

These inherent conflicts between cultural values do not necessarily mean that the core ethical principles of the student affairs profession must be changed. After all, these ethical principles for student affairs are found in the context of the United States and naturally reflect the dominant values of that culture. However, the essence of these underlying ethical principles must be examined for cultural bias, and there is a need for ongoing professional dialogue about how to make these ethical principles meaningful and appropriate for all individuals.

Unless there is an effort to understand and value diverse cultural perspectives and values, ethical issues and concerns will only perpetuate the ongoing invisibility of multicultural issues in higher education today. The assumptions underlying our ethical principles and virtues must be deconstructed and understood if we hope to build an ethical framework and professional codes that truly embrace diverse cultures and values as well as strategies for addressing ethical conflicts or dilemmas. Multicultural issues must be infused into ethical principles and guidelines for the student affairs profession, deliberately and thoughtfully. Until now, the ethics of student affairs have been presented and implemented under the presumption of value-neutral or universal perspectives, when in fact such cultural neutrality is unlikely, and may even be undesirable (Dalton, 1993).

If ethical principles and underlying values are unable to address the concerns of all members of the higher education community, then the ethical decision-making process is weakened and less valuable as a tool to create civility and community. Given that "being just" is one of the core ethical principles of the profession, we must consider what justice means for all members of the community. If it is seen as expedient to reduce the budget of the multicultural affairs office at a predominantly White university rather than reduce the number of resident assistants in the residence halls, then we must ask if justice is being served. If a secretary in a student affairs office is known for being openly homophobic with students, but we do not fire her for fear of conflicts with the union, then we must ask ourselves, Are our actions benefiting others? For all students, staff, and faculty to believe in and invest in the community, thorough and meaningful dialogue is necessary, which implies remembering that universal and sometimes simplistic responses to ethical concerns are not always productive or expedient (Fried, 1997).

The multicultural nature of higher education today appears to be at the core of many current ethical challenges. There are multiple communities, each with its own principles and beliefs, trying to find common goals and language to resolve conflict. Brown (1985) stated that the challenge of higher education seems centered on finding balance between what is good for the individual or group and what is best for the common good. Ethical dilemmas are often at the intersection of conflicting values, beliefs, and realities (Fried, 1997). Since change seems constant in diverse and dynamic communities, any personal or professional ethic must evolve to fit the changing context of higher education (Sundberg & Fried, 1997).

Multicultural Competence in Ethics and Professional Standards

To be competent and ethical student affairs professionals, practitioners must explore multicultural considerations in all aspects of their work. This exploration ultimately leads to a reconceptualization of what is viewed as core attitudes, knowledge, and skills. This redefinition process must also occur in the development of our professional ethics and values. Even though there is no analytical framework available to accomplish this task, it is vital that the underlying assumptions and fundamental skills in applying ethics to diverse situations and populations be explored and clarified.

According to Canon (1996), there are many important issues to be considered in resolving any ethical dilemma. Among them are being able to recognize ethical dilemmas and knowing the ethical principles and professional codes necessary to guide one's responses. Two other key issues that may be even more challenging involve knowing if, how, and when to get involved in a situation as well as knowing how to work well with others in addressing a dilemma.

Competence in ethical decision making requires that several key characteristics be considered before reconceptualizing how multicultural issues fit within an ethical framework. There are primarily two types of knowledge requisite to being an ethical professional: self-knowledge and knowledge of relevant ethical principles, values, codes, and legal considerations. Self-knowledge means understanding the personal context, including cultural values and assumptions, which influences the decision making process. Knowledge of the specific ethical values and requirements of the profession is also essential in being an effective and ethical practitioner. In addition to the knowledge base, professionals need some model or process for ethical decision making that helps them sort out how to respond to any ethical dilemma. Such ethical scholars as Elfrink and Coldwell (1993), Kitchener (1985), Young (2001), Cooper (1998), and Cottone and Claus (2000) have offered various ethical decision-making models to consider in evaluating ethical dilemmas.

Young (2001) highlighted a model of reflection-in-action from the Harvard University Program in Ethics and the Professions, which emphasized the need for ongoing revision of ethical principles to keep them relevant and meaningful. Reflection-in-action involves questioning one's assumptions and actions even after a decision has been made. Young identified six primary aspects of ethical reflection:

1. Be specific.
2. Reflect on experience.
3. Involve others in the process.
4. Understand general ethical principles.
5. Test alternative solutions.
6. Reflect-in-action (p. 22).

Ultimately, true reflection-in-action may require changing the underlying theories, beliefs, and ethical principles used to resolve the conflict. This model offers an ideal process for challenging and exploring the core cultural assumptions that are embedded within an ethical framework.

Young identified several more components to ethical reflection that contribute to the veracity and meaningfulness of ethical decision making and action. He suggested that professionals develop their own personal definitions of ethics, allowing them to reflect and act from a moral center rather than being pulled by external guidelines, rules, and laws. It is important that professionals have a thorough understanding of their role in the various relationships and contexts in which they operate (employee, supervisor, mentor). Modeling, mentoring, and motivating are key approaches that professionals can take when striving to live consistently, make meaningful and moral decisions, and apply ethical principles within the context of the community in which they work (Young, 2001).

Community Collaboration and Multicultural Ethics

Many student affairs scholars have highlighted the role of community in addressing ethical issues (Canon, 1996; Fried, 1997; Roberts, 1993; Young, 2001). In considering the diverse needs, perceptions, and values of the many communities that currently constitute higher education today, one finds that such community collaboration and consensus seems necessary. According to Fried, forging a new paradigm in ethical decision making means focusing on "the power of relationships, nonlinear information, the unpredictability of change, and the power of context" (1997, p. 9). This process requires that multiple points of view and belief systems be considered simultaneously in rendering a just, meaningful, and effective solution to any ethical dilemma. Ethical principles and standards are only meant to serve as a guide through difficult and sometimes contradictory circumstances.

Before student affairs rely on these standards and professional codes, extensive conversations and dialogue need to occur within the diverse and sometimes fragmented community (Canon, 1996; Fried, 1997). If a community of students, staff, and faculty can reach consensus about core values and visions on the campus that includes exploration of the relevance of culture and context in all conversations, then ethical concerns and dilemmas will constitute more exploration of those earlier discussions. Unfortunately, these conversations rarely happen, and when an ethical dilemma does occur on a campus (in a private or a campuswide manner) there is little common ground upon which to resolve the issues. The result is more reliance on the principles and codes and less on the community and the process of making meaning of contradictory values, goals, and needs. Canon (1996) emphasized the importance of creating an environment or community that promotes ongoing exploration of ethical issues and concerns: "The resolution of ethical problems is an imprecise task requiring personal reflection, community concern, and, above all, tolerance for ambiguity and appreciation for the complexity of the human social condition" (p. 107).

Therefore, addressing ethical issues and resolving ethical dilemmas is much more than doing the right thing and making appropriate and ethical decisions. Sundberg and Fried (1997) viewed creation of a mutual and respectful community as one of the fundamental goals of ethical dialogue. Such goals fit well with the development of a multiculturally sensitive and inclusive community. Ultimately, campuses that are truly ethical *and* multicultural may require more of a focus on the process of building a community of common dreams, values, and expectations rather than concentrating on such outcomes as ethical decisions or the racial makeup of the campus.

Developing Values and Ethics of Students

In addition to focusing on building community and consensus, other student affairs scholars have concentrated on the ethical responsibility of developing the values of students (Blimling, 1998; Brown, 1985; Canon, 1996; Clement, 1993; Dalton, 1993; Saltmarsh, 1997). According to Canon, the student affairs profession is committed to developing ethical behavior, one part of which is contributing to the moral and ethical development of students. This focus on the development of individual character and values seems to be a natural outcome of the larger focus on creation of ethical and multiculturally sensitive communities. Dalton (1993) suggested that student affairs should adopt values-centered leadership as a means of assisting practitioners in making moral and ethical choices as well as guiding students in their own development. Embracing values clarification or education may make some professionals uneasy, but Dalton argued that student affairs practitioners are continuously transmitting values in their decisions, actions, and role modeling. Thus, the challenge is not whether to advocate specific values but to choose which values and how they should be expressed and taught.

Dalton (1993) further suggested that expressing values helps individuals associated with an institution feel a sense of purpose and pride. Once those values are openly expressed, they are more easily integrated into routine services and practices. Dalton specified how such values can be taught or transmitted: through role modeling, communicating values, disseminating policies and procedures, personal advocacy, and celebrating shared traditions. All of these actions help to bring a diverse community together. Making a personal and public commitment to diversity, as an illustration of values-based leadership, may be the best way to encourage others in the organization or institution to endorse those same values.

Saltmarsh (1997) offered a specific illustration of how such values education can be integrated into student affairs through the use of service learning. From his perspective, community service learning has the potential to transform students through reflection, purpose, action, and compassion. Through an exploration of "connected knowing" (from Belenky, Clinchy, Goldberger, & Tarule, 1986), he advocated focusing less on ethical reasoning and more on ethical knowing and relating. Belenky and colleagues suggested that integrative learning is most likely to occur in experiential and relational experiences that foster opportunities for interaction and emotion. Reciprocal relationships are central to this type of development and can lead to empathy, multicultural sensitivity, self-knowledge, and self-confidence in both students and staff. This relational and affective approach supports Noddings's ethic of caring (1984). Noddings suggested that true caring means being able to set aside our own point of view in order to understand the needs, feelings, concerns, and expectations of another person. This same type of immersion has also been suggested as an approach to developing multicultural sensitivity (Pope-Davis, Breaux, & Liu, 1997).

Using the work of Dewey as inspiration, Saltmarsh (1997) advocated for a justice orientation as part of an ethics education approach in which students are taught to consider the well-being of society as becoming more connected to their own well-being. Service learning is not about doing *for certain others,* as much charity work is often conceived; rather, it is about seeing the interconnectedness of life and striving to do what is right *for all.* Using a multicultural lens, this means that Whites should not fight racism in order to help people of color but rather build more genuine and honest relationships with people of color. It is not enough for men to speak out against sexism and violence against women because of how it affects the women they love. Ideally, men are driven to fight sexism because it affects how women relate to men and how men view themselves. Society free from oppression benefits everyone, not just those who are the target of the oppression. As the concept of ethics is reconceptualized, the connections in building ethical and multiculturally sensitive communities become stronger and more obvious.

Exemplary Multicultural ETHICAL PRACTICES in Student Affairs

The particular exemplary practices described here are not intended to be an inclusive or exhaustive list but rather to suggest some of the important multicultural awareness, knowledge, and skills necessary for making ethical decisions and choices as well as integrating ethics into all aspects of one's work in student affairs. The goal in exploring these exemplary practices is to create a more complex, concrete, and meaningful understanding of multicultural competence.

A student affairs professional is attentive to all aspects of campus life and strives to be aware of when ethical principles or codes are not being honored or followed. A multiculturally sensitive professional looks beyond her own worldview to build connections with colleagues and students who are culturally different from her. Through those relationships she is able to more fully understand others' perceptions and understand how their values are affected every day. This professional understands that groups may interpret a given event differently and therefore have differing reactions.

Our values and beliefs about the world may be regularly challenged in the higher education setting, but we are not always aware when such challenges constitute an ethical dilemma. Canon and Brown (1985) and others have highlighted the importance of addressing the ethical problems that occur within daily practice. More than likely, we rely on what the professional codes and standards tell us is an ethical dilemma rather than rely on the voices of students, colleagues, and even ourselves. We need to be more vigorous in our effort to listen and understand the experience of students if we hope to gain access to the core conflicts they face. We must face the assumptions and beliefs that interfere with our ability to perceive an event as an ethical dilemma. For example, in the vignette described previously where some resident assistants feel torn between their commitment to their job and supervisor (to be faithful) and their belief that there is an injustice occurring within their residence hall (being just), the supervisor needs to be sensitive to their struggle rather than just demanding that they meet their job requirements and expectations.

Part of the process of recognizing the full range of ethical concerns that students experience is to learn how their cultural and life experiences influence their beliefs about themselves and the world around them. It is not good enough to wait until there is a conflict if we want students to feel valued and understood. We need to spend more informal time with students and make the effort to understand who they are and how they think. Our jobs, with all of their administrative and programmatic demands, generally allow little time for truly getting to know students so that we can appreciate and make meaning out of their thoughts, expectations, and actions. Barr (1993a) suggested that, instead of spending 80 percent of our time with 20 percent of our students, we reprioritize and take the time to enjoy all of our students and what they bring to our institutions and our lives.

A student affairs professional is cognizant of the ethical principles and guidelines of the profession. A multiculturally sensitive professional actively deconstructs the ethical code and understands the relative and subjective nature of the values that underlie the professional standards and guidelines. Through peer supervision and in-depth discussion with one's peers, he can begin to appreciate how the codes, as they are often interpreted, may not honor the reality and experiences of all students.

Unless the student affairs profession can examine its underlying values and assumptions, it will be difficult to expand our notions of what is ethical. Part of the process may mean participating in national forums, sponsored by professional associations, in which we explore these difficult questions. Embracing the complexity of determining what is harm, what is justice, and how we define autonomy is not easy, and we may not agree on all matters. It is important to acknowledge that just because a culture sanctions a certain belief or behavior, it will not always be appropriate and acceptable in higher education. For example, imagine a student raised in an evangelical church who ends up with a gay roommate and uses language and behavior that are not acceptable by the residence hall guidelines. Those beliefs may be valid and acceptable in his own community, but he needs to be aware of the community standards in the residence hall that do not allow individuals to mistreat each other. The residence hall staff members have to appreciate and value the importance of that student's belief system, while at the same time making sure that he can accept and live by the community expectations and standards set by the residence halls and supported by the institution.

Ethical codes inherently make statements about the values and beliefs of a profession and a campus community. Individuals involved in those worlds must understand and accept those values if they want to participate in those communities. They don't always have to agree with those values, but they must embrace the expectations for behavioral standards in a living and learning environment. Again from the previous example, even if the resident director agrees with the values of the evangelical resident, it is still her duty to enforce those standards and ensure that every member of that living community feels welcomed and affirmed. The ethical dilemma is quite acute when an individual has to choose between being faithful to a personal value system and the values of the institution and profession. As professionals, if we are unable to embrace the values of our profession and accept the professional standards, then we might need to consider if we are working in the correct profession.

A student affairs professional must know how to apply ethical principles to her work with students and colleagues. A multiculturally sensitive professional strives to be consistent and fair in how she applies these codes and realizes that her efforts to be fair and just in her actions do not determine how various groups or individuals perceive the effort. It is never enough to simply say that one has tried; it is the effect and outcome that matter more than the intent.

To be effective, multiculturally sensitive professionals need an ethical decision-making process that they value and that seems to work. Fried (2003) suggested "we must continually attend to our own ethical practice, to the creation of communities that support ethical dialogue and to the process of ethics education that we conduct with students on a daily basis" (p. 118). As stated previously in this chapter, the ethical decision-making process cannot occur in a vacuum if we want it to be successful and build an ethical and just community. All voices and points of view must be acknowledged and included in the process.

Having a decision-making process that is consistent, thorough, and inclusive is the key to effectively resolving ethical dilemmas. The process of addressing multiple and sometimes conflicting perspectives about an ethical conflict requires that professionals have plans or models and feel confident using them. Reflection and introspection are vital aspects of the process and help ensure that individuals respond preventively rather than reactively.

Young (2001) identified a valuable model of reflection-in-action that emphasized the importance of community and dialogue in resolving ethical conflicts. Ethical reflection requires that we consider ethical issues more frequently, not just when an obvious conflict or problem exists. Fried (2003) also proposes a dynamic ethical model that includes the importance of considering many factors from the larger context (time frame, phenomenology, culture) in the ethical decision-making process.

Fried (2003) suggests, as did Young (2001), that the best way to teach ethics and values to students is through what we say and the choices we make. If we tell students that they should value diversity and engage with all students on the campus, yet they observe us relating on a social level to professionals who are like us, they will wonder about the veracity of our words. However, if we are active advocates on campus for diversity issues and work in coalitions with students, faculty, and staff across cultural groups, students are more likely to value our multicultural education efforts. How can we truly expect students to change their lives if we have been unwilling to change our own?

A student affairs professional views ethical issues and principles as being at the center of all the work he does. A multiculturally sensitive professional attempts to integrate a reconceptualized view of ethics in all aspects of teaching, training, and professional development.

Since training is one of the primary ways any profession puts forth its beliefs and values, it is essential that reconceptualization of ethics and incorporation of multiculturalism into the ethical principles and decision-making process of student affairs occur within graduate training. To truly examine and alter our expectations of the role of ethics and our role as ethical role models in higher education today, we must begin with individuals as they are being socialized into the profession. Inevitably, we all learn the complexity of professional work once we leave graduate school and work in the diverse world of higher education. As new professionals are beginning to conceptualize "what is" and how they should respond, they need to think in the most complex way possible. If we try to keep it simple and teach graduate students about ethics more didactically and dualistically, their ability to think with increasing complexity and see the value of dialogue and community is diminished. Graduate school is the time when most new professionals develop a formative understanding of what to expect in the field. Central to that understanding is the need for appreciation of complex cultural realities and belief systems and how they influence everything we do.

A student affairs professional, through her appreciation and knowledge of the experiences and expectations of college students, views herself as an advocate for their beliefs and concerns. A multiculturally sensitive professional understands that being detached and uninvolved in the campus dialogue about multiculturalism serves only to reinforce the status quo. An ethical practitioner sees it as her responsibility to use her voice and power to advocate for all students, especially when their perceptions and needs are not being addressed.

As student affairs professionals, unless we engage with the campus community and attempt to promote alternative perspectives to what the dominant culture presents, we are preventing the rich diversity of our campus from coming together and forming a dynamic and powerful community. Attempting to be neutral or to somehow foster a value-free environment only sends a message contradicting the core values of our profession. As Dalton (1993) stated, it is not possible to be value-free in our work, and even if it were, is that the direction we want to go? If we use a values-centered leadership approach as advocated by Dalton, then the higher education community understands what is expected and how they can contribute.

If we are advising a student group that elects only male students to leadership roles, what is our responsibility in helping these students understand how women's voices have been historically silenced in leadership? Yes, we can allow the democratic process to occur naturally, thus permitting the dominant values of our community to determine the outcome, or we can attempt to educate students about power and leadership. Many scholars believe it is our role as professionals to challenge students to become more complex thinkers (Blimling, 1998; Canon, 1996; Dalton, 1999); what better way to challenge them than to engage them in dialogue about multicultural issues?

As professionals, it is not enough to engage in the multicultural change process on our campuses if we do not also get involved in our own profession. According to Dalton, "Responses to values issues associated with increasing diversity and pluralism on campus will continue to shape our profession" (1993, pp. 94–95). Participating in leadership positions within our professional associations is a powerful way to influence the values, theories, and practices of student affairs. We cannot expect advocacy to occur on our campuses if it is not happening within our profession. Pope, Reynolds, and Cheatham (1997) and others have suggested significant areas of change for the student affairs profession. Changing organizations and institutions is demanding, humbling, and never-ending work that needs to be ongoing.

Summary

The diverse priorities, needs, expectations, cultural assumptions, and values within higher education mean that ethical dilemmas are inevitable. However, this inherent conflict should not be viewed as a problem to be solved or overcome but rather as an illustration of the challenges and demands of addressing the concerns and issues of a diverse student body within an increasingly complex institutional structure and world. According to Dalton (1993), addressing the value-laden issues of diversity and pluralism on our campuses will continue to be at the center of student affairs work.

Brown (1985) identified the need for the student affairs profession to develop an ethical agenda to fulfill its mission of being the conscience of the campus. To be successful, it is essential that multicultural issues be incorporated into all aspects of ethics, from how we determine what is an ethical dilemma to how we resolve those important conflicts inclusively and meaningfully. Being aware of any inequities of race, gender, social class, or sexual orientation existing in higher education is a fundamental aspect of competence within student affairs (Canon, 1996). Reconceptualizing what it means to be ethical and effective student affairs professionals is an important aspect of that competence.

Developing a new paradigm that embraces culture and community is the foundation of building a more humane and affirming campus environment. As stated so clearly by Roberts (1993), "Community making is our heritage, and now we must attempt to find ways to fulfill the vision that has been ours from the inception of student personnel work" (p. 44). Embracing the multiple values and belief systems that exist in higher education is the first step toward creating this new framework. Dialogue among diverse communities within higher education is an excellent tool for creating understanding, consensus, empathy, and respect. This notion of ethics becoming a process within a complex and dynamic community can replace old and static ideas of using ethical guidelines and codes as the foundation of ethical decision making. Brown (1985) envisioned an ethical community that was formed by the efforts and commitment of student affairs professionals and built on caring and responsible relationships, self-knowledge and affirmation, and a humane and compassionate environment.

Chapter Seven

Multicultural Competence in Teaching and Training

I am a new member of my campus diversity team. We are not affiliated with a particular program or department, and our team consists of people who are genuinely committed to multicultural work. We provide diversity training across campus to students, staff, and faculty. Despite a wide range of training experience in the group, we work very well together. However, lately I have been concerned about several team members. Even though they have gone through extensive multicultural training, I feel their personal issues, especially their White identity, are affecting their ability to be effective. I am not sure if I should speak with them directly or talk with the team coordinator first. It isn't enough that we care about these issues, right? I thought we had to have our own act together first. (White female career counselor)

This is my first year as an assistant professor, and I am excited to finally be teaching in a graduate program. The job search process was challenging, and I feel lucky that I found a program that really wanted me. Now that I am here it has become clear that I am expected to develop and teach a new course on multicultural issues in higher education. It is not that I have a problem with the course. I wish my doctoral program had offered that type of course. I am just worried they are assuming that multicultural issues are my area of expertise just because I am a person of color. I don't want to be pigeonholed as the diversity expert when I have so much more to offer. (Asian American male professor in student affairs program)

I have been working for years to recruit a diverse orientation staff, and for the first time almost half of my student staff identify as diverse either because they are students of color or lesbian, gay, or bisexual students. This is really exciting for me but I am unsure how to design our multicultural training. I had done it one way when my staff was predominantly White and heterosexual, but I am not sure that type of training will work with this staff. I don't know whether to focus on multicultural awareness and have them work on understanding themselves and each other more. Or maybe I should focus more on skills and how to work with students who may be culturally different from them. Now that I have the diverse staff I always dreamed of, I realize that I don't have a lot of the skills that I think I need. (African American male orientation director)

Student affairs professionals have always been responsible for encouraging student learning and development as well as for contributing to the academic mission of the college or university (Terenzini, Pascarella, & Blimling, 1999). Although student affairs professionals have historically focused on the out-of-class experiences of students, many student affairs scholars have argued that education is the "fundamental domain of student affairs administration" (Winston, Creamer, & Miller, 2001, p. 8). This out-of-classroom education essentially serves the same goal as classroom instruction, which is to contribute to students' development to prepare them for life and work after college. As colleges and universities have become more complex and the roles of faculty have grown more specialized with increasing emphasis on research and related tasks, student affairs administrators take on more of an educational role (Creamer, Winston, & Miller, 2001). Furthermore, since student development theories and practice were introduced and became a cornerstone of student affairs practice, increasing attention has been focused on how students develop and learn.

Research has increasingly shown that a number of out-of-classroom conditions and experiences affect the academic achievement of students (Terenzini, Pascarella, & Blimling, 1999). For example, students who are members of a living-learning residence hall environment perform better than students living in a more conventional residence hall setting. Extensive scholarly work has demonstrated that many diverse experiences—residence hall living environment, fraternity and sorority involvement, athletics, employment, faculty and peer interaction, and other co-curricular activities—shape and influence how college affects students (Astin, 1993; Kuh, 1995; Pascarella & Terenzini, 1991). Although the impact of these experiences can be positive or negative, overall it appears that co-curricular activities have a positive influence on the academic and cognitive learning of college students (Terenzini, Pascarella, & Blimling, 1999). Active student involvement and opportunities for well-developed interpersonal interactions with faculty and peers also seem to have a powerful influence on students (Astin, 1993; Terenzini, Pascarella, & Blimling, 1999).

On the basis of its understanding of the rich history of student affairs professionals as educators who contribute to the academic and intellectual development (as well as moral, emotional, and psychosocial) of students, the American College Personnel Association created the Student Learning Imperative (ACPA, 1994). The goal of this initiative was to emphasize, for the student affairs profession as well as others in the academic community, the importance of the role of student affairs in promoting student growth and development. By focusing intentionally on creating conditions and responsibilities within the profession that positively contribute to the learning and development of students as well as to the overall academic mission of the institution, the student affairs profession can strengthen its role in creating policies and practices that benefit students.

Roper (1996) emphasized the role of student affairs professionals as educators and student development professionals. Student affairs practitioners are involved in education both formally and informally, as in offering training opportunities for student staff, staff members, and faculty; providing educational programming for students; and interacting with students every day as advisor, supervisor, counselor, and mentor. Rhoads and Black (1995) offered the view of student affairs practitioners as transformative educators who have the opportunity to play a major role in restructuring the campus community. According to those authors, "The most important arena for teaching by student affairs administrators lies in the compelling requirements for creating and sustaining multicultural communities on campus" (1995, p. 15).

The purpose of this chapter is to explore the awareness, knowledge, and skills that are required by student affairs practitioners in their central role as educators in transforming higher education into a multiculturally sensitive environment. This chapter examines the underlying beliefs and assumptions that influence the teaching and training practices of student affairs. The chapter highlights what constitutes competency in teaching and training and what happens when multicultural issues and assumptions are not incorporated into both the formal and informal educational efforts carried out by student affairs. Examples of what happens when multicultural issues are not infused into teaching and training interventions are shared. Teaching and training competence is redefined to include multicultural issues, and strategies for developing the necessary multicultural awareness, knowledge, and skills are also explored. Finally, good-practice exemplars that incorporate those strategies are presented.

Teaching and Training in Student Affairs

According to Malaney (2002), teaching is the most common and most essential form of scholarship in higher education. Through their own education and experiences as student affairs professionals, many practitioners have developed some of the behavioral characteristics of teachers. Rhoads and Black (1995) identified some of these important skills: lecturing, demonstrating, coaching, modeling, designing, advising, facilitating, learning, researching, evaluating, structuring, and collaborating.

Student affairs professionals have experience teaching in and out of the classroom. Direct teaching experiences include teaching within a graduate-level student affairs or higher education program; conducting training and professional development workshops for students, faculty, and staff members on a variety of topics; and teaching courses to undergraduates, such as freshman year or orientation to college courses, leadership courses, or resident assistant or peer helper courses. Indirect teaching incorporates an even wider array of programs and services provided to students: creating positive learning environments within the residence halls and student government, teaching parents and new students about what to expect during college, developing effective policies that help shape meaningful and appropriate relationships among students through campus activities, and teaching campus values and community norms through judicial affairs (Rhoads & Black, 1995; Roper, 1996). This type of informal teaching and daily involvement in student lives, even though abundant in educational values, demands a particular mind-set to be successful. Student affairs, despite its rich history and background in student development theories, cannot carry on developmental or transformational efforts unless such interventions are intentionally planned and implemented with specific educational goals and outcomes in mind (Rhoads & Black, 1995). Fried (2002) suggested the importance of developing an "integrated learning environment in which student learning is the focus of all staff members" (p. 126).

According to Fried (2003), training is how most of the teaching done within student affairs should be described; it is becoming an increasingly important role for student affairs professionals. Training is often viewed as a way to improve the performance of individuals or organizations, and like teaching it may be offered in a variety of formats: workshops, teleconferences, credit-bearing courses, consultations, and so on. Training may aptly describe many of the out-of-classroom educational experiences that student affairs practitioners facilitate, but the underlying competencies for both teaching and training appear essentially the same. According to Roper (1996) and Davis (1993), effective teaching and training require in-depth knowledge of the subject matter; organizational skills; positive attitude and enthusiasm; empathy for students; presentation or stand-up skills; ability to give feedback and evaluate the performance of others; effective advisement and mentoring; good use of media, technology, and other teaching aids; and knowledge of student development and learning style theories. Additional essential knowledge and skills are facilitating team building; the ability to facilitate active, cooperative, and collaborative learning; and understanding and teaching to multicultural populations (Roper, 1996). Finally, on the basis of her model of intellectual development, Baxter Magolda (1992) emphasized the importance of teaching responsively to different ways of knowing. Roper (1996) also suggested that to provide stimulating, enriching, and dynamic educational experiences, an effective teacher has to be able to respect "diverse talents and ways of thinking" (p. 322).

There has been a significant critique of college teaching over the years; many scholars believe that higher expectations must be set for educators. According to Boyer (1990), teachers must study extensively in their own disciplines, know the literature of other disciplines, and be intellectually engaged with the course material and students. This task is not always easy because, as Weimer (2001) suggested, most faculty members (or student affairs educators) have not been trained as teachers and have a limited understanding of pedagogy. Even the educators who are successful at teaching students a new knowledge base or set of skills may not have mastered the expertise necessary to enhance the students' critical thinking or to teach them how to evaluate, understand, and when necessary transform themselves and the surrounding social structures that limit growth, exploration, and diversity. According to Roper (1996), "one of the major challenges facing higher education today is to create positive learning environments that support diversity" (p. 330). Few, if any, educators have been taught how to develop learning environments that truly affirm diversity in thought, values, and identity. Some scholars believe that our traditional means of teaching in the United States do not allow or support such transformative views or styles of teaching (Fried, 2002; Giroux, 1983; hooks, 1994; Rhoads & Black, 1995). Specifically, Fried (2002) suggested that the student affairs profession, and higher education in general, must change its views about teaching and learning if it is to make education relevant, meaningful, and valuable for today's students.

Multicultural Competence and Strategies in Teaching and Training

Reconceptualizing our vision of what constitutes education and redefining the core competencies expected of educators in the diverse and complex twenty-first century is an essential and necessary task for higher education professionals. For student affairs professionals, in particular, this task requires a broad and inclusive understanding of our educational role. It is important to examine the direct and indirect types of teaching and training that we accomplish on campus so we can more fully understand what may need to be changed. Amidst our diverse teaching and training opportunities with undergraduate or graduate students, staff, and faculty, we must be concerned with not only *what* we teach but *how* we teach.

Multicultural competence in teaching and training within the student affairs profession needs to be explored within student affairs preparation programs as well as the range of educational interventions offered on campus by student affairs practitioners. Both are dealt with in this chapter, and strategies for infusing multicultural awareness, knowledge, and skills are identified.

Curricular Transformation

For the past thirty years, educators have been challenging the teaching status quo by suggesting that traditional teaching content and methods were not inclusive, dynamic, or collaborative enough to engage learners in a meaningful and empowering process (Freire, 1970; Giroux, 1983; hooks, 1994). Different schools of thought—feminism, postmodernism, critical theory, and multiculturalism—have adopted distinctive perspectives and formulated unique analyses of society, human behavior and relationships, and education (Rhoads & Black, 1995). In spite of their differences, these diverse points of view have embraced key beliefs and ideals, prominent among them being inclusive, emphasizing collaboration and equal relationships, challenging traditional organizational structures, and affirming cultural differences. The goal is to develop a critical consciousness that enables individuals to reflect actively and critically about themselves, their assumptions, and the world around them.

The Reflective Judgment model, proposed by King and Kitchener (1994), has suggested similar goals and explored how such critical thinking can be encouraged within the classroom. King and Shuford (1996) further suggested that "faculty can play a key role in developing learning environments that enhance the process of learning to think more reflectively by providing adequate challenge matched by adequate supports" (p. 158). Faculty members also play a vital role in helping students understand and make meaning of their experiences, assumptions, and beliefs on a personal level (King & Shuford, 1996; Meacham, 1996). Once students understand how their personal experiences, identities, values, and emotions affect how they interpret information, form opinions, and perceive and relate to others, they are better able to comprehend complicated, controversial, and dynamic concepts such as multiculturalism (King & Shuford, 1996; Meacham, 1996).

Acknowledging how these individual and cultural influences affect people is especially important. Some scholars, notably Baxter Magolda (1992) and Gilligan (1982), have found empirical support for gender differences in how men and women make meaning and value judgments about various issues and concerns. Other differences and life experiences, less obvious or measurable, may also shape how individuals perceive and interpret information and behavior; this self-knowledge is essential to true reflective and critical thinking.

Many scholars believe that the goal of education is to actively construct or expand knowledge rather than passively accept information from teachers or other expert sources (hooks, 1994; Meacham, 1996; Rhoads & Black, 1995). Passive education encourages a certain detachment and lack of passion about others and the world around them, whereas active education, with emphasis on critical thinking, supports students' interest and activity in creating a more just, democratic, and inclusive society (Freire, 1970; Giroux, 1983; hooks, 1994). The dynamic, complex, and controversial nature of multicultural issues demands that students be actively involved in the process of critiquing assumptions and knowledge and the creation of new ideas and voices. White (2002) suggested that students and scholars work jointly to develop new perspectives and create knowledge and understanding. If all students believe that it is important to contribute to the educational process rather than merely accept and absorb the knowledge of others, then education has the potential to be a liberating force in their lives (hooks, 1994; White, 2002).

Student affairs scholars such as Manning (1994a) and Rhoads and Black (1995) suggest that student affairs practitioners have an important role to play in higher education as transformative educators. Rhoads and Black presented six principles to guide student affairs professionals in their efforts to have an impact on individual students, their groups, and the larger campus community. Their principles focused on such areas as influencing the values and direction of the campus community, empowering students to develop a connection with others and make a commitment to a fair and just community, embracing diverse values and voices in all levels of decision making, respecting cultural differences and being willing to take risks to challenge others, building affirming and equalitarian relationships with students, and viewing conflict and value differences as unique opportunities to create individual understanding and organizational change.

By fostering critical, interactive, and creative thinking, we create learning opportunities for both teacher and student. Talbot (1996b) stated that this type of pedagogy "emphasizes the need for all participants to be active and responsible both for educating and being educated" (p. 387). Manning (1994a) emphasized the need for collaborative discussion, honest dialogue, and nonjudgmental exchange of feelings and ideas as the foundation for true learning. Few teachers or students have much experience in this type of learning, either in or out of the classroom, yet it is essential that we find new ways to reach and educate students. In acting as transformative educators, student affairs professionals have the opportunity to "prepare students to lead socially and professionally meaningful lives in a changing and challenging world" (Roper, 1996, p. 323).

Many scholars have emphasized the importance of incorporating multicultural issues into the curriculum and training of the student affairs profession (Fried, 1995; McEwen & Roper, 1994a; Pope & Reynolds, 1997; Sanlo, 2002; Talbot, 1996b; Talbot & Kocarek, 1997). Sanlo took that suggestion one step further by imploring the student affairs profession to retrain current faculty so as to create new ways of teaching. Although there is evidence that multicultural issues are being included in the curriculum of student affairs preparation programs (Talbot, 1996a), most student affairs graduates, faculty members, students, and practitioners have received little training in multicultural issues and have limited multicultural knowledge and experiences (Hoover, 1994; McEwen & Roper, 1994b; Pope & Reynolds, 1997; Talbot, 1996a; Talbot & Kocarek, 1997).

Multicultural Issues in Student Affairs Preparation Programs

Since multicultural issues appear to be prominent and permanent themes on most college campuses today, scholars such as Meacham claim that "not to engage students in a critical examination of these issues would be an abdication of our responsibilities as college and university faculty" (1996, p. 112). Pope and Reynolds (1997) and others (McEwen & Roper, 1994b; Talbot, 1996b) have emphasized the ethical responsibility of student affairs professionals to incorporate multicultural knowledge and experiences into the curriculum and expectations of the field. According to Meacham, the question is no longer whether to incorporate multicultural issues but "how to teach these issues in a way that maximizes critical thinking and productive learning on the part of our students" (1996, p. 113).

Infusing multiculturalism into graduate student affairs preparation programs is especially powerful because of their role in shaping the values, knowledge and experiential base, and culture of new student affairs professionals. The influence of these academic programs is strongly felt in their design of the overall curriculum, program requirements, and structure of individual courses. According to Talbot and Kocarek (1997), "student affairs graduate faculty shape their profession . . . through pedagogy, role modeling, and personal and professional characteristics" (p. 278).

Reynolds (1995a) highlighted the importance of examining how multicultural learning was structured within an academic program. Copeland (1982), in her exploration of multicultural issues in counseling training programs, offered four possible program designs:

1. Stand-alone multicultural course
2. Area of concentration model
3. Interdisciplinary approach
4. An integration model

Ridley, Mendoza, and Kanitz (1994) also identified additional models for developing multicultural training programs. There has been some criticism of the various multicultural training models. Some multicultural experts worry that the approach of using separate multicultural courses may reinforce certain stereotypes about groups and not encourage students to view multicultural knowledge as integral to their professional knowledge and skill base. In addition, these courses are often not required and suffer criticism as the area of concentration model, which assumes that it is appropriate and sufficient for some individuals to develop multicultural expertise but unnecessary for all professionals to develop multicultural competencies. Some scholars support the integration model because it encourages integration and generalization of multicultural awareness, knowledge, and skills; however, there are some concerns that this model may be inadequate because there is not enough time or opportunity to create deeper learning and understanding. Many multicultural experts within counseling psychology have proposed that academic programs combine a variety of designs, as in mandating a separate course yet also integrating multicultural content and experiential opportunities in all other courses (LaFromboise & Foster, 1992; Lewis & Hayes, 1991; Ridley, Mendoza, & Kanitz, 1994).

McEwen and Roper (1994a) suggested using Pedersen's five-step multicultural training model (1988) as a framework for infusing multiculturalism into student affairs preparation programs:

1. Needs assessment
2. Objectives
3. Design
4. Implementation
5. Evaluation

Systematic and thorough assessment of individual attitudes, needs, and perceptions of students and faculty is a necessary first step in creating a multiculturally inclusive academic program. Exploring the overall environment—curriculum, practicum experiences, examinations, research, and any support services—is also essential. Specifying goals, objectives, and desired outcomes for any multicultural training program is paramount to an effective preparation program. Reexamining the core attitudes, knowledge, and skills that are expected of new professionals is vital to the assessment process.

The next critical step involves the redesign of the curriculum to meet the needs and desired outcomes of the training program. There are many available curriculum transformation models to assist faculty members with their efforts (AACU, 1995; Musil, 1996; Musil, Garcia, Smith, & Moses, 1995; Schmitz, 1992; Schuster & Van Dyne, 1985; Williams, 1994). An approach that focuses on transforming underlying beliefs, assumptions, and knowledge bases rather than merely adding content should create the opportunity to reexamine the priorities and values of a preparation program. Implementation is the next step and requires time and commitment from the entire faculty as well as from all the individuals who contribute to, interact with, and benefit from the preparation program, such as practicum supervisors. The final step in creation of a multicultural training program, according to Pedersen (1988), involves evaluating the curriculum transformation effort at various stages of the development process. Information gained from the evaluation process can then be used to strengthen or change the preparation program.

Meacham (1996) identified five key factors for effective multicultural teaching:

1. Course content
2. Student makeup
3. Faculty makeup
4. Intellectual tools
5. Classroom dynamics

What content is to be taught and how it is taught are essential components in multicultural training. Understanding the backgrounds, beliefs, experiences, and identities of students and faculty members is essential because these factors have a profound effect on how they perceive and make meaning of the course content (Meacham, 1996). Intellectual tools, among them conceptual frameworks, theories, vocabulary, research methods, and evaluations, allow students to integrate knowledge and understanding deeply and meaningfully. Finally, the ability to understand and incorporate classroom dynamics into the learning process enriches the experience for all involved. According to Meacham, "The classroom itself should become a model for living with diversity, so that both the students and the teacher need to strive to listen with respect and to understand, even if they do not agree with, what others have to say on controversial issues" (1996, p. 119). McEwen and Roper (1994a) suggested preparation programs serve as a laboratory, "an intense learning environment, for engaging in and embracing multicultural awareness, knowledge, skills, and attitudes" (p. 49).

In addition to considering how to structure program curriculum and requirements and design individual courses, it is equally important to explore individual attitudes, knowledge, and skills for faculty members to use in incorporating multicultural issues or teaching multicultural courses. Davis (1993) offered some general strategies to assist faculty members in addressing diversity issues in the classroom. This is her list of considerations:

1. Recognizing personal stereotypes or biases that exist and may be used unintentionally in the classroom
2. Treating and respecting students for their individuality
3. Changing any language that may offend, exclude, or diminish specific cultural groups
4. Using terminology for specific cultural groups and related terms that are current and sensitive to the overall sensibilities of the group
5. Assessing students' comfort level with the climate and tone of the classroom
6. Using departmental meetings to discuss diversity issues that are relevant and meaningful to the program

Fried (1995) also suggested two specific skills that faculty may require to be effective within a multicultural training program: separating facts from cultural assumptions and beliefs about those facts, and teaching students how to shift perspectives and adopt another's point of view.

Davis (1993) highlighted how diversity issues must be considered within every aspect of a course, from content and material to how discussions are structured, what types of assignments and exams are used, and advising and mentoring activities that can significantly affect students. There are numerous types of teaching strategies for effectively incorporating multicultural learning: experiential exercises, didactic approaches, reading and writing assignments, participatory learning, observational learning, supervised practica or internships, and research (Ridley, Mendoza, & Kanitz, 1994). According to Reynolds (1995a), the type of strategy used depends on the focus of the multicultural training. She suggested six design elements that should be considered in the development of multicultural courses:

1. Content: information oriented
2. Cognitive: worldview or cognitive filter
3. Affective: feelings or emotions
4. Experiential: hands-on activities
5. Skills
6. Process: interpersonal dynamics and focus on the here and now

Using a range of design elements heightens the chance that the diverse needs, learning styles, personal issues, and cultural assumptions of the various students will be taken into account. In addition to consideration of particular design elements in creating a multicultural course or a multicultural intervention within another type of course, numerous activities and exercises have been explored and suggested within the literature (Evans, 1997; Pope-Davis, Breaux, & Liu, 1997; Stage & Manning, 1992; Strange & Alston, 1998). Faculty members are encouraged to adopt or adapt any of these activities to meet their needs.

Teaching multicultural courses or infusing multicultural content or interventions into other student affairs preparation courses is a complex and challenging task. Even when faculty members study the multicultural teaching and training literature and make informed decisions, there are always personal dynamics and issues on the part of faculty and students that most likely need to be explored and addressed. Higginbotham (1996), Ridley and Thompson (1999), and Chan and Treacy (1996) explored the role of resistance in the teaching and training process, while Wolfe and Spencer (1996) identified how stereotypes and prejudice can shape and influence the classroom.

There are additional design elements to be considered within multicultural education and training. Most training programs tend to focus on some combination of multicultural awareness, knowledge, and skills, which are often based on the values, goals, and assumptions of the training program and individual faculty members. Many multicultural scholars, among them Carney and Kahn (1984), Christensen (1989), and Lopez et al. (1989), have suggested the importance of using a developmental perspective when conceptualizing or designing multicultural interventions. Understanding developmental differences in how individuals learn about multicultural issues is a necessary perspective when exploring how to actually structure the learning environment (Reynolds, 1995a). Appreciating how developmental theory can be used to design multicultural educational interventions is as important as knowing about multicultural resources and how to match them to meet the needs of individual students (Reynolds, 1995a).

Multicultural Issues in Outreach and Training Efforts

Incorporating multicultural learning into the classroom has many similarities to infusing such materials into a training and outreach approach. Assessment of workshop and training designs is an important first step in evaluating the ability of all outreach and training programs to be inclusive and multiculturally sensitive. There are opportunities to create and implement stand-alone diversity training for a variety of programs, offices, and student groups across campus. Multicultural training for student staff, as for resident advisors or orientation leaders, is a common strategy for increasing their effectiveness on the job. The development of this type of multicultural training should be evaluated and its effectiveness assessed. The goals, design, and ground rules might differ markedly when dealing with an intact group versus a group of individuals who specifically seek out the diversity training.

Likewise, it is also possible to explore programming on campus and assess the degree to which multicultural issues, context, and dynamics can be incorporated. Even though many workshops may seem unrelated to multicultural issues, it is possible to examine issues unique to a variety of groups within almost any content area. For example, when conducting a workshop on relationships, staff members must be sure not to presume heterosexuality and use nonspecific gender pronouns when exploring relationship issues. Or if one is leading a workshop on time management, grief, or safer sex, it is vital to understand that members of certain cultural groups may approach the topics of time, grief, and sex from different belief systems and experiences. Having a knowledge and experiential base about how various cultural groups address certain issues is necessary for creating and implementing culturally sensitive and relevant educational interventions across campus. In addition to better meeting the needs of diverse groups, incorporating diverse examples and considerations within one's design also has the effect of educating other members of the audience about the diverse life experiences, cultural beliefs, and opportunities of various cultural groups. Challenging their assumptions is a powerful intervention by itself. Minnich (1990) emphasized the power of challenging our hidden assumptions, including the normality and commonality of our experiences, especially if we are members of a specific dominant group such as heterosexuals, men, or Whites.

Exemplary Multicultural Competence in Teaching and Training

The particular exemplary practices described here are not intended to be an inclusive or exhaustive list but rather to suggest some important multicultural awareness, knowledge, and skills necessary for infusing multicultural issues into all aspects of teaching and training within student affairs. The goal in exploring these exemplary practices is to create a more complex, concrete, and meaningful understanding of multicultural competence.

A student affairs professional gathers enough knowledge and resources to be able to infuse cultural diversity issues and content into all aspects of curricular and training designs. A multiculturally sensitive professional realizes that without intentional effort to transform the design, assignments, evaluations, and advisement involved in teaching and training, the educational interventions may be incomplete, inaccurate, and irrelevant to student affair practice.

Issues of culture need to be integrated into all student affairs preparation courses, from student development theory to history and foundations, to research, to practicum experiences. Whether it is the theories used, the readings assigned, or the type of examples and assignments used, cultural diversity issues are always relevant and often powerful in adding understanding and complexity to any issue. It is not enough to just assign a few readings or use a cultural diversity activity in class. An additive approach is never complete because it doesn't explore the underlying values, beliefs, and literature base upon which the original course was established. To be effective and meaningful, the entire course design must be reconceptualized and redeveloped from an expanded view of the subject matter (Schuster & Van Dyne, 1985).

The first step to this process involves consulting with the literature and selected professionals to see how others have incorporated diversity issues into a particular course. There are limited resources available to assist in the curricular transformation effort, but some literature (for instance, McEwen & Roper, 1994a) has been developed to assist faculty members in their efforts to expand

and rethink their curriculum. In addition to addressing each course, it is essential that every aspect of the course—assignments, classroom norms, readings, out-of-classroom experiences, and course evaluation—incorporate diversity-related ideas, questions, and activities. It is suggested that faculty members, whenever possible, borrow from other disciplines, such as counseling psychology or education, that have spent the last decade or so addressing these issues. These same steps hold true for any staff or faculty training, campus outreach, or related educational endeavor on campus.

A student affairs professional thoroughly evaluates all multicultural educational interventions within a curriculum or training program to assess the effectiveness, meaningfulness, and value of those efforts. A multiculturally sensitive professional assesses student attitudes, needs, and perceptions before and after any classroom interventions, practicum and research experiences, and advisement and mentoring opportunities.

Curricular transformation requires appropriate planning and evaluation at all stages of the change process. Prior to any change effort, it is appropriate, and most likely necessary, to fully assess the attitudes, needs, and perceptions of students and faculty alike. Such information offers important insight into what is needed to assist undergraduate and graduate students, staff members, and faculty in their attempts to more fully appreciate, understand, and use multicultural awareness and knowledge in their daily lives. Completing thorough assessment before, during, and after a course or training program allows the teacher and trainer to fully appreciate the impact of any multicultural interventions. Such formative and summative evaluations can assist educators during the process and help them make meaning of the content, design, and requirements of the course or training program. It is equally important to evaluate the effectiveness of any practicum site or research project to assist the students or trainees in their efforts to expand their multicultural competence.

A student affairs professional actively assesses the comfort level of students in examining their own values, assumptions, resistance, and skill level and explores how multicultural issues affect classroom dynamics. A multiculturally sensitive professional is able to openly address those interactions and dynamics within the classroom in a responsive and heuristic manner.

Within any classroom or training intervention there are always intrapersonal and interpersonal dynamics influencing the learning process. It is vital that teachers and trainers have the insight and ability to address these issues directly and, when appropriate, incorporate them into the coursework or workshop. Active listening, using effective open-ended questions, and being able to intervene on the group level are just a few of the unique skills that educators need when infusing diversity into the classroom. Since multicultural issues are often complex, emotional, and easily influenced by the perceptions, values, and experiences of individuals, teachers and trainers should assume there may be process or interpersonal issues that are brought out by the course content. For some students, addressing diversity issues brings forth complex emotions and sometimes resistance to self-exploration, which may need to be addressed within the classroom. Being able to assess students' comfort level as well as the effect of individual or collective resistance in the classroom is an essential competency for educators. Knowing how or when to address these issues within teaching or training usually requires additional training, supervision, consultation, and mentoring as well as work and life experience.

It is helpful for student affairs professionals who are teaching multicultural content in their courses or trainings to actively consult with other colleagues involved in similar efforts by way of personal correspondence, electronic mail, conferences, or professional association interest groups. Having access to additional support and resources is vital to the success of any effort to transform coursework or workshop design.

A student affairs professional is able to integrate developmental concepts in the design and implementation of teaching and training efforts. A multiculturally sensitive professional strives to effectively address how developmental needs and learning styles influence students' ability to learn.

Much of the multicultural training literature within counseling psychology has emphasized the heuristic value and meaningfulness of using a developmental approach in incorporating diversity issues. According to Lopez et al. (1989), an individual's overall developmental level affected the ability to incorporate multicultural information. They suggested that a trainee or new professional with limited multicultural experience might feel overwhelmed, intimidated, or resistant to addressing multicultural issues in the classroom or at work. Finding a proper balance of challenge and support allows individuals to take risks yet not feel over-whelmed by the new content and classroom dynamics that come with multicultural training. In addition, using a range of activities and teaching styles helps to assist diverse learners in the process of adding new information, challenging old knowledge, and mak-ing new meaning out of one's knowledge, assumptions, and inter-ventions.

A student affairs professional is able to deconstruct how various indi-vidual and social issues such as racial identity and demographic and expe-riential characteristics influence the manner in which students perceive and react to multicultural interventions. A multiculturally sensitive profes-sional realizes that individuals are always affected by their cultural assumptions, life experiences, and worldview.

Whether we are conscious of it or not, we all have beliefs and assumptions about the world that affect our interpretation of infor-mation, experiences, and relationships with other people. Our assumptions are not value-free or neutral, no matter how much we desire them to be so (Minnich, 1990). As educators, we must real-ize there are many individual and social factors that influence how people make meaning of the world. This is true in all matters, but it seems especially so in situations with multicultural dynamics. There is a growing literature base about the influence of racial iden-tity on multicultural competence and one's worldview (Mueller & Pope, 2001; Ottavi, Pope-Davis, & Dings, 1994; Pope-Davis, Reynolds, & Dings, 1994; Pope-Davis, Reynolds, Dings, & Nielsen, 1995). It is important for any educator to understand that how individuals view their own race as well as the race of other individ-uals has a significant impact on their self-esteem and relationships with others. Although limited work has explored how other social identities (gender, sexual orientation) might influence multicul-tural competence, it is expected that those identities would have similar effects on the perceptions and values of individuals.

In addition to racial identity, other demographic and experi-ential variables influence how individuals perceive, address, and make meaning of multicultural issues. Factors such as whether one has had much experience living or working with individuals of other races or sexual orientations or had any opportunities to receive multicultural training or supervision can influence the perceptions, attitudes, and multicultural competence of individuals (Mueller & Pope, 2001; Pope-Davis & Ottavi, 1995).

A student affairs professional always attempts to be inclusive and sensitive in his language usage as well as the specific terms he uses when exploring multicultural issues. A multiculturally sensitive professional is knowledgeable about current and common terminology and language used to describe specific groups and makes every effort to incorporate that knowledge into his teaching and training interventions.

Language is a powerful tool that consciously and unconsciously indicates our assumptions, values, and attitudes about the world. In an effort to be inclusive and respectful of all individuals, educators must consider their use of language in any teaching or training endeavor. Using nonsexist language is a perfect example of the importance of being inclusive because of the power of the modeling that occurs when a teacher or trainer uses *she* and *he* rather than just *he*. It is also important not to use language that is offensive or disempowering—such as "wheelchair-bound," which many people with disabilities view as being insensitive. Davis (1993) emphasized the importance of recognizing one's assumptions about the audience, as in making statements such as "when your parents were in college" or assuming that all students in the room are heterosexual. Examples, case studies, and personal stories should include the full range of cultural identities and life experiences to minimize making any group or individual feel invisible or inferior.

In addition to attending to the language and examples we use, Davis (1993) suggested that educators must be sensitive to the most current terminology used by various cultural groups. This practice is not meant to make teachers and trainers overly cautious or defensive in their use of terms for various groups (Latinos versus Hispanics) but rather to raise the awareness of the importance of letting groups name themselves. It is also vital to acknowledge that there will always be many differences—individual, geographic, or generational—in how people choose to label themselves. Asking students and colleagues as well as keeping current with the literature are just some of the ways to be aware of any terminology trends for various cultural diversity groups. To be open-minded and nondefensive, it is helpful to acknowledge the changing nature of terminology and be willing to accept the diverse opinions of those around us in our role as educators.

A student affairs professional encourages critical thinking, group interaction, and collaboration in all teaching and training. A multiculturally sensitive professional is able to use experiential activities and interactive discussions to heighten the awareness, knowledge, and skills of students, staff, and faculty.

Given that one of the goals of higher education is to expand the critical thinking abilities of students as well as to enhance their ability to work with individuals who are culturally different from them, it is essential that teachers and trainers within student affairs learn what types of intervention, activity, and collaboration heighten the opportunity for this type of learning. Many multicultural scholars, notably Manning (1994a), Fried (1995), Meacham (1996), and Reynolds (1995a), have emphasized the importance of creating a collaborative, interactive, and experiential-oriented learning environment to enhance the abilities of students to expand or change their worldview as well as to understand the values and perceptions of others. Using theories such as the Reflective Judgment model as explained by King and Shuford (1996), or the more specific suggestions of Meacham (1996), offers educators the knowledge base and strategies for encouraging critical thinking in the classroom.

Summary

Student affairs professionals have always been educators and have assisted college students in their efforts to learn and grow. Our primary responsibilities as student affairs professionals have included facilitating student growth and development as well as supporting the educational mission of our colleges (Roper, 1996). These efforts have occurred in the classroom as well as in an array of venues—residence halls, student government, campus activities, career centers, and more. As our campuses have become more complex and diverse, teaching and training in an affirming, inclusive, and meaningful way grows more challenging.

As educators, student affairs professionals are in an ideal position to assist in transforming higher education into a more multiculturally sensitive environment. We interact with students in a variety of settings, in a range of roles, and this allows us to observe their developmental process and intervene appropriately and meaningfully. As we observe and build relationships with students, we can begin to infuse multicultural content and understanding into our educational interventions, thus allowing students the opportunity to see the relevance of multicultural issues and dynamics in all aspects of their lives. Such efforts seem to require that we transform our notions of education and what constitutes an educated person to include multiculturalism.

Part Two

Research and Practice Implications of Multicultural Competence

In Part Two, we turn our attention to the applications and implications of this model for research and practice. Although multicultural competence research is an emergent area of research with few published studies, it is important to review the current research and explore what implications these studies have for student affairs practice. In addition, by thoroughly addressing the practical applications of the core competency model through the use of case studies, readers discover how multicultural competence can enhance their effectiveness as student affairs professionals. Using case studies offers opportunities for each reader to explore multiple perspectives when problem solving as well as simulate "real-life" situations, thus preparing the student affairs professional to more effectively address the complex and ever-changing multicultural dynamics in higher education.

Chapter Eight

Multicultural Competence Research and Practical Implications

Theory, research, and practice are highly interrelated concepts that are arguably inseparable from one another. In any profession, practice identifies problems and related questions that theory attempts to explain. Theories may offer insights and recommendations for future practice, but they can also constitute a framework for research that validates and refines the theory and ultimately leads to improved practice. The theory of multicultural competence, which through research has been transformed into knowledge and practice in the counseling profession for more than a decade, has only recently been introduced into the student affairs profession. The construct of multicultural competence in student affairs offers a plausible conceptualization for practice, as described in the first portion of this book. It also lays a promising foundation for a whole new body of knowledge translated from research. This chapter describes the current state of research on multicultural competence in student affairs and some of the preliminary implications of this research for student affairs practice. In addition, the chapter offers suggestions for a research agenda on multicultural competence in student affairs.

Building on Counseling Psychology Research

As noted earlier in this book, the concept of multicultural competence within the counseling psychology profession dates back to just before 1982. Since that time, there has been broad agreement among counseling psychologists that the multiculturally competent therapist must possess proficiency in three areas: awareness, knowledge, and skills (Atkinson et al., 1989; Carney & Kahn, 1984; Pedersen, 1988; Ponterotto, 1988; Sue et al., 1982; Sue et al., 1992). Similarly, within the student affairs profession, discussions have emerged in the literature about the need to prepare and train practitioners to develop skills to work effectively with culturally diverse populations and with multicultural issues (Ebbers & Henry, 1990; McEwen & Roper, 1994b; Pope & Reynolds, 1997; Wright, 1987). These scholars argued that the concepts and models from the counseling psychology literature serve as an appropriate place for student affairs professionals to begin a discussion of multicultural competence. By extension, then, a review of the multicultural competence research in counseling psychology can offer a useful framework for discussing the current multicultural competence research in student affairs, the implications of this research, and future directions.

A survey of the literature in counseling psychology, with respect to multicultural counseling competence, reveals scholarship in several broad categories: conceptualizations and the theory development of multicultural competence (Atkinson et al., 1989; Carney & Kahn, 1984; Christensen, 1989; Lopez et al., 1989; Pedersen, 1988; Sue, 1981; Sue et al., 1992); the development of instrumentation to measure multicultural competence (D'Andrea et al., 1991; LaFromboise et al., 1991; Ponterotto et al., 1993; Sodowsky et al., 1994); the demographic and educational predictors of multicultural competence (Pope-Davis et al., 1994; Pope-Davis et al., 1995); the relationship between racial identity and multicultural competence (Fulton, 1994; Ottavi, 1996; Ottavi et al., 1994); and supervision and training issues in multicultural counseling (Brown & Landrum-Brown, 1995; Chen, 2001; Constantine, 1997; Ladany, et al., 1997; Martinez & Holloway, 1997).

It is clearly beyond the scope and purpose of this chapter to summarize the findings and assertions from the large volume of journal articles, books, and chapters that contain details on these categories. Still, it is important to note that much of the information gained in the counseling psychology profession has application to the student affairs profession, and the research questions and methodologies can serve as a useful model for multicultural competence research in student affairs. In particular, two areas of counseling psychology research have immediate relevance: measuring multicultural competence and examining predictors of multicultural competence. Both areas can expand our conceptualization of multicultural competence in student affairs practice.

Measuring Multicultural Competence in Counseling Psychology

Although there has been a considerable amount of literature on multicultural competence since the early 1980s, it has been only in the past ten years that efforts have been launched to empirically investigate the construct. Instruments designed to measure multicultural competence have made two important contributions to the work of counselors and educators. First, these instruments are important tools for researchers who seek to understand demographic and educational variables related to multicultural competence (Ottavi et al., 1994; Pope-Davis & Dings, 1995; Pope-Davis et al., 1994; Pope-Davis et al., 1995). Second (and some would argue more important), instruments such as these may allow practitioners to evaluate their training and preparation programs, their overall competence, and the effectiveness of their interventions (Ponterotto & Pedersen, 1993; Pope & Reynolds, 1997).

Within the field of counseling psychology, four notable instruments of counselor multicultural competence have been developed. Three are self-reporting:

1. The Multicultural Counseling Inventory (MCI), developed by Sodowsky et al. (1994)
2. The Multicultural Counseling Attitudes Scale Form B-Revised (MCAS-B), developed by Ponterotto et al. (1993)
3. The Multicultural Awareness Knowledge-Skills Survey (MAKSS), developed by D'Andrea et al. (1991)

The fourth instrument of multicultural competence, the Cross Cultural Counseling Inventory-Revised (CCCI-R), developed by LaFromboise et al. (1991), differs from these three in that it is not self-reporting; instead, it is meant to be used by a supervisor who observes and scores the multicultural competence of a counselor trainee.

Each of these instruments has not only made significant contributions to the research of counseling multicultural competency but also informed the development of a self-report instrument used to quantify multicultural competence of student affairs practitioners: the Multicultural Competence in Student Affairs-Preliminary Form 2 (MCSA-P2), developed by Pope and Mueller (2000).

In a review of the counseling psychology literature on multicultural competency assessment, Ponterotto, Rieger, Barrett, and Sparks (1994) argued that more precise definitions of multicultural counseling competence are needed to develop effective measures and that these measures can benefit from further investigation of their psychometric properties. To that end, they recommended that the counseling profession's understanding of multicultural competence should not rely solely on quantitative measurement but also be facilitated by the development of qualitative approaches.

Sue, Ivey, and Pedersen (1996) explicitly advocated use of qualitative research approaches to understand how multicultural competency is operationalized within a counseling context. Pope-Davis et al. (2002) assumed the challenge in a study designed to investigate the client's perspective of multicultural counseling competency. Initially, the investigators questioned whether data gathered by having clients complete an instrument designed to measure preexisting constructs such as the counselor's multicultural awareness, knowledge, and skills "would be a meaningful representation of the client's experiences" (p. 360). In response, the researchers designed a qualitative study to collect the data (using two sets of semistructured interviews with the participants) and to analyze the data (employing concept coding, category generation, and axial coding).

The study yielded a model of the counselor's cultural competence from the perspective of the client. The authors suggested that a qualitative research design can "produce a different understanding of multicultural competencies . . . that can both inform and propel quantitative research" (p. 361). Ponterotto (2002) and Constantine, Kindaichi, Arorash, Donnelly, and Jung (2002) commended these researchers for employing a qualitative approach to further the counseling profession's understanding of multicultural competence—a complex construct that has until recently been studied almost exclusively with quantitative research methodologies. Although research on multicultural competency in student affairs is in its fledgling stages, it is worth noting and learning from the evolution of this particular line of inquiry in the counseling profession.

Predictors of Multicultural Counseling Competencies

One initial area of interest in researching multicultural counseling competence was identifying the demographic variables (age, gender, race, and so forth) as well as educational variables (for example, courses and internships), factors that were related to multicultural competence. Another variable that has been of particular interest to researchers within the counseling psychology field is the relationship between a counselor's racial identity and her or his multicultural counseling competence.

With regard to demographic variables, the findings across many studies have indicated that age and gender are not significant predictors of multicultural competence (Ottavi et al., 1994; Ponterotto et al., 1994; Pope-Davis et al., 1995; Sodowsky et al., 1994). However, other studies have evidenced a significant, though mild, relationship between multicultural competence and age (Fulton, 1994; Ottavi, 1996; Pope-Davis et al., 1994) as well as gender (Ottavi, 1996; Pope-Davis et al., 1994). When examining race as a predictor, results indicated that Asian American, African American, and Hispanic counselor trainees reported higher levels of multicultural competence than their White counterparts (Ponterotto, et al., 1994; Pope-Davis, 1995).

Results from studies that examined educational and clinical experiences as predictors of multicultural competence indicated that those who did counseling with racially diverse clients reported higher levels of competence (Pope-Davis et al., 1995; Sodowsky et al., 1994). In addition, those who had multicultural coursework and attended multicultural workshops reported higher multicultural competence (Ponterotto et al., 1994; Pope-Davis et al., 1995).

Studies that have examined racial identity, particularly White racial identity, have indicated a relationship between it and multicultural counseling competence. Ottavi et al. (1994) found moderate correlations between the two constructs among counseling students, suggesting that within-group difference among White counselors with regard to their racial identity explained significant variance in self-reported multicultural competence. In a later study, Ottavi (1996) again found a significant relationship between the two constructs. Likewise, while studying a similar relationship, Fulton (1994) concluded that racial identity is a predictor of self-reported multicultural competence.

Multicultural Competence RESEARCH in Student Affairs

Since the general idea of cultural competence was first introduced to the student affairs profession by Ebbers and Henry (1990) and more explicitly articulated and defined as multicultural competence by Pope and Reynolds (1997), research on measuring and better understanding the construct has been under way (see King & Howard-Hamilton, 2000; Pope & Mueller, 2000; Mueller & Pope, 2001). Ebbers and Henry (1990) were among the first to argue that student affairs and academic affairs professionals need to work together to assess and evaluate the cultural competence of their personnel and the effectiveness of their programs. Ebbers and Henry further argued that baseline information was needed to measure how well the academy is doing so that appropriate program goals and objectives can be determined to address deficit areas. Later, Pope and Reynolds (1997) echoed Ebbers and Henry by suggesting that research on multicultural competence was "urgently needed" (p. 274) so that the awareness and skills of student affairs professionals could be expanded. This research could also assist graduate preparation faculty and student affairs supervisors in their efforts to determine the success of their own multicultural educational and training efforts.

Measuring Multicultural Competence in Student Affairs

Pope and Reynolds (1997) suggested that an important starting point in this new research area in student affairs is the development of a valid and reliable measure of multicultural awareness, knowledge, and skills in student affairs. In response, Pope and Mueller (2000) developed a measure of student affairs multicultural competence with the Multicultural Competence in Student Affairs-Preliminary

Form 2 (MCSA-P2). Building on the specific characteristics of a multiculturally competent student affairs practitioner as identified by Pope and Reynolds, Pope and Mueller conducted two studies to develop the instrument and investigate its reliability and factor structure and then to furnish initial evidence of the instrument's validity.

In developing the instrument, the researchers took deliberate steps in assembling diverse teams of graduate students, practitioners, and scholars to participate in all aspects of development. Dawis's rational-empirical approach of scale construction (1987) was adopted in the development of the instrument. This approach was similar to the multicultural competence measurement research done in the counseling psychology profession by LaFromboise et al. (1991) and Ponterotto et al. (1996). The rational-empirical is a multistep approach to scale construction involving item development, card sorting, content and face validity checks, item analysis, and factor analysis. The research teams were particularly useful in the item development and content validity aspects of the instrument's construction.

Once the first iteration of the instrument was done, it was administered to a heterogeneous sample (in terms of race, gender, age, professional experience, and areas of responsibility on campus) of 253 student affairs practitioners, graduate students, and program faculty. The results of this study indicated that the instrument had very good internal consistency (alpha coefficient = .92). A factor analysis was also conducted and indicated that the instrument was measuring a single factor that the researchers termed "general multicultural competence." Although this single factor seems inconsistent with the tripartite model of multicultural competence (that is, multicultural awareness, knowledge, and skills), as a finding it is consistent with the counseling psychology literature on multicultural competence assessment research, which, according to Ponterotto et al. (1994), has found that multifactor conceptual models tend to be unidimensional or bidimensional in structure, largely because of substantial overlapping of the three domains in multicultural competence. Another study of the instrument's factor structure, by Mueller (1999), lent additional support to the measure's one-factor interpretation.

On the basis of the findings in the first study, the instrument was revised to yield an instrument with thirty-four items arranged using a Likert-type self-report scale, measuring individual responses to items where 1 equals "Not at all accurate" and 7 equals "Very accurate." The instrument, referred to as the Multicultural Competence in Student Affairs-Preliminary Form 2, or the MCSA-P2, was then investigated in a second study to assess its reliability and convergent validity. For this study, a nationwide sample of 190 student affairs practitioners was collected. The MCSA-P2 showed a satisfactory level of internal consistency, with an alpha coefficient of .91. Statistically significant correlations with the Quick Discrimination Index (Ponterotto et al., 1995), which measures attitudes about racial diversity and gender equality, provided support for the construct validity of the MCSA-P2.

Multicultural Competence Research in Student Affairs

The MCSA-P2 has been used in two documented studies since it was first introduced to the profession as measurement of student affairs multicultural competence. Each study is summarized and discussed in greater detail here.

In one study, Mueller and Pope (2001) attempted to further our understanding of multicultural competence by examining the construct in relation to White racial consciousness (Choney & Behrens, 1996; Rowe, Behrens, & Leach, 1995; Rowe, Bennett, & Atkinson, 1994). White racial consciousness describes a typology of the attitudes held by White people about the significance of being White and the related attitudes toward people of color. The model comprises seven "types," which, briefly described, are *avoidant* (no exploration of or stance on racial issues), *dissonant* (confusion about racial issues), *dependent* (superficial and unreflective position on racial issues largely influenced by others), *dominative* (a strong ethnocentric perspective that places Whites in a dominant position), *conflictive* (competing perspectives of egalitarianism versus maintenance of White dominance and privilege), *reactive* (compelling need to respond to racism and White privilege), and *integrative* (realistic and complex perspective on race issues and how to address them). The Oklahoma Racial Attitudes Scale, or ORAS-P (Choney & Behrens, 1996), gives researchers a means to assess the racial consciousness of White persons (Rowe et al., 1995).

The findings from the study suggest a strong relationship between racial consciousness and multicultural competence among White student affairs practitioners, particularly among the avoidant, dominative, conflictive, and reactive subscales of the ORAS-P. Mueller and Pope (2001) concluded that less avoidance of, less uncertainty about, and less ethnocentric attitude toward racial issues appear to be related to multicultural competence. In addition, a greater intellectual understanding of racism is related to multicultural competence. Finally, the researchers learned, in the process of identifying the unique relationship between racial consciousness and multicultural competence, that several other variables were strongly related to multicultural competence among White practitioners: self-identified membership with a marginalized group (for example, gay and lesbian); experience with multicultural education, programming, or policy development; discussions with supervisors about multicultural issues; and, finally, interest in and a desire to work with diverse students and colleagues.

In a second study, King and Howard-Hamilton (2000) used the MCSA-P2, along with other assessment instruments, to examine the multicultural competencies of three distinct groups: self-identified diversity education specialists, professional student affairs practitioners, and graduate students in student affairs preparation programs. The sample, drawn from four campuses, comprised 132 participants, of which nearly one-quarter were people of color. The methodology employed both quantitative (that is, self-report measures) and qualitative approaches (such as case study and focus group discussions).

The researchers reported that the diversity educators scored the highest level of multicultural competence and that the graduate students scored lowest on the measures. Similar rankings were reported for the three groups with regard to expectations of what multicultural competence involves. With respect to race, students of color scored significantly higher in multicultural competence measures than their White counterparts. The researchers also reported that among all three groups, respondents scored themselves highest in multicultural awareness and lowest for multicultural knowledge.

Implications for Practice in Student Affairs

Although there has been limited research conducted in student affairs on multicultural competence, some practical implications of the extant research are beginning to emerge. In addition, a number of scholars in student affairs have been exploring related constructs that, although not termed "multicultural competence," have similar implications for student affairs work. The implications of this research for practice are discussed next.

The overarching implication of the existing research has to do with professional preparation and professional development of student affairs practitioners. Komives and Woodard (1996) argued that developing competence in student affairs is an ongoing process of "knowing, being, and doing" (p. 295). It begins with graduate preparation, with a focus on knowledge acquisition, but it must extend into one's professional tenure in which the practitioner seeks out learning opportunities, mentoring, and ways of getting feedback on her or his growing competencies (Carpenter, 1990). We suggest that these same principles apply to developing the more specific multicultural competencies of knowledge, skills, and awareness as practitioners.

Professional Preparation

The significant role student affairs preparation programs can play in developing multicultural competencies has been examined and discussed by a number of scholars (King & Howard-Hamilton, 2000; McEwen & Roper, 1994a; Mueller & Pope, 2001; Pope & Reynolds, 1997; Talbot, 1992, 1996a; Talbot & Kocarek, 1997). Talbot's research (1992) suggested that the role of diversity in graduate preparation programs varied greatly by topic (race, gender, sexual orientation) as well as by the self-reported comfort level of the faculty on these topics. Race issues were more commonly addressed, while sexual orientation issues were less frequently explored. The comfort level of the faculty was reflected in the curriculum content; the diversity of the student body; and in the self-reported knowledge, comfort, and skill levels among these students. In addition, diversity issues, when addressed, were more likely to be found in theory courses than in practicum courses.

Closer examination of faculty by Talbot and Kocarek (1997) echoed Talbot's earlier findings (1992) and brought more depth to the issue. A clear implication of this work is that if multicultural competency begins with graduate preparation, and if the faculty members in such programs are central to this endeavor, then greater attention to faculty competencies must be addressed. To this end, Talbot and Kocarek made several suggestions. First, greater efforts must be made to mentor and recruit a more diverse population of faculty members, who tend to be female, White, and heterosexual. Faculty in student affairs preparation programs, who espouse the core value of multiculturalism in the student affairs profession, must work harder than other academic colleagues and departments to promote diversity in their own ranks. Next, more opportunities and incentives (such as tenure and promotion processes) must be created for faculty members to invest time and energy in gaining self-awareness and knowledge about diversity, which can ultimately lead to improved teaching and better learning environments for all students. Finally, Talbot (1996b) suggested that faculty need to "walk their talk" in emphasizing the importance of diversity in their teaching. That is, students want to see diversity integrated into course content and pedagogy—and see it reflected in faculty's personal and professional lives.

With regard to students in graduate preparation programs, King and Howard-Hamilton (2000) suggested that although graduate students are eager to gain more multicultural experiences, they are uncomfortable in situations where they must work and respond to multicultural issues and people unlike themselves. The authors suggested that meaningful and stimulating discussions about multiculturalism competence could effectively address this quandary. The table entitled "Characteristics of a Multiculturally Competent Student Affairs Practitioner" found in Pope and Reynolds (1997, p. 271; also see Table 1.1 in this book) might prove effective in framing these discussions and helping students see and appreciate the relationship among multicultural knowledge, skills, and awareness. Additionally, preparation faculty can play a significant role in fostering the multicultural competencies of graduate students by articulating expectations for multicultural knowledge and skill attainment and by creating opportunities for them to explore multicultural issues throughout the curriculum.

Furthermore, preparation programs must offer opportunities through course assignments, study groups, and practicum experiences that allow students to engage in cross-cultural and interracial experiences, thereby enhancing their multicultural awareness, knowledge, and skills (McEwen & Roper, 1994b). Each of the chapters in Part One of this book presented core competencies that are reflected in most curriculums in student affairs preparation programs. Content from each chapter can be integrated into individual courses so that students can begin to see and understand how multicultural competence in student affairs can enhance such core competencies as research and evaluation, management and administration, and teaching and training.

Given that some initial research has shown that multicultural competence may be related to one's own racial identity (see Fulton, 1994; Mueller & Pope, 2001; Ottavi, 1996), some specific recommendations for professional preparation can be suggested. Student affairs preparation programs that emphasize multiculturalism and multicultural competencies would benefit by including opportunities for students to explore their racial attitudes and to process their past racial experiences (Mueller & Pope, 2001). Exploration of one's racial attitudes is particularly relevant since there may be a tendency to take action on racial issues without examining one's personal responsibility for racism. Training and development on multiculturalism too often focuses on knowledge about other racial groups or about the conceptual aspects of oppression without encouraging self-awareness. Within the context of the Multicultural Intervention Change Matrix (see Table 3.1 in this book), Pope (1995) argued that in addition to "content-focused" training on multicultural issues, there must also be "cognitive-restructuring," which challenges the individual's assumptions and beliefs about the world, other races, and oneself as a racial being. Learning-as-practice texts, which foster the opportunity for individual reflection and group discussion, such as those authored by Helms (1992), Katz (1978), and Okun, Fried, and Okun (1999), can be useful in helping learners move beyond intellectualizing racial issues.

Similarly, Reynolds (1995a) discussed a set of components that she argues are central to designing effective multicultural training and education programs and that encompass a range of educational interventions:

- Content (providing information on cultural differences and concepts such as oppression and acculturation)
- Cognitive (understanding and challenging our ways of seeing the world)
- Affective (exploring feelings, attitudes, and values)
- Experiential (presenting hands-on activities that move learners beyond content toward greater sensitivity)
- Skills (teaching learners culturally responsive skills and interventions)
- Process (paying attention to group dynamic and emphasizing the role of modeling)

Finally, since Mueller and Pope (2001) also found that identification with a marginalized group may be related to multicultural competence, it is useful to allow students to explore and understand their many social identities as both oppressors and oppressed (Jackson & Hardiman, 1986). An examination of one's multiple identities can lead to greater integration of these identities (Reynolds & Pope, 1991) as well as a greater understanding of the interaction between one's personal identity and more externally defined dimensions such as race, gender, and religion (Jones & McEwen, 2000), thus laying a foundation for greater understanding of the complexity of diversity issues as well as one's own multicultural competencies.

On a broader level of graduate preparation, Wallace (2000) called for change in multicultural education at graduate schools. In addition to challenging academic administrators and faculty to incorporate multicultural competence into their institutional and departmental missions, she supplies a provocative set of questions that can be asked of and answered by individuals who are either well versed in or relatively new to multicultural education. Questions such as these can be useful in framing discussions around reconceptualizing our graduate preparation programs as incubators for multiculturally competent practitioners.

Professional Development

The process of developing multicultural competence need not start with graduate preparation, and certainly it does not end when one's professional life begins. Developing multicultural competence is a lifelong undertaking and can and should be integrated into one's professional development objectives. Everyone, at various leadership levels within the student affairs profession (including seasoned professionals), can benefit from greater exploration of their racial attitudes and the role this exploration might play in their ability to work with racial issues on campus and with students and staff of color (Mueller & Pope, 2001). Therefore, the suggestions noted here about graduate preparation can be readily applied to professional development and training programs.

Developing multicultural competence in professional settings can also occur outside of professional development and training. Research indicates that the development of multicultural competence is related to discussions about multicultural issues with one's supervisor, and it is also related to opportunities to implement diversity programs and policies (Mueller & Pope, 2001). The practical implications of these findings are apparent. As King and Howard-Hamilton (2001) noted, supervisors can—and should—play a significant role in fostering the multicultural competencies of their supervisees by communicating expectations for acquiring and demonstrating multicultural knowledge and skills and by promoting opportunities for them to explore multicultural issues. Such opportunities need not be limited to professional development training workshops but can also include weekly one-on-one supervisory meetings as well as staff meetings where multicultural issues are addressed. Multiculturalism should be addressed not just in response to campus issues and crises that might arise but also as part of standard discussions in which the supervisor is assisting in the development of all professional competencies. Furthermore, supervisors can offer access for their staff to participate on campus committees that address diversity issues through programming and policy development. Of course, the supervisee's comfort level in working on such a committee varies with the individual, and the supervisor may need to monitor closely and provide support as needed.

Suggestions for Future Student Affairs Research

The research on multicultural competence in student affairs is severely limited and is about ten years behind the research in counseling psychology. Attempting to catch up to the pace of the counseling psychology profession may seem an insurmountable task, so perhaps we should regard their work as a source of inspiration and as a foundation for our own. The volume and depth of research conducted thus far in counseling psychology constitutes a model and framework for continued research in our own profession. Borrowing from the investigation of multicultural competence in counseling psychology, a research agenda for multicultural competence in higher education emerges in three broad areas. First, to pluralize our understanding of multicultural competence through research, measurement of the construct needs to be expanded and validated. Next, demographic, experiential, and educational predictors of multicultural competence should be explored since these variables may become targets of intervention through programs and policies designed to enhance graduate preparation, professional development, and supervision. Finally, given the assumption that multicultural competence must be infused into the array of professional competencies delineated by Pope and Reynolds (1997), the relationship between and integration of multicultural competence and the other professional competencies noted in this book has to be explored. We now look at each of these research areas in greater detail.

Measurement

Currently, one measure of multicultural competence in student affairs exists—Multicultural Competence in Student Affairs-Preliminary 2 (MCSA-P2) (Pope & Mueller, 2000). Initial research on the instrument demonstrates satisfactory reliability and validity, but additional research is needed to further examine these psychometric properties. Studies investigating test-retest reliability as well as construct-related, discriminant, and predictive validity are warranted. Such research will strengthen the instrument for continued use in research and for eventual use in student affairs program evaluation.

Diversifying how multicultural assessment in student affairs is conducted is also advisable. This might include objective, comparative, or outcome assessments of the practitioner's competence from supervisors, professors, peers, supervisees, and students. Student affairs may also benefit by measuring multicultural competence at the institutional level, as illustrated by the work of Grieger's Multicultural Organizational Development Checklist for Student Affairs (1996) and Reynolds, Pope, and Wells's Student Affairs MCOD Template (2002; see Table 3.2 in this book). Finally, Pope and Mueller (2000) argued that measurement of a construct as complex and fluid as multicultural competence needs to be broadened. Similar to recent advances in the counseling profession, measurement of multicultural competence in student affairs research can only be enhanced by considering employment of qualitative research approaches. Methodologies that employ qualitative techniques may reveal greater depth and new dimensions to our understanding of multicultural competence (Pope-Davis et al., 2002; Ponterotto, 2002), or they can be triangulated (Stage & Russell, 1992) with quantitative approaches.

Predictors

Contributing to the amplification of our understanding of multicultural competence are those studies that explore the variables related to multicultural competence. There is some preliminary evidence suggesting that certain variables, such as experience with training and implementation of multicultural programs and policies, personal identification with a socially marginalized group, and racial identity, are related to multicultural competence (Mueller & Pope, 2001). Future research could examine these variables more closely to help us better understand why and how they relate to one another.

Beyond this, there are many other variables worth investigating for a possible relationship with multicultural competence. These include, but are not limited to, socioeconomic status, varied roles and position levels within the profession, racial composition of coworkers and supervisors, organizational culture, institutional type, the frequency of discussion on multicultural issues with colleagues, and climates they influence and are responsible for maintaining.

As greater comprehension of these relationships emerges, practitioners will have better understanding of their work environments, which can guide their interventions in pursuit of creating a more multiculturally sensitive campus staffed with more multiculturally competent professionals.

Core Competence

A premise of this book is that multicultural competence can and must be infused into the other professional competencies of a student affairs practitioner (Pope & Reynolds, 1997). This seems easier said than done. Fuertes, Bartolomeo, and Nichols (2001) proposed that, in the counseling psychology profession, the basic competencies of a profession may need to be in place (and almost at an expert level) to "meaningfully engage and use multicultural competencies" (p. 10). Other researchers in the counseling profession have described the interrelatedness of basic counseling skills with multicultural counseling skills and have suggested that the latter are a more refined and sophisticated set, developed only after basic skills are established (Coleman, 1998; Fuertes & Brobst, 2002). It is unclear if this is true for the student affairs profession. The model of competence developed by Pope and Reynolds (1997) creates fertile ground for further examination so we can better understand how, when, and by what processes multicultural knowledge, skills, and awareness can be integrated into the other competencies of the profession.

Summary

A significant development in our profession's attempt to address multicultural issues has been the introduction of the concept of multicultural competence (Ebbers & Henry, 1990; McEwen & Roper, 1994a; Pope & Reynolds, 1997). The advancement of this concept in the counseling literature is quite impressive and offers useful insight into our professional practice, but there is a limit to what can be translated from the counseling profession to our own. It is time for our own profession to explore this concept as it relates to our goals, organization, personnel, practices, and competencies. Considering that the research done in the counseling profession has nearly a ten-year head start on our own, we can use their research as a model and guide for our own research agenda. As a profession, we have broken ground on multicultural competence research and have been able to articulate some implications of these early findings, but there is much more to be done. This chapter has discussed some of the multicultural competence research being carried out in our profession and the implications of that research for practice; it has raised some questions for further research activity in this important area.

Chapter Nine

Multicultural Competence: Reflection and Practice

From the Preface of this book to the end, we assert that for truly effective student affairs practice, multicultural competence—that is, multicultural awareness, knowledge, and skill—is essential. Multicultural awareness and knowledge can be acquired through a methodical amalgamation of research, reading, study as well as sessions at professional associations, training, staff meetings, work shops, coursework, personal reflection, and journaling—all of which must then be combined with personal experiences, honest communication, and increased and prolonged interaction with individuals different from oneself and with others on a similar journey. Conversely, building upon the solid foundation acquired from all of these experiences, we see that developing multicultural *skills* requires occasions to practice specific behaviors, tasks, and interventions.

The use of case studies can present such occasions. Case studies encourage consideration of multiple perspectives, allow simulation of real-life practice, and yet simultaneously reduce anxiety because the stakes are not nearly as high as in an actual work situation. Stage (1993) gave a particularly apt description of the benefits of using case studies when she stated: "Through vicarious analysis of realistic cases, the administrator or future administrator can practice with the theoretical tools of the trade. While case analysis cannot replicate a sense of danger or urgency (no one will lose a job for a weak analysis of a case), it can provide useful practice for future administrative decision making" (p. 16).

Case studies have been used voluminously in student affairs and a variety of other fields, among them medicine, social work, the military, business management, and other areas of education. In the student affairs literature alone, there has been wide variation in the content, format, and scope of the presentation of case studies (see, for example, the work of Blimling, Whitt, & Associates, 1999; Sandeen, 1991; Stage & Associates, 1993). The case studies presented in this chapter are designed to stimulate involvement and simulate real-life situations using the concepts discussed in Part One of this book. Although it is highly appropriate to simply read through the case studies presented in this chapter, we believe it is far more advantageous for you to engage with others in a group or class setting to discuss these concepts and complete the case studies and guided discussion questions. If you are not currently in a class using the book, we encourage you to join or establish a study group with colleagues to complete the accompanying "case exploration activities."

The case studies in this chapter are based on situations that have actually happened on campuses across the nation and are presented as realistically as possible. They vary in length and scope. Most of them are limited in terms of background information. You may desire additional information about the history of the institution, the surrounding community, or political issues currently facing the state in which the institution is based, but this is not essential for the resolution of the problems posed. If, however, these case studies are used for class or group discussions and the instructor or group leader desires it, one could easily adapt a case to a particular institution by adding applicable information, either demographic or situational.

While reading the case studies, you should look for ways to apply relevant concepts from Part One of the book rather than merely react to the events described. The case exploration activities (adapted from Snowden & Gorton, 2002) for each case are categorized under five headings: "Analyze the Case," "Identify and Categorize the Multicultural Competencies," "Propose a Solution," "Evaluate Your Solution," and "Examine Your Campus."

Case Exploration Activities

Prior to presenting the case studies, a detailed discussion of the components of the case exploration activities is presented to assist you in better understanding the various tasks involved in the case analysis and resolution. Using the case exploration activities effectively involves understanding and performing the tasks suggested under each heading

Case Analysis

Prior to analyzing the case, you should consider these key questions: (1) What multicultural issues and dynamics play a role in this scenario? (2) What ideas, theories, or strategies from Part One of this book might be useful in exploring the case? The cases focus on significant issues or problems within student affairs. There are many factors to consider when exploring these cases, including but not limited to how and in what order the events occurred and what the attitudes, perceptions, and reactions of the participants were to the various aspects of the case. It is important to notice if, and then how, the initial actions and reactions of student affairs staff, students, faculty, or other university personnel influence the direction and magnitude of the problem. In every case, there are always improvements (such as better communication and decision making) that could have improved the outcome. Understanding concepts such as power, organizational culture, social influence, and organizational change adds to an in-depth analysis of any case or problem involving dynamic and sometimes complicated human interaction and organizational structures. Case studies involving diversity issues require this type of vigorous analysis.

To effectively analyze any case, it is vital to consider the perceptions of all of the individuals involved. This is probably true in most situations but particularly so in a situation involving multicultural dynamics. What becomes relevant is not just what happened but also how our cultural background and experiences influence how we interpret the events. Thus, "what happened" has various levels of truth and accuracy. An example might be helpful here. A familiar but unfortunate occurrence on campus is the occasional fistfight between male students. If the men are from different races and cultures, the fight—which might just as well have occurred for the very same transgression between two men of the same race—may take on additional complexity. In Kochman's book on cultural miscommunications between Blacks and Whites (1981), he makes clear the cultural conflict that is present even in determining when the fight began. In White communication style, according to Kochman, the fight begins when the first punch is thrown. When two White men begin to argue, as the intensity of the argument rises, the men may get very close to each other and even bump chests. This may or may not escalate to punches being thrown. If it does, often the instigator of the fight is viewed as the individual who threw the first punch. In Black communication style, according to Kochman, the fight begins when *the level of threat is raised*, not when the first punch is thrown. Presumably, if two students argue, one White and the other Black, when the White student follows his norm in an argument of stepping closer to the Black student, he might be surprised by a punch. In the Black student's mind, the fight began when the White student stepped closer to him, initiating a perceived threat. Campus judicial systems, typically grounded in White communication style, demonstrate their preconceived interpretation of the beginning of the fight when staff members ask, "Who hit whom first?" In a campus judicial system that incorporates cultural realities and experiences, when the students are asked to explain what happened, their individual and cultural perspectives are acknowledged and honored. Thus, using a multicultural perspective to analyze this situation, both students contributed equally to the conflict and the fight that ensued.

Clearly, our perceptions are influenced by our worldview, life experiences, and cultural identity. We must acknowledge and examine this reality closely as we interpret the cases presented in this chapter; even more important, in the complex situations that occur daily on our campuses we must also remain open to expanding our understanding of others, the world around us, and ourselves.

At the conclusion of each case, we pose questions created to begin the critical thinking and problem-solving aspect of case analysis. They are by no means inclusive and are meant to stimulate other questions. This analysis can occur individually or within a classroom or group discussion. It is unlikely that these exact cases will be replicated in a professional's life, but it is hoped that they encourage ideas about how to handle a similar situation. One goal of thorough analysis and discussion is deep appreciation of the challenging nature of multicultural competence.

Identify and Categorize the Multicultural Competencies

The case studies selected for this chapter are intended to highlight the complexity of the multicultural issues on our campuses. There is already considerable evidence that issues of student and staff diversity significantly affect campuses. In going through the case studies, you are asked to detect how multicultural awareness, knowledge, and skills are demonstrated. You are also asked to classify what specific areas of multicultural awareness, knowledge, and skills are missing in the student affairs professionals' actions. For example, would the residence hall director handle the situation differently if he had additional knowledge about the cultural implications of pointing a finger in the face of a student from a particular cultural background? Or how might self-reflection and increased awareness assist the faculty member in her interaction with a female Muslim student whose worldview and religious beliefs are contrary to her own view on the role of women?

In addition, you are asked to determine which area or areas of the Dynamic Model of Multicultural Competence, presented in Part One, are relevant to each case. At times—as is often true in real life—the cases involve more than one competency. Finally, you are asked to identify specific content knowledge—theories, literature, and research—that may offer assistance in addressing the case.

Propose a Solution

Initially, when analyzing the various aspects of case studies, it is essential to categorize the multicultural dynamics and their influence on the process. Understanding the various components of the case study and knowing how one might respond in this situation is crucial. The beliefs, concepts, and theories presented in Part One of this book can assist practitioners in the case analysis process and help them clarify what they might do in this situation. Evaluating the various options for responding to the cases and resolving the problems involved is a foundational step in the case analysis process. Two steps in developing an effective solution are (1) making a decision on how to respond and (2) creating a tangible plan to resolve the issues.

Evaluate Your Solution

The solution evaluation section of the case exploration activities is probably one of the most important processes involved in effective use of case studies, but it is also one of the most underused. Too often, individuals, classes, or groups who use case studies tend to just generally describe a solution without fully considering the range of possible reactions or consequences to a suggested plan. Occasionally, a more systematic and careful attempt to successfully resolve the problem in a case is developed, yet success is too often determined by whether the solution is one that other individuals in the class or discussion group view as realistic and appropriate. In other words, success is determined by the approval of the group. However, in the daily practice of student affairs, our solutions often create reactions that can be viewed as positive or negative. Our ideas or action plans may be accepted, rejected, or somewhere in between. The proposed solution may ultimately improve, worsen, or have no effect on the original problem.

The solutions we suggest to these cases or to real-life challenges inherently produce insight into our core beliefs and assumptions about people, events, and strategies. These underlying assumptions have implications for how we perceive the situation, how we interact with the individuals involved, and what type of outcome we believe is possible or necessary. Testing or experimenting with possible outcomes may make our assumptions more visible and help us better understand them. A vital part of problem solving is anticipating the reactions of others and their possible responses to our proposed solutions before they actually happen. Therefore, this type of exploration should be a significant component of any problem solving, whether in real life or as part of a case study exercise.

To enhance the effectiveness of these case studies, it is helpful if the individual or groups involved develop possible scenarios and role-play the potential results of one or more suggested solutions. The case studies offered in this chapter provide little information about how the individuals or actions might evolve as the situation unfolds. Participating in role playing or other related activities might stimulate the thinking and problem solving of the individuals analyzing the case. For example, in the case study of the vice president for student affairs and the residence hall staff interacting after a highly controversial and public racial incident in the residence halls, a role play might be created and implemented. The specific details of the role play are left for the case study group to develop; hopefully they are varied enough to test possible outcomes. This type of role play can give the individuals involved in the case study activity some general ideas about how to address possible follow-up problems and concerns about the original matter.

Another type of role play might involve clues to possible scenarios that the case study group wants to implement. For example, in that same role play, several alternatives regarding the reactions of the residence hall staff or vice president could be suggested, thereby giving the case study group a general idea about the type of situation that might develop.

To be effective, these role-playing activities require commitment and involvement from everyone. If this is to be more than just an exercise, participants must see the value in actually testing a possible solution. If they are uncomfortable role-playing and have difficulty anticipating how others might respond, then the simulation is unlikely to be successful. Being an effective problem solver requires willingness to take risks and test proposed solutions. The value of activities of this kind is that they create opportunities for self-improvement and professional growth.

Examine Your Campus

The learning activities suggested in this section have been created to involve you or other members of the case study group as fully as possible. The issues that occur in responding to a campus problem have implications for any college or university. For each case study, there are several questions meant to suggest follow-up activities for the case study group members to investigate and apply the proposed solutions to their own campus. This type of explorative process is meant to anticipate and prevent possible problems later on. These questions may challenge you to more fully understand the implications for campus policy, state law, ethical standards, community expectations and demographics, administrative procedures, and the endless possible reactions and views of the various constituent groups involved. For this to be effective, you need an adequate knowledge base to solve the specific case studies. Many individuals are unaware of campus policies or unique features of their campus population that are outside of their daily work responsibilities. However, because of the interrelated and synergistic nature of campus life, problems in one unit may have implications for others, and student affairs professionals must be prepared for such possibilities. Participants are encouraged to fully explore the relevant policies and procedures as well as useful and meaningful cultural information regarding the case studies presented in this chapter.

Case Studies

In this section, we have prepared several case studies for you to read, analyze, and design appropriate interventions. Immediately following the case studies, questions are posed, using the previously described format, to aid you in analyzing the cases.

Case 1—Orientation Skit Flap

Benson State University (BSU) is a large, urban, public university with an excellent reputation for science and engineering programs. Although it is clearly a predominantly White institution, it has a diverse student body served by a highly reputable staff of student affairs administrators. This summer, however, the vice president for student affairs, Sam Infantino, has had more than his share of headaches, as has the director of student life, Brenda Giarc, who is responsible for, among other things, new student orientation.

The difficulties start after the second of six orientation sessions offered during the summer. Each session lasts three days and two nights and is administered by a staff of twelve undergraduate orientation guides and a graduate orientation coordinator, Deb Kane. On the second night of each orientation session, the guides lead small-group discussions on diversity and multiculturalism at BSU. In the past, the guides have complained that the students do not "get into" these discussions, no matter what they try to do. This year, the guides, in consultation with Deb, have decided that they will do a skit before the discussions to get the new students to think about the many situations that can occur on such a diverse campus. The set-up for the skit is "a typical day in a residence hall suite." Each guide plays a particular type of student: an African American woman, an Asian woman, a Latino, two lesbians, a student who uses a wheelchair, a White man and woman, and a student with a learning disability. The skit lasts twenty minutes and involves a range of jokes and imitations, all of which are intended to exaggerate stereotypes of the various groups represented by the choice of characters.

During the first orientation session of the summer, the audience of new students chuckles uncomfortably as the guides perform the skit. By the end of the skit, however, many are laughing uproariously. Following the skit, the guides break down into their respective groups to lead discussions, qualifying their behavior by stating that they needed to "play up the stereotypes in order to get our point across." At the end of the discussions, the guides are pleased with their work and the lively discussions that followed.

However, the guides do not get such favorable reviews after their skit with the second orientation group. There is less laughter in the audience, and many of the guides report to one another—and to Deb—that they spent most of the discussion time justifying and defending their skit and never had the opportunity to discuss any diversity issues. In one group, two students leave the discussion in anger. Several days later, the senior student affairs administration of the university receives two angry phone calls, three letters, and several e-mail messages from new students and parents about the "racist," "sexist," "homophobic," and "insensitive behavior" of the guides. The director of student life, Brenda, investigates the incident and learns for the first time about the skit. She requests that the guides do the skit for her and the VP. Following the skit, the VP, Brenda, and Deb meet to discuss the incident. The vice president reports that the president has requested that the skit be discontinued but that some diversity discussion should still take place. Deb explains that the guides put the skit together, and although she was somewhat uncomfortable with it, she felt it was important that the guides take ownership and responsibility for their work. Regardless, the vice president decides to enforce the president's request.

When Deb and Brenda meet with the guides later that day, most of them get upset and say that the students and their parents have missed the point and are blowing the whole thing out of proportion. They remind Brenda and Deb that there was no problem with the first group, who seemed to enjoy the skit and the ensuing discussion. Several days later, five of the guides send a letter to Brenda indicating that they will quit "on principle" if they are not allowed to do the skit.

Case Analysis

- What multicultural issues and dynamics play a role in this scenario?
- What beliefs, theories, or strategies from Part One of this book are useful in exploring this case?
- What are possible explanations for why the two orientation groups have reacted differently to the skits?
- Was this situation preventable? If so, what might have been done to prevent it?
- What is your evaluation of the strengths and weaknesses of the orientation guides' plan to encourage discussion on diversity topics?

Identify and Categorize the Multicultural Competencies

- In what ways are multicultural competencies demonstrated in this case?

  - How is multicultural awareness demonstrated in this case? By whom?
  - How is multicultural knowledge demonstrated in this case? By whom?
  - How is multicultural skill demonstrated in this case? By whom?

- What specific areas of multicultural competence are missing from this case?

  - How is multicultural awareness missing from this case?
  - How is multicultural knowledge missing?
  - How is multicultural skill missing?

- Which area(s) of the Dynamic Model of Multicultural Competence is (are) the focus of this case?

Propose a Solution

Assume that you are Brenda Giarc, the director of student life.

- What decisions need to be made and steps taken to resolve this situation?
- What multicultural awareness, knowledge, and skills does Brenda need?

Evaluate Your Solution

To test your thinking about the problems in this case, the group or class should create and role-play one or more of these situations:

- A meeting with Brenda Giarc, Deb Kane, and the five orientation guides who have threatened to quit if the skits are discontinued.
- Brenda's next supervisory meeting with Deb. Assume that this meeting will be to discuss this specific incident and also broader multicultural issues.
- A meeting between Deb and students from several multicultural groups on campus: the Black Student Union, Hispanic Student Association, GLBT, United Asian-Pacific American Students, and Students Against Racism. The students call her office requesting a joint meeting to discuss what they heard about the orientation skits.

Examine Your Campus

Describe the criteria and process used on your campus to approve student-designed and -facilitated programs for the public, including prospective students, their parents, and the local community. How are student leaders—RAs, orientation guides, peer advisors, and others—on your campus trained to facilitate diversity discussions?

Case 2—Equal Opportunity Employer in Search of "Good" Diverse Candidates (Written by Deidre Marriner)

Franklin Roberts College is a four-year, highly selective, private institution located in central New York. There are roughly thirty-five hundred students in attendance, and approximately one thousand live on campus in the residence halls. Although the college offers approximately seventy majors, the largest academic programs on campus are engineering, biology, and psychology. The demographic makeup of the institution is 72 percent White, 14 percent Asian, 8 percent Black, 4 percent Hispanic, and 2 percent Native American.

Tammy Wu, a senior in the chemical engineering program, has been coming to see Diane Campbell for career counseling for a few months as she gears up for her postcollege job search. They have worked together to perfect Tammy's resume and reviewed the job search resources available to all students at Franklin Roberts. Diane is aware that Tammy has submitted her resume for several on-campus recruiting interviews and that she has been selected for most of them. So far she has not made it past the first round of interviews, and Diane doesn't understand why. Tammy is a bright, hardworking student who has done very well academically (with a GPA of 3.79) and has been involved in several co-curricular activities. She is on the executive committees of the Asian American Student Association (AASA) and Women in Engineering (WIE). Tammy is feeling discouraged about her job search and is thinking of going to graduate school because she isn't sure she is going to get a job.

Diane has been a career counselor in the University Career Planning Center for the past three years. She has been assigned to work primarily with students majoring in engineering, math, and science. She also coordinates on-campus recruiting for those career fields. Still thinking about Tammy's stalled job search, Diane decides to followup with John Marshall, a recruiter that she has worked with for the past few years, who is on campus today. She takes him to lunch, as is customary, and during their conversation she mentions that she has worked with a student named Tammy who seems like a great candidate. She wonders if he has formed an opinion after meeting her that morning in a series of screening interviews. John pauses and then, after further recollection, says: "Oh, yes, that Asian girl. I couldn't get anything out of her. Basically, she just wasn't able to sell herself. It's too bad because we could use some minorities. The boss is on our back to hire more women and other minorities, but I won't consider it if they can't present themselves well. We are not in the business of hiring a minority just to fill a quota!"

Dumbfounded, Diane asks him to clarify what he sees as the major issues for Tammy. John replies: "I asked her several questions about her leadership and her ambitions, and she was unable to tell me much about herself. She talked about what her 'group' did for class, what activities her 'club' initiated, and what her 'family' thinks—more than she did about herself. I simply got the impression that she wasn't a go-getter and that she didn't seem as though she would be able to step up to bat when her work group needs a leader. To top it all off, she just will not maintain eye contact.

Personally, I have difficulty reading people who don't have a firm handshake and who aren't self-assured enough to look you in the eye."

Diane begins to respond and then decides not to push the issue further.

Upon returning to the office, Diane initiates a conversation with her supervisor, Sally Church, the director of the Career Planning Center. Sally has served in that post for five years and is Diane's direct supervisor. In Sally's office, Diane explains the conversation that she had with John over lunch and asks if the staff at the Career Planning Center should begin to think about strategies or interventions to work with the recruiters, some of the Asian American students, or both. Sally, who is distracted by the task she was already working on, looks up and says, "There is nothing we can do about it. The recruiters will hire whom they see fit, and we shouldn't interfere because we can't afford to lose our relationship between the businesses and the school. We have enough on our plates this year; do we really have time for additional programming?" Diane shrugs and walks out.

Case Analysis

- What multicultural issues and dynamics play a role in this scenario?
- What beliefs, theories, or strategies from Part One of this book are useful in exploring this case?
- Assess Diane's discussion with her supervisor, Sally. What was done well? How could Diane have handled the situation differently?
- What is Diane's role, as a student advocate and as a campus representative, during her discussion with the recruiter?

Identify and Categorize the Multicultural Competencies

- In what ways are multicultural competencies demonstrated in this case?

  - How is multicultural awareness demonstrated in this case? By whom?
  - How is multicultural knowledge demonstrated in this case? By whom?
  - How is multicultural skill demonstrated in this case? By whom?

- What specific areas of multicultural competence are missing from this case?

  - How is multicultural awareness missing from this case?
  - How is multicultural knowledge missing from this case?
  - How is multicultural skill missing from this case?

- Which area(s) of the Dynamic Model of Multicultural Competence is (are) the focus of this case?

Propose a Solution

Assume that you are Diane Campbell. What are your next steps to respond to this issue?

What multicultural awareness, knowledge, and skills might Diane need to respond appropriately?

Evaluate Your Solution

To test your thinking about the issues in this case, the group or class should create and role-play one or more of these situations:

- A conversation between Diane Campbell and Tammy Wu the next time they meet to discuss Tammy's job search.
- Sally Church meets individually twice a month with each member of her staff. During these regular meetings, they discuss progress toward individual goals, future directions, and current or potential problems or concerns.
- At Diane's next meeting with Sally, Diane again raises the issue of diversity and the recruiters. She requests that the Career Planning Center staff discuss the issue in the near future.
- Two weeks later, John Marshall is back on campus to meet with students. Sally again takes him to lunch.

Examine Your Campus

What type of multicultural or diversity training do the career counselors on your campus receive? On your campus, in this type of situation, who would be considered the client or customer: the students searching for employment or the recruiters looking for employees?

Do the recruiters on your campus receive diversity or multicultural training either in their own workplace or from your campus? If so, describe the type and extent of the training. If not, describe the type of training and education on-campus recruiters should receive to enhance their interaction with all students.

Case 3—Looking for a Place to Be All of Me (Written by Katherine Frier)

Sutton University is a four-year, private, liberal arts institution located in a large northeastern city. This institution of nearly eight thousand undergraduates boasts an above-average distribution of racial and ethnic groups thanks to the extraordinarily large number of international students attending the institution as the sons and daughters of diplomats assigned to the United States. Here is the breakdown: 3 percent American Indian, 12 percent African American, 10 percent Latino American, 22 percent Asian, and 53 percent White. Nearly 60 percent of the incoming class scored 1050 or better on the SATs. The most sought-after programs of study at Sutton are international relations, public service and administration, business administration, and communications. There are approximately 250 faculty members on campus, of which 22 percent are faculty of color; this is due to the exceptional efforts of the provost's office to recruit a faculty that closely represents the diverse population of the university.

In addition to the international atmosphere at Sutton, there has always been an exceedingly large population of students from the New Jersey, New York, Long Island region. A large number of these students come from Jewish homes. Many of the women from this area are stereotyped as "Jewish American princesses" (or "JAPs") by both Jews and non-Jews, in part because of their metro New York or New Jersey accents and their high socioeconomic status. Because all students are permitted to select the residence hall of their choice, many of these students live together in the same residence hall.

Although the Greek system at Sutton is not quite as visible as on some other campuses, there are several fraternities and sororities that actively recruit members. The campus administration is tolerant of the Greek system because of its traditional roots but does not devote a lot of professional support to students who show interest in or join the fraternities and sororities.

Lisa Lowenstein, who is Jewish, is a first-semester student from Long Island. Her mother, Mona, is an alumnus of Sutton and former president of the Kappa Gamma Delta sorority.

Lisa is absolutely miserable at Sutton after just one week of classes. She believes she was pushed into going to Sutton by her mother and is now sure that she has made the worst decision in her life. Although Lisa strongly believes in her Jewish faith and heritage, she is tired of being stereotyped as a Long Island JAP (a label she detests) and would like nothing more than to go out and meet and befriend some of the international students who fascinate her. Although her mother insisted that she declare herself as a communications major, Lisa is determined to change her major to international service so she can travel the world and have new experiences as an interpreter, or even a member of the diplomatic service.

Lisa's roommate, Sondra Bloomberg, appears to take much pride in being viewed as a "Jewish American Princess" and has been continuously pressuring Lisa to rush the sorority to which "all the girls belong," Kappa Gamma Delta. Sondra has no interest in meeting anyone on campus other than those living in their residence hall and insists that Lisa is "missing all the fun that all the other girls are having." Lisa's mother agrees with Sondra and strongly encourages Lisa to join her beloved KGD.

Looking for guidance, Lisa approaches her resident advisor, Jennifer Adams, for advice. She explains her interest in broadening her horizons outside of the Long Island group and asks for suggestions on how she can meet different people. Jennifer, a senior at Sutton, is very busy planning her wedding this semester and has little advice to give Lisa. Jennifer offers her opinion that Lisa will probably be happiest if she goes along with her roommate and joins in the social activities in which "all the girls like you" participate. Lisa reluctantly decides to follow Jennifer's advice and rushes Kappa Gamma Delta, but inwardly she vows to continue her attempts to meet other people and join other groups on campus.

Several weeks into the semester, Lisa, now a pledge of KGD, is more miserable than ever. She has made several attempts to participate in some of the political activities and international clubs around campus but has felt alienated and rejected because of obvious stereotyping and political undercurrents. She tries to downplay her Long Island accent and even avoids giving her last name at meetings, but she continues to feel like an outsider.

Last week, for the first time, Lisa spoke with Cassandra Williams in the Office of Student Activities about her feelings. Cassandra is the university liaison for Greek affairs with whom Lisa has been developing a good relationship because of her membership in KGD. Lisa shares how she is feeling isolated and depressed: "The semester is almost over, and I still don't feel like I belong anywhere on this campus. Everyone seems to have already decided who I am and where I belong. When do I get to decide? Don't get me wrong, I'm proud of being Jewish. It is an important part of who I am, but I am also more than just Jewish. I want to meet people who are different than me. I want to explore other ways of being and learn from other people. How do I do that?" Cassandra indicates to Lisa that as an African American woman who attended a predominantly White university she has had some similar personal experiences and can understand Lisa's dilemma. At the same time, Cassandra says she does not have any particularly helpful advice to offer other than to persevere in her attempts to integrate with other groups on campus. Cassandra also points out that the current political climate (both local and international) holds potential hazards for a Jewish American woman to attempt to engage in broad international circles and that she should proceed with caution. As Lisa leaves, Cassandra makes a mental note to call the hall director in Lisa's building to fill her in on Lisa's feelings.

Analyze the Case

- What multicultural issues and dynamics play a role in this scenario?
- What beliefs, theories, or strategies from Part One of this book are useful in exploring this case?
- What is your evaluation of how the various student affairs staff members have responded to Lisa's feelings and concerns?
- What barriers exist on this campus that are making it difficult for Lisa to fully express herself and discover who she is?

Identify and Categorize the Multicultural Competencies

- In what way are multicultural competencies demonstrated in this case?

  - How is multicultural awareness demonstrated in this case? By whom?
  - How is multicultural knowledge demonstrated in this case? By whom?
  - How is multicultural skill demonstrated in this case? By whom?

- What specific areas of multicultural competence are missing from this case?

  - How is multicultural awareness missing from this case?
  - How is multicultural knowledge missing from this case?
  - How is multicultural skill missing from this case?

- Which area(s) of the Dynamic Model of Multicultural Competence is (are) the focus of this case?

Propose a Solution

Assume that you are Cassandra Williams. What are your next steps to respond effectively to Lisa?

- What multicultural awareness, knowledge, and skills might Cassandra need to most effectively assist Lisa?

Evaluate Your Solution

To test your thinking about the issues in this case, the group or class should create and role-play one or more of these situations:

- A follow-up conversation between Cassandra and Lisa in which Lisa asks more directly for assistance.
- A meeting between Cassandra and Lisa's residence hall director.
- A telephone conversation between Cassandra and Mona Lowenstein (Lisa's mother). Mrs. Lowenstein has called to express her concern that "Someone at the Sutton University is trying to make my daughter hate Jews and hate herself because she is Jewish. Before she went away to Sutton, she was proud to be a Jew. But now, she has an attitude if it's Jewish, it's not good enough."

Examine Your Campus

Investigate the diversity plans that exist on your campus to assist staff and faculty in meeting the needs of the diverse student body. What type of helping skills training do staff members in each student affairs office receive to more effectively and empathically respond to students? Describe the community building activities and multicultural training that occur for students on your campus. How do these activities allow or encourage students to interact with students who are different from them?

Case 4—The New Hate Speech: Using New Technology for Old Messages

At Camden State, a large, predominantly White, midwestern state university, the campus newspaper, *The Daily Collegian,* has printed an article concerning an e-mail message that was sent out to the entire campus community. The message rants about students from the Middle East, particularly Muslims. It lists reasons Muslim students should not be allowed on campus or in the town. It further describes, with violent language, what should be done to eliminate Muslim students from the campus. The entire message is filled with stereotypes and violent images. In reporting the incident, the campus newspaper has also printed the actual e-mail message.

The incident has outraged much of the campus community. Letters and editorials from individual students and faculty members have filled the campus newspaper editorial pages since the article's original publication more than three weeks ago. The overwhelming majority of the printed letters and editorials have offered support to the Muslim community and belittled the cowardice of the anonymous author(s). The most recent letters have also criticized the campus administration for not publicly condemning the anonymous authors or the content of the e-mail message. There has also been criticism of the *Collegian* staff and accusations of sensationalism for printing the actual e-mail message.

Concurrently, numerous occurrences of anti-Muslim graffiti painted on campus buildings and sidewalks and various flyers supporting the sentiments expressed in the original e-mail message have also appeared. Many Muslim students, faculty, and staff, and several individuals who were assumed to be Muslims, feel threatened. Several cases of harassment, property damage, and one case of physical assault also have been reported.

The Campus Computing and Information Systems office is working with campus police to identify the creators of the e-mail message. Although the campus police and all other university administrators have refused to comment on the ongoing investigation, the campus newspaper reports that sources close to the investigation have confirmed that individual(s) on the campus created the message. The paper also reports that the investigation indicates a number of students know the identity of the perpetrators but are unwilling to divulge that information and cooperate with the investigation. A rumor is circulating on campus that within two days, members of the Delta Omega Sigma fraternity will be identified as the perpetrators of the original e-mail message.

Analyze the Case

- What multicultural issues and dynamics play a role in this scenario?
- What beliefs, theories, or strategies from Part One of this book are useful in exploring this case?
- Evaluate the response of the campus administration at this point in the investigation.
- Examine the decision of *The Daily Collegian* to print the original e-mail message.

Identify and Categorize the Multicultural Competencies

- In what way are multicultural competencies demonstrated in this case?

  - How is multicultural awareness demonstrated in this case? By whom?
  - How is multicultural knowledge demonstrated in this case? By whom?
  - How is multicultural skill demonstrated in this case? By whom?

- What specific areas of multicultural competence are missing from this case?

  - How is multicultural awareness missing from this case?
  - How is multicultural knowledge missing from this case?
  - How is multicultural skill missing from this case?

- Which area(s) of the Dynamic Model of Multicultural Competence is (are) the focus of this case?

Propose a Solution

Assume that you are the vice president for student affairs.

- What decisions need to be made and steps taken to resolve the components of the case under your jurisdiction?
- What multicultural awareness, knowledge, and skills might the vice president need to draw on?

Evaluate Your Solution

To test your thinking about the issues in this case, the group or class should create and role-play one or more of these situations:

- A meeting of the Muslim students, faculty, and staff (total of thirty people) and the vice president for student affairs.
- The advisor for *The Daily Collegian* schedules a meeting with the editorial staff of the paper to review the decision the staff made in printing the e-mail message in its entirety in the paper.
- A letter and petition addressed jointly to the president of the university and the vice president for student affairs has just been delivered to your office. The letter accuses both you and the president of complicity with the perpetrators of the original e-mail message as well as the graffiti, harassment, and abuse. The letter states: "Your failure to immediately condemn these actions and to state unequivocally that bigotry and harassment of this type is antithetical to the idea of a university and will not be tolerated here, has led to a lack of confidence in your leadership. Therefore, we the undersigned, demand that you both resign effective immediately." A total of 362 students, faculty, and staff have signed the letter.

Examine Your Campus

Investigate your campus administration's policy and procedures and past practices in regard to public responses to incidents on campus. When does the administration comment? How soon? Are there different procedures or timelines for criminal investigations? What are your campus policies and practices regarding graffiti? Are there separate policies for bias-related graffiti? On your campus, what is the relationship between the campus administration and the campus newspaper? Who is the paper's advisor, and what influence does she have over editorial practices?

Case 5—Just an Average White Guy (Written by Nigel Marriner)

Cartier University is a medium-sized, private, liberal arts university in the Northwest with approximately eight thousand students. It is known for its challenging undergraduate education and students who tend to come from the top 15 percent of their class. The campus is racially diverse: 66 percent White, 4 percent American Indian, 11 percent African American, 9 percent Asian American, and 10 percent Latino/Latina American students.

Students at Cartier University are very satisfied with their campus. Generally, the staff and students are open, thoughtful, and receptive to all students. The culture of the institution is such that it is a sign of prestige or inclusion to be involved in one or more of the student clubs funded by the Student Association (SA). Participation in a student club is on par with the prestige imparted by being involved in Greek societies at other institutions. There is a high level of student activism on campus, which may be the result of the liberal nature of the institution. Students are known to ask tough questions and demand quick responses. They are not likely to wait to allow things to work themselves out. Students are known to take the initiative on things if they see a need.

Joe Walsh, a middle-class White student, has formed a club he wants to call the "Average White Guys." He wants to do so for a group of students he feels wouldn't feel comfortable participating in the activities of other ethnic groups. He would like to get the SA to give the group some start-up money just as they have done for numerous other ethnic and special interest clubs on campus. Their application states that they "want to explore issues of 'masculinity' and 'Whiteness' on the campus and elsewhere."

Cheryl Tobin, an American Indian and president of the SA, has officially spoken against formation of this club. She has released a statement on behalf of the SA, that they believe this group would be exclusionary, either consciously or unconsciously, and as a result funding cannot be provided. The official stance of the Student Association is that no group will be chartered if it is not open to all members of the university population. Unofficially, Cheryl has been saying that she refuses to support this initiative when "every day is White-guy day."

Joe knew there would be reactions of this type. His response is that everyone seems to be part of a special interest group receiving special support and programming, except for the average White students. His prepared arguments include the fact that high-income students, who have more access to elite high schools, tend to do better academically and have their honors program. Low-income students have Educational Opportunity Program, with its extended orientation and cadre of full-time counselors. He also states that "there is a minority services program to assist students dealing with bigotry, ignorance, and acceptance on campus. However, where do I go when I struggle with what it means to be both White and a man? . . . There are no specifically labeled, full-time professionals on campus to help me."

In addition, there is a women's studies program on campus but no men's studies, or even gender studies. He feels there are few avenues available to help him explore the impact and history of being White and male in a modern society. This initiative is one way he feels he can help himself and others like him.

He recognizes and believes that there are inherent rewards to being White, things that he doesn't deal with or have to struggle through. However, he is paying the same amount of tuition and fees as Asian American and African American students, and they receive support in ways that are realistically not available to him. He wouldn't feel comfortable going into the minority services office and asking for assistance.

He is starting to become concerned with where this conversation is going in general. Joe entered into this situation with the best of intentions, but he finds he must constantly defend himself, sometimes voraciously, just to get people to listen to him. He really wants to learn more about being male and being White, but it feels as though others are labeling him as insensitive and maybe even racist. "Why is it OK for every other racial or ethnic group to explore what it means to be who they are or to seek support for their race and not for Whites?" he asks. He's beginning to doubt if his desire to start a new club is worth it anymore.

Carl Cunningham, an African American who has served as the dean of students since being hired at Cartier twelve years ago, has been informed of this situation and is troubled by what is beginning to emerge. He would like to see the situation resolved as quickly as possible.

Analyze the Case

- What multicultural issues and dynamics play a role in this scenario?
- What beliefs, theories, or strategies from Part One of this book are useful in exploring this case?
- What is Dean Cunningham's responsibility in this situation?

Identify and Categorize the Multicultural Competencies

- In what way are multicultural competencies demonstrated in this case?

    - How is multicultural awareness demonstrated in this case? By whom?
    - How is multicultural knowledge demonstrated in this case? By whom?
    - How is multicultural skill demonstrated in this case? By whom?

- What specific areas of multicultural competence are missing from this case?

    - How is multicultural awareness missing from this case?
    - How is multicultural knowledge missing from this case?
    - How is multicultural skill missing from this case?

- Which area(s) of the Dynamic Model of Multicultural Competence is (are) the focus of this case?

Propose a Solution

Assume you are Dean Cunningham. What are your next steps in responding to and resolving this issue?

- What multicultural awareness, knowledge, and skills might the dean need to respond appropriately?

Evaluate Your Solution

To test your thinking about the issues in this case, the group or class should create and role-play one or more of these situations:

- A conversation among Dean Cunningham, Cheryl Tobin, and Joe Walsh to discuss the proposed new club.
- If your solution dictates that the SA approve the new club, use scenario A. If your solution dictates that the SA not approve the new club, use scenario B.
- Scenario A. The SA has approved the club proposed by Joe Walsh. The first meeting is just about to begin, and Joe Walsh is reviewing his opening remarks to detail the purpose and

goals of the club. He scans the room, excited that so many people have attended; there are approximately thirty-five men in the room. All of them are White. He recognizes a couple of the guys from his residence hall floor and one or two guys from his sociology class. Joe also notices three guys he's not seen before, standing in the back of the room even though there are several seats available. These men have shaved heads and are wearing green fatigue jackets. Joe steps to the front of the room, ready to begin the meeting.

• Scenario B. The SA has not approved the club proposed by Joe Walsh. The student newspaper has written an editorial stating that the decision by the student association was indefensible and clearly "reverse discrimination." Joe has filed an appeal and a grievance and has requested that all SA funds be frozen until a decision is made on his grievance. The panel that will hear the appeal comprises two SA representatives, two faculty members, the advisor of SA, and two additional student affairs staff members. Dean Cunningham is an ex-officio member of the panel.

Examine Your Campus

How are student monies controlled on your campus? Do students actually have the final say in both policy and practice? Can administrators step in? If so, according to what criteria? Describe how new student groups are formed and funded on your campus.

Case 6—Just Watching TV

Kevin Brownell, an activities coordinator in the Office of Student Union and Activities at City Community College, is taking a break from his office to watch TV in the union lounge, where he finds several students from various groups watching a network news program. He knows the eight students in the lounge, because he is an advisor to their groups, so he takes a moment to greet each of them. After the commercial break, there is a story on the differential treatment Whites and Blacks receive in employment and housing. The reporters use hidden cameras to show how two men, one Black and one White, have very different experiences when looking for apartments, submitting job applications, and getting bank loans.

During the next commercial, one of the White students states that the story was grossly one-sided and inaccurate and explains how he was once discriminated against in obtaining a summer internship. A Latino student who says that White people cannot possibly understand what discrimination feels like, even in that situation, interrupts him. The discussion gets more heated, with neither student relenting. The rest of the students just sit there watching the argument, as does Kevin. Finally, the White student leaves in anger. Another student turns to Kevin, shrugging her shoulders, as though she is asking, "Well, what are you going to do about that?"

Analyze the Case

What multicultural issues and dynamics play a role in this scenario?

- What beliefs, theories, or strategies from Part One of this book are useful in exploring this case?

Identify and Categorize the Multicultural Competencies

- In what way are multicultural competencies demonstrated in this case?

  - How is multicultural awareness demonstrated in this case? By whom?
  - How is multicultural knowledge demonstrated in this case? By whom?
  - How is multicultural skill demonstrated in this case? By whom?

- What specific areas of multicultural competence are missing from this case?

  - How is multicultural awareness missing from this case?
  - How is multicultural knowledge missing from this case?
  - How is multicultural skill missing from this case?

- Which area(s) of the Dynamic Model of Multicultural Competence is (are) the focus of this case?

Propose a Solution

Assume you are Kevin Brownell. What decisions, if any, need to be made and steps taken to resolve this situation?

- What multicultural awareness, knowledge, and skills might Kevin need to draw on?

Evaluate Your Solution

To test your thinking about the issues in this case, the group or class should create and role-play one or more of these solutions:

- If your solution is that Kevin Brownell does nothing, use scenario A. If your solution has Kevin immediately responding to the students involved, use scenario B.
- Scenario A. Over the next week or so, Kevin begins feeling as if he is getting the cold shoulder from some of his students in the groups he advises. It is particularly noticeable with the students of color. Finally, he pulls one of these students aside and asks her what's going on. After much hesitation, she finally begins to open up. "The word is that you were present when a White student was saying some really inappropriate stuff and that you just sat there and listened. Some of us feel betrayed," she said.
- Scenario B. Kevin asks the Latino student who has been arguing if he will wait in the lounge for him because he wants to talk with him, but first he has to take care of something else. The student agrees. Then Kevin follows the White student into the hall and asks him to stop and talk about what has just happened in the lounge. After about ten minutes, Kevin and the White student return to the lounge. What happens next?

Examine Your Campus

What type and amount of multicultural training are provided for student affairs staff and faculty on your campus? How often does it occur, who administers it, and is it mandatory? Does it differ among departments? What mediation services exist on your campus? What happens when students are unable to resolve their difficulties?

Case 7—Diversity Training for Student Leaders (Written by Matthew J. Weigand)

The Institute for Student Leadership (ISL), sponsored by the Student Leadership Development Center at Central State University, is a three-day program designed to create opportunities for student leaders to enhance their leadership skills, meet and network with other student leaders, identify campus resources, and design and implement individual and group goals for the academic year. Over the years, ISL and the Student Leadership Development Center have gained an impressive reputation on the campus and throughout the state system for its effective training of student leaders. Even though components of the ISL continue to evolve and change as the needs and desires of the student leaders emerge, there remains no apparent diversity awareness or multicultural component to the ISL. Kara Thomas, the director of the center, believes diversity is important, but she has spent most of her time on other priorities (acquiring additional funding for ISL, scheduling nationally recognized speakers for the institute, and working with various academic departments to allow students to obtain academic credit for their participation at ISL).

Kara has, however, attempted to infuse multiculturalism into ISL in subtle ways, though with limited success. She works to recruit a diverse group of graduate and undergraduate students on her staff but has found that she gets few applications from particular demographic groups. For example, she has been unable to hire a Black male in the last two years. In another attempt to include multiculturalism in the work of the center, Kara and others occasionally suggest books for the student leaders' book club (a mandatory club that meets twice a semester to discuss assigned books dealing with leadership issues) that are relevant to diversity issues.

This year, one month before the ISL is scheduled, Corlisse Jordan is hired as the new coordinator of multicultural affairs at CSU. Kara asks Corlisse to assist in training the ISL student staff. Kara requests that Corlisse introduce herself and her office to the staff and facilitate a discussion about the importance of respect for diversity as it applies to their role as student leaders, frontline university representatives, and role models for new students. Corlisse happily agrees and conducts a well-received and thought-provoking session for the student staff.

In a later discussion, Corlisse mentions that she has a relatively short activity she would like the student staff to facilitate with the new student leaders during the ISL. Unfortunately, since the ISL is now less than two weeks away, it is impossible to adjust the schedule. However, Kara thinks the student staff may be able to incorporate the activity into an existing discussion time. Kara tells Corlisse she will get back to her, and then she decides to talk with Eric Jiang, one of her graduate assistants, about the options available.

In previous conversations with Kara, Eric has expressed interest in multicultural issues, particularly those related to race. As a person of Asian descent attending a predominantly White institution in a mainly White community, he is particularly aware of issues of oppression and the importance of feeling welcome and comfortable in one's environment.

When Kara brings up Corlisse's request for incorporating the diversity activity, Eric is at first silent. After a few minutes and with considerable encouragement, he tells Kara he thinks it is a bad idea. He believes that trying to squeeze in a brief diversity activity into an already set schedule is inappropriate, ineffective, and even insulting. He says it would be better to have no diversity component in the ISL than to have such a small, perhaps "token" component. There will be little, if any, time to get into a meaningful discussion about real diversity issues, and so just skimming the surface could potentially do more harm than good, he says.

Kara thanks Eric for his honesty and insight. As he leaves, she realizes she has a complicated decision to make.

Analyze the Case

What multicultural issues and dynamics play a role in this scenario?

- What beliefs, theories, or strategies from Part One of this book are useful in exploring this case?
- Compare and contrast the relative merits of Corlisse and Eric's contradictory views on the training activity.

Identify and Categorize the Multicultural Competencies

- In what way are multicultural competencies demonstrated in this case?

  - How is multicultural awareness demonstrated in this case? By whom?
  - How is multicultural knowledge demonstrated in this case? By whom?
  - How is multicultural skill demonstrated in this case? By whom?

- What specific areas of multicultural competence are missing from this case?

  - How is multicultural awareness missing from this case?
  - How is multicultural knowledge missing from this case?
  - How is multicultural skill missing from this case?

- Which area(s) of the Dynamic Model of Multicultural Competence is (are) the focus of this case?

Propose a Solution

Assume you are Kara Thomas. What decisions, if any, need to be made and steps taken to resolve this situation?

- What multicultural awareness, knowledge, and skills might Kara need?

Evaluate Your Solution

To test your thinking about the issues in this case, the group or class should create and role-play one or more of these solutions:

- A follow-up meeting takes place between Kara and Corlisse in which Kara outlines Eric's concerns and asks Corlisse for her response and suggestions.
- Kara sets her next supervisory meeting with Eric, in which she questions Eric's perspective and suggests that doing something is better than doing nothing.
- Two weeks later, during discussion time, the student staff introduces the activity suggested by Corlisse to the new student leaders attending the ISL. The student staff is now sharing what happened during the activity with Kara, Eric, and Corlisse.

Examine Your Campus

What type of multicultural training, if any, do student leaders on your campus receive? How often does it occur, who carries it out, and is it mandatory? Does it differ among departments? On your campus, how are diversity or multicultural programs presented? Are the programs presented as short activities, a long workshop, a combination of the two, something in between, or not at all? Are they the same for all groups?

Chapter Ten

Conclusion

The concept of multicultural competence is relatively new and unexplored in the student affairs literature. In this book, we have endeavored to define the term not only in an academic sense but also in practical terms through exemplars and case studies. The concept of multiculturalism has been tricky for practitioners. It appeals to our good intentions of being just and fair. But becoming multiculturally competent remains elusive for many of us; we simply do not know how to make it part of our practice. In short, we're often looking for easy answers to complex issues. A challenge in writing this book has been striking a balance between offering a conceptualization of incorporating multiculturalism into our work and suggesting practical ways this can be done. It is our hope that this balanced approach has strengthened the reader's appreciation for the complexity of multiculturalism while at the same time furnishing some tools for enhancing their skill set.

What we have attempted to do is several things. First, we have extended the literature from the counseling psychology profession to the student affairs profession to help expand and deepen our understanding of multicultural awareness, knowledge, and skills. Second, we have demonstrated how multicultural competence can and should be infused into the array of competencies needed by student affairs practitioners. It may seem deceptively easy to comprehend multicultural competence in helping and advising skills, but we should ponder what it has to do with conducting assessment on campus, or in training our student staff, or in supervising and managing resources. We hope that we have added a new dimension to the multiple competencies required for effective practice. Finally, we have shown the many ways in which multicultural competence can be infused into our practice through the examples interspersed in this book, and in particular through the case studies presented in Chapter Nine. Our overall goal has been to present you with a conceptual model and examples of the awareness, knowledge, and skills needed to enhance practices and interactions with students and colleagues in the ever-more-diverse higher education setting.

As Levine and Cureton (1998) stated, "Multiculturalism remains the most unresolved issue on campus today" (p. 91). Given that society is in flux as demographics change and new ideologies emerge to challenge existing ones, the need to consistently address multicultural issues may always be around, and what works now may not be a fitting approach in the future. Therefore, our hope is that we have offered suggestions on new ways of thinking and viewing the world so you can anticipate and see the ever-changing multicultural world and have the vision to respond accordingly.

In this final chapter, we wish to summarize the key points of each of the preceding chapters. From this review, we wish to highlight some of the recurrent themes that have emerged from the discussions there. Finally, as a means to connect some of the recurrent themes, we offer suggestions and resources from the literature to begin or continue the process of creating more multicultural organizations and becoming more multiculturally competent practitioners.

Summary of Key Points

Since the Dynamic Model of Student Affairs Competence (Pope & Reynolds, 1997) lays out the framework for much of this book, it serves as an appropriate framework for summarizing the key points. We start by restating the key features of the model. First, the model assumes that all student affairs practitioners, to be most effective in their work, should have basic competence in each of the seven areas. Beyond the basic level of competence, some practitioners may develop expertise in one or more of the core competency areas. Second, this model intentionally includes multicultural competence as a core competency and not as a marginal dimension or simply an area of expertise. Thus, the model insists that *all* student affairs practitioners should have some fundamental awareness, knowledge, and skills with regard to multicultural issues. Finally, this model suggests that there is a dynamic and integrative relationship among the seven competencies. The work of student affairs professionals is so complex that to carve up the roles, responsibilities, and practice into seven neat categories is artificial. Still, there is heuristic value in doing so. The reality is that in most situations and interactions in our work, various competencies come into play and do so integratively. Multicultural awareness, knowledge, and skills interact with the other competencies on a day-to-day basis. We urge readers to consider multicultural competence not as a separate feature of student affairs practice. All student affairs practice is multicultural.

To further review the Dynamic Model of Student Affairs Competence, let us briefly examine each of the competencies and summarize the key points.

Multicultural Awareness, Knowledge, and Skills

Multicultural competence, as a distinct competency, includes awareness, knowledge, and skills. Multicultural awareness includes an understanding of one's values, beliefs, attitudes, and assumptions and the influences they have on one's work with students who are culturally different. Multicultural knowledge includes knowledge of the dynamics of oppression in higher education as well as information (history, traditions, values, and customs) about the many cultures that participate in higher education. Multicultural knowledge also includes knowledge about the limitations of standard student development theories as they apply to students of color as well as an understanding of models of identity development and acculturation. Finally, multicultural knowledge includes a thorough understanding of the history of higher education and how institutional barriers have limited and continue to limit access to and success in higher education for members of oppressed groups. Multicultural skills in student affairs include a range of abilities needed in one's practice to create and maintain multicultural campus environments: communicating effectively across cultures, expanding one's cross-cultural interactions, developing campus programs and policies that are culturally sensitive and appropriate, rebounding from inevitable cultural mistakes, and incorporating new and previous learning in new situations.

Multicultural Competence in Theory and Translation

Most practitioners are not theoreticians in the formal sense, but we develop and rely on personal theories to help us understand and explain campus phenomena as much as we rely on the formal theories we have learned, if not more so. Applying multicultural competence to theory and translation means that we do more than learn newer theories that uniquely describe the identity development of underrepresented groups or learn the recently revised theories that attempt to incorporate the values and perspectives of those groups. We must also critically examine and identify the assumptions and beliefs that are the basic tenets of our theory base and their limitations. This becomes an important skill to learn and practice. It can be partly accomplished by obtaining knowledge through reading, training, and personal interactions with the various cultural groups that our new and existing theories attempt to describe. Such knowledge can help us appreciate the within-group differences that enrich our understanding of and ability to apply theory in both culture-specific ways and more universally.

Multicultural Competence in Helping and Advising

Learning how to effectively relate to and help others who are culturally different demands a lot from us. First, we cannot overemphasize the powerful act of becoming more aware of our own biases, misinformation, and comfort zones. This self-awareness either enhances or hinders our interactions with others who seek guidance, reassurance, or a place to explore. In addition to knowing ourselves is knowledge of the history, traditions, beliefs, concerns, and resources of various cultural groups. This can help us be more empathic, a key to effective helping. Knowledge about various groups' experiences in higher education and on our own campus can further enhance our empathy. Knowledge about how individuals within groups identify to varying degrees with and respond to their identity group and the majority group (which in some cases are the same thing) can also further enhance our helping interventions. The knowledge of ourselves and of the individuals we are trying to help, when combined, informs the basic skills we use in helping and advising, such as listening, responding, and attending.

Multicultural Competence in Administration and Management

Management and administration practices in student affairs face a difficult challenge: attempting to create and maintain multicultural campus and administrative environments while using administration and management principles and practices that have generally been steeped in a single (that is, the dominant) culture's perspective. A set of approaches and models are needed that facilitate change throughout student affairs divisions and departments. Multicultural competence in student affairs administration and management involves awareness needed to recognize practices and policies (supervision, resource allocation, goal setting, and so forth) that reflect a dominant cultural perspective. Multicultural competence also involves gaining knowledge about the varying needs, conflicting interests, and contributions of a diverse staff as well as knowledge about organizational development frameworks that address these needs, interests, and contributions. Finally, multicultural competence in administration and management involves using models to make systemic change at the individual, group, and institutional levels across the multiple responsibilities of student affairs administration.

Multicultural Competence in Assessment and Research

At first glance, one may wonder how multicultural competence can be infused into the scientific and systematic process of inquiry we call research. Still, the assumptions we hold that affect how we translate theory and helping can also affect the process of data collection and interpretation. Researchers must bear in mind the assumptions they hold about what they consider normal behavior, thoughts, and feelings and the role these assumptions play in the research questions we ask and how we interpret data. In addition, researchers should be aware of the cultural variables affecting both the research process and the interactions within the populations they are studying throughout their data collection procedures. These cultural variables include, but are not limited to, differences in time orientation, a variety of communication styles and languages, and the degree to which the population being studied tends to be individualistic or collectivistic. Researchers must also carefully consider the instruments they select for data collection to guard against insensitivity inherent in the content of the instrument as well as the cultural bias in the process of establishing norms for the instrument. Finally, researchers are urged to explore alternate approaches to collecting data that might attract and affirm a wider range of respondents.

Multicultural Competence in Ethics and Professional Standards

The thorniest ethical dilemmas on campus often involve diversity issues, whether we are aware of it or not. What we communicate through our decision-making process when confronting these dilemmas reflects our core assumptions, ethics, and values. Even though ethical codes and principles can guide us through difficult dilemmas, we must consider how cultural assumptions are embedded in any ethical framework. Multicultural competence in ethics requires that we explore the sometimes simultaneous and conflicting needs, goals, and values of a diverse community and attempt to make meaning of those differences in establishing common ground for resolving issues. Multicultural competence in ethics also involves teaching and transmitting values and ethics to our students through role modeling, communicating values, and personal advocacy.

Multicultural Competence in Teaching and Training

All student affairs professionals are educators. Some of us have explicit responsibilities for teaching and training, but all of us share in the educational enterprise with respect to our students and one another. Multicultural competence in teaching and training is as much about *how* we teach as *what* we teach. Therefore, as we infuse this competency into our teaching and training we are challenged to create learning environments that are inclusive, collaborative, and dynamic and that affirm cultural differences. One of the ultimate goals of embracing multicultural competence in our teaching and training is that everyone in the learning process (teacher and student alike) be actively engaged in critiquing assumptions and knowledge in pursuit of new perspectives. Multicultural competence in teaching and training urges us to examine department curriculum and workshop designs to ensure that (1) developmental differences among learners are addressed by appropriate challenges and supports; (2) the cognitive, affective, content, experiential, skill-building, and process domains are balanced; and (3) cultural sensitivity is applied to the content of the learning experience through inclusive language and examples as well as through readings and activities.

Themes

In writing about the infusion of multicultural competence into the six other competencies, we see that several themes have emerged requiring closer attention before we conclude this book. First is the powerful act of challenging our assumptions. Next is viewing people as individuals while at the same time honoring their membership in multiple identity groups along with the histories, traditions, beliefs, and worldviews that are embedded in these group identities. Finally, and perhaps least obvious, is examining the process of infusing multicultural awareness, knowledge, and skill into a competency area. This examination may lead to the question, Does one need to have fully developed the competency before multicultural competence can be infused, or can this occur simultaneously? Let us look at each of these themes more closely.

Challenging Our Assumptions

In each of the competency areas identified in the Dynamic Model of Student Affairs Competence, the infusion of multicultural competence requires that we question our assumptions and at times deconstruct our underlying beliefs and values. At some level, this is hard to comprehend and even harder to do. Our assumptions and beliefs have served us well and have given us the perspective we need to accomplish what we have accomplished. For many people, challenging them sounds like letting them go and entering an uncharted area. We argue instead that challenging our assumptions is not about letting go of what is familiar in favor of something new and unknown. It is about changing our cognitive structures and making room for new understandings. This is akin to taking off blinders that have limited our view of the world and seeing the world anew.

Challenging our assumptions involves awareness, knowledge, and skill. We must be aware of our existing assumptions, values, and beliefs. This is not an easy task because they are so embedded and taken for granted. It is not until someone points them out to us or we are confronted by a new set of assumptions that we realize what our own are and how much they guide our behaviors and attitudes. Challenging our assumptions also involves learning about other cultural groups and the beliefs and values that underlie their actions, traditions, and views of the world. This knowledge can serve us in becoming more aware of our own. Challenging our assumptions is exceedingly difficult. We are being asked to observe, analyze, make meaning, and restructure our mind to accommodate new learnings.

Responding to the Individual or Culture (or Both)

An ongoing dilemma in the discussion on multiculturalism in professional practice is the *etic* versus *emic* argument. Essentially, the debate can be stated as universal versus culture specific. The etic perspective assumes that our experiences are unrelated to our cultural background or experience. For example, everyone experiences interpersonal conflict, regardless of race, or gender, or class. In other words, the experience of interpersonal conflict, according to the etic perspective, is culture-free. The emic perspective, by contrast, views our experiences as culture specific. How we deal with conflict in interpersonal relationships may be learned within a culture and is specific to that culture.

Practicing from the emic perspective can be challenging if individuals attempt to recognize the differences among cultures and try their best to respond to those differences accordingly. However, a potential pitfall is when practitioners, in their attempt to honor cultural differences, assume that all members of that culture share a particular cultural perspective. This can lead to stereotypes. Consensus decision making, for example, is highly valued in Native American culture. It is important to know this cultural perspective (emic). However, it is also important to note that not all Native American students or staff members endorse this approach to decision making; some may prefer hierarchical or democratic approaches . The point is this: when working with different cultures, it is important to learn and know the various culture-specific ways of seeing and interacting in the world. It is important to get to know the individual, to understand the degree to which she or he is characteristic of that culture. Knowledge of the variables influencing individual perspectives is also vital, as with acculturation, racial identity, geographic locations, and educational experiences. What is most needed is *diunital* reasoning, or the ability to understand and respond to seemingly contradictory ideas so as to fully embrace the complexity of human beings.

Multicultural Competence and Traditional Competencies

A final theme—or perhaps it is a question—that is raised when examining this model is, Does one already need to have some skill in the other six competency areas before multicultural competence can be infused? In the counseling psychology profession, some argue the possibility that multicultural competencies represent "higher order, more specific and sophisticated counseling knowledge and skills, which may be developed only after sound training in basic counseling competence" (Fuertes, Bartolomeo, & Nichols, 2001, p. 10). In this book, we have raised a similar question as a potential area for research. The question is provocative and worthy of study, but we argue that it supports the notion of multicultural competence as an add-on, learned only after the other skill sets (such as management or assessment) are acquired. Our argument is that developing multicultural awareness, knowledge, and skill can and should be incorporated with the development of each competency area in the Dynamic Model of Student Affairs Competence. For several decades now the student affairs profession has treated multicultural competence as an add-on, and the results have been uneven and fragmented (Cheatham, 1991; Pope, 1993a). Let's now learn how to integrate multicultural competence and conduct research to see the effectiveness of this approach.

Becoming a Multiculturally Competent Professional

In this book, we have attempted to expand on the Dynamic Model of Student Affairs Competence (Pope & Reynolds, 1997) by describing in great detail each of the competency areas and how each area is enhanced by incorporation of multicultural awareness, knowledge, and skills. It is our sincere hope that these descriptions and the numerous examples have proven useful to professionals who seek to become more multiculturally competent. At the same time, we recognize that becoming more multiculturally competent is a developmental process requiring challenge (from within ourselves and from our work environments) as well as support. Given this assumption that all of us are at various levels of competency, the questions raised might be, "How do I start?" or "What do I continue doing in my pursuit of becoming a multiculturally competent professional?" We suggest that these questions need to be asked and answered on the personal level as well as the professional. We offer several suggestions for addressing these questions.

Professional Level

Developing multicultural competence must occur at the individual level, but the efforts to become multiculturally competent have to be supported and sanctioned by a commitment at the professional level of student affairs. In particular, we refer to our professional associations, our graduate preparation programs, and our individual campus divisions and departments of student affairs. Let us examine each more closely.

Professional Organizations

In 1997, Pope, Reynolds, and Cheatham presented a report summarizing the accomplishments of an ACPA task force charged with developing initiatives to promote multiculturalism within ACPA and the broader higher education community. The report reflected on the seven goals of the association and articulated how the diversity issues and concerns could be integrated into each of the goals. From this framework, six initiatives to promote multiculturalism were proposed:

1. Establish a document and a process (similar to Tomorrow's Higher Education, or T.H.E project) with a focus on multiculturalism
2. Establish a national institute on multiculturalism to promote a research agenda and national discussions and to identify programming and financial resources

3. Establish and disseminate multicultural professional standards and guidelines for use in professional preparation and practice
4. Prepare publications that facilitate accomplishment of individual and organizational goals in multiculturalism
5. Offer ongoing and systematic professional development programs at the national and regional levels
6. Produce and disseminate videotapes and other technological tools to enhance the education of practitioners

Although the authors of this report made these suggestions for a specific association (that is, the ACPA), many of the same principles could apply to professional associations for specific functional areas (for example, the Association of College and University Housing Officers—International or the National Association for Campus Activities) or regional and state division organizations. The report and the proposals have no less utility now than they did when first proposed. This may be the time to investigate the degree to which these initiatives have been turned into action and to revive some of these ideas.

Graduate Preparation Programs

As we've noted several times throughout this book, graduate preparation programs are an important place to begin the process of developing multicultural competence in student affairs. It is our hope that the contents of this book can be a useful resource for initiating and guiding discussions on multicultural competence across the curriculum. Readers are also encouraged to review McEwen and Roper's comprehensive set of recommendations (1994a) for integrating multicultural knowledge and experiences in student affairs preparation programs. Using the Council for the Advancement of Standards for Student Services/Development Programs (1986) as a guide and basing their review and analysis on student affairs literature, the authors made specific recommendations for incorporating multicultural content and experiences into standard courses in student affairs preparation programs: student development theory, history of higher education, the American college student, research, individual and group helping skills, administration, and supervision. The authors also proposed a set of recommendations for the academic and student services offices that support these graduate preparation programs.

Institutional and Departmental

Interventions at the institutional and departmental levels could more directly and consistently influence current practitioners than the graduate preparation programs or professional associations do. The application of organizational development models is important as institutions and departments move toward becoming more multicultural. Pope's Multicultural Change Intervention Matrix (or MCIM; 1993b, 1995) offers a useful conceptualization to classify the range of activities used by student affairs departments in addressing diversity issues. The model proposes that interventions at the individual, group, and departmental/institutional levels are strengthened when systemic and systematic change is made (that is, when challenging assumptions and examining underlying goals and values of the organization).

Another useful tool in multicultural organizational development comes from Grieger (1996), who applied principles of multicultural organization development in the form of a checklist to specific activities of student affairs divisions, such as goal setting, policy development, staff recruitment, training and development, and program evaluation. The final assessment tool yields fifty-eight possible long-term multicultural objectives that can be initiated and measured.

A final useful tool in MCOD is the Student Affairs MCOD Template by Reynolds, Pope, and Wells (2002; Figure 3.2 in this book). The template identifies ten specific key targets for multicultural intervention, among them mission statement, policy review, and multicultural competency expectations and training. It also highlights the purpose or importance of those key areas, and it identifies specific components to be included within a diversity plan.

Individual Level

As we move toward the end of this book, we return to its primary target: the individual practitioner. Developing multicultural competence is a challenge that requires unrelenting commitment. Each practitioner must establish for herself a program of lifelong learning through formal education and training as well as a personal investment in self-exploration and increasing the circle of multicultural interactions. Here is a list highlighting some views on developing multicultural competence and offering some suggestions.

- *Developing multicultural competence is a call to personal action.* Developing multicultural competence is much more than learning a new skill or understanding more about cultural groups. It is about making a personal commitment to address social injustice in our daily lives. It is not enough to engage in this process on an intellectual level. To be multiculturally competent, we must involve all aspects of ourselves. This includes recognizing our multiple identities (race, gender, sexual orientation, and so forth), our multiple roles (educator, parent, partner or spouse, neighbor, and so on), and the broader dimensions of our being (spiritual, political, social and community, and the like). A personal call to action involves being committed to infusing the principles of multiculturalism into all of those aspects of us. The benefits of doing so can be mutually reinforcing across all our identities, roles, and responsibilities. A personal call to action need not be a lone venture. Joining with others and thereby gaining support and becoming part of a growing effort to build communities of justice can enhance one's commitment. Finally, a personal call to action need not be overly ambitious. It should involve setting realistic goals that lead to change in our own spheres of influence (such as our families, our neighborhoods, our faith communities, and our workplace).
- *Developing multicultural competence is a process.* As lifelong learners we recognize that increasing self-awareness, acquiring knowledge, and developing skills are ongoing processes. Developing multicultural competence is very much the same. If we view multicultural competence as an end point at which only a few (in other words, the "experts") will arrive, then the energy, time, and resources spent seem futile. It's simply not possible to know everything about all the cultural groups that we need to know at one time, but every little bit we add to that knowledge helps. We must remember that the process involves risk taking, and it inevitably involves mistakes. We must move beyond our fears and our defenses and appreciate the small steps we take on this journey. We will amaze ourselves when one day in the future we see how far we've come.

- *Developing multicultural competence takes place from the inside out.* If there is one thing we want the reader to get from this book, we hope it is recognizing that our actions and behaviors in addressing multicultural issues are a necessary part of the process. By themselves they are insufficient. Developing multicultural competence across all of these competencies involves more than trying to be culturally sensitive, attending cultural events, or reading diverse authors. It also involves examining our assumptions and how we see the world. It involves uncovering our biases and stereotypes. It is both a paradigm shift and an ideology that influences and permeates our work. If we develop multicultural competence from the inside out, we overcome feelings of guilt, anger, hurt, resentment, obligation, and hypersensitivity to political correctness; we can establish genuine relationships with students and colleagues in a multicultural setting.
- *Developing multicultural competence involves multiple sources of learning.* Our efforts to become more multiculturally competent are enhanced when we broaden our sources of learning. For many practitioners, this can include (and is sometimes limited to) reading, attending workshops and seminars, and consulting with experts. Many of us tend to overlook, or take for granted, the learning that can *also* take place from expanding and enriching our day-to-day relationships with our colleagues and students. Creating and maintaining genuine contacts with others and legitimizing them as sources of knowledge can lead to developing self-awareness and knowledge. Depending on our life experiences and level of identity, these relationship networks may be vastly different for each of us.
- *Developing multicultural competence is a deliberate act.* Developing multicultural competence does not begin and end when we are in our office. Developing multicultural competence is about transforming how we live our lives; our role as student affairs professionals is only one portion of how we live our lives. Developing multicultural competence is enhanced when we look at the totality of our lives and see where and how we deliberately place ourselves in a position to explore, reflect, examine, and challenge our ways of seeing the world. We must consider our social circles, our faith communities, our families, and our ongoing educational experiences and see who is

a part of those spheres of influence. To what degree do we limit ourselves to those who look, think, and act most like us? Do we take the risk to interact across boundaries to gain knowledge and new insights? In this book we emphasize that most of the people we regard as multiculturally competent did not follow a process that existed in a vacuum. Becoming multiculturally competent means obtaining knowledge, increasing awareness, practicing new behaviors in multiple settings, and applying what we've learned to new and different settings.

Summary

In *Multicultural Competence in Student Affairs,* we have endeavored to examine closely the core competencies of our profession using principles of multiculturalism as our lens. What may have been revealed in this process, we hope, are new insights and ways of thinking about the work we do. We hope that we have answered questions about what multicultural competence might look like in our daily practice. We also hope that we have challenged our readers to raise new questions; to evaluate values and assumptions; to risk letting go of absolutes and certainties; and to envision new relationships, roles, and responsibilities. Creating and maintaining a multicultural learning and work environment is difficult work, but it is not impossible. We must acknowledge the many competencies we already bring to our work. Infusing multicultural competence is not about adding a new competency; it's about revitalizing, enriching, and refocusing the ones we already have.

References

Alvarez, A. N. (2002). Racial identity and Asian Americans: Supports and challenges. In M. K. McEwen, C. M. Kodama, A. N. Alvarez, S. Lee, & C.T.H. Liang (Eds.), *Working with Asian American college students* (New Directions for Student Services, no. 97, pp. 33–43). San Francisco: Jossey-Bass.

American College Personnel Association (ACPA). (1993). Statement of ethic standards. *Journal of College Student Development, 34,* 89–92.

American College Personnel Association (ACPA). (1994). *The student learning imperative: Implications for student affairs.* Washington, DC: Author.

American Psychological Association (APA). (1993). Guidelines for psychological practice to ethnic, linguistic, and culturally diverse populations. *American Psychologist, 48,* 45–48.

American Psychological Association (APA). (2000). Guidelines for psychotherapy with lesbian, gay, and bisexual clients. *American Psychologist, 55,* 1440–1451.

American Psychological Association. (2001). *Publication manual of the American Psychological Association* (5th ed.). Washington, DC: Author.

Arredondo, P., Toporek, R., Brown, S. P., Jones, J., Locke, D. C., Sanchez, J., & Stadler, H. (1996). Operationalization of the multicultural counseling competencies. *Journal of Multicultural Counseling and Development, 24,* 42–78.

Association of American Colleges and Universities (AACU). (1995). *American pluralism and the college curriculum: Higher education in a diverse democracy.* Washington, DC: Author.

Astin, A. W. (1984). Student involvement: A developmental theory for higher education. *Journal of College Student Personnel, 25,* 297–308.

Astin, A. W. (1992). *Minorities in American higher education.* San Francisco: Jossey-Bass.

Astin, A. W. (1993). *What works in college?* Four Critical Years *revisited.* San Francisco: Jossey-Bass.

Atkinson, D. R., Morten, G., & Sue, D. W. (Eds.). (1989). *Counseling American minorities: A cross cultural perspective* (3rd ed.). Dubuque, IA: Brown.

Attinasi, L. C., & Nora, A. (1992). Diverse students and complex issues: A case for multiple methods in college student research. In F. K. Stage (Ed.), *Diverse methods for research and assessment of college students* (pp. 13–27). Washington, DC: American College Personnel Association.

Axelson, J. A. (1985). *Counseling and development in a multicultural society.* Belmont, CA: Wadsworth.

Barr, D. J., & Strong, L. J. (1988). Embracing multiculturalism: The existing contradictions. *NASPA Journal, 26,* 85–90.

Barr, M. J. (1993a). Becoming successful student affairs administrators. In M. J. Barr (Ed.), *The handbook of student affairs administration* (pp. 522–529). San Francisco: Jossey-Bass.

Barr, M. J. (Ed.). (1993b). *The handbook of student affairs administration.* San Francisco: Jossey-Bass.

Baxter Magolda, M. B. (1992). *Knowing and reasoning in college: Gender-related patterns in students' intellectual development.* San Francisco: Jossey-Bass.

Belenky, M. F., Clinchy, B. M., Goldberger, N. R., & Tarule, J. M. (1986). *Women's ways of knowing: The development of self, voice, and mind.* New York: Basic Books.

Bills, T. A., & Hall, P. J. (1994). Antidiscrimination laws and student affairs. In M. D. Coomes & D. D. Gehring (Eds.), *Student services in a changing federal climate* (New Directions for Student Services, no. 68, pp. 47–66). San Francisco: Jossey-Bass.

Blimling, G. S. (1998). Navigating the changing climate of moral and ethical issues in student affairs. In D. L. Copper & J. M. Lancaster (Eds.), *Beyond law and policy: Reaffirming the role of student affairs* (New Directions for Student Services, no. 82, pp. 65–75). San Francisco: Jossey-Bass.

Blimling, G. S., Whitt, E. J., & Associates (1999). Identifying the principles that guide student affairs practice. In G. S. Blimling and E. J. Whitt (Eds.), *Good practice in student affairs: Principles to foster student learning* (pp. 1–20). San Francisco: Jossey-Bass.

Blocher, D. (1978). Campus learning environments and the ecology of student development. In J. Banning (Ed.), *Campus ecology: A perspective for student affairs* (pp. 17–24). NASPA monograph. Washington, DC: NASPA.

Boyer, E. L. (1990). *Scholarship reconsidered: Priorities of the professoriate.* Princeton, NJ: Carnegie Foundation for the Advancement of Teaching.

Brown, C. (1991). Increasing minority access to college: Seven efforts for success. *NASPA Journal, 26,* 85–90.

Brown, M. T., & Landrum-Brown, J. (1995). Counselor supervision: Cross-cultural perspectives. In J. G. Ponterotto, J. M. Casas, L. A. Suzuki, & C. Alexander (Eds.), *Handbook of multicultural counseling* (pp. 263–286). Thousand Oaks, CA: Sage.

Brown, R. D. (1985). Creating an ethical community. In H. Canon & R. Brown (Eds.), *Applied ethics in student services* (New Directions for Student Services, no. 30, pp. 67–80). San Francisco: Jossey-Bass.

Canon, H. J. (1993). Maintaining high ethical standards. In M. J. Barr (Ed.), *The handbook of student affairs administration* (pp. 327–339). San Francisco: Jossey-Bass.

Canon, H. J. (1996). Ethical standards and principles. In S. R. Komives & D. B. Woodard (Eds.), *Student affairs: A handbook for the profession* (3rd ed., pp. 106–125). San Francisco: Jossey-Bass.

Canon, H. J., & Brown, R. D. (1985). How to think about professional ethics. In H. J. Canon & R. D. Brown (Eds.), *Applied ethics in student services* (New Directions for Student Services, no. 30, pp. 81–88). San Francisco: Jossey-Bass.

Caple, R. B. (1991). Expanding the horizon. *Journal of College Student Development, 32,* 387–388.

Caple, R. B., & Newton, F. B. (1991). Leadership in student affairs. In T. K. Miller & R. B. Winston (Eds.), *Administration and leadership in student affairs: Actualizing student development in higher education* (pp. 111–133). Muncie, IN: Accelerated Development.

Caple, R. B., & Voss, C. H. (1983). Communication between consumers and producers of student affairs research. *Journal of College Student Personnel, 24,* 38–42.

Carney, C. G., & Kahn, K. B. (1984). Building competencies for effective cross-cultural counseling: A developmental view. *Counseling Psychologist, 12,* 111–119.

Carpenter, D. S. (1990). Developmental concerns in moving toward personal and professional competence. In D. D. Coleman & J. E. Johnson (Eds.), *The new professional: A resource guide for new student affairs professionals and their supervisors* (pp. 56–72). Washington, DC: NASPA Monographs.

Carter, R. T. (1995). *The influence of race and racial identity in psychotherapy: Toward a racially inclusive model.* New York: Wiley.

Carter, R. T., & Qureshi, A. (1995). A typology of philosophical assumptions in multicultural counseling and training. In J. G. Ponterotto, J. M. Casas, L. A. Suzuki, & C. M. Alexander (Eds.), *Handbook of multicultural counseling* (pp. 239–262). Thousand Oaks, CA: Sage.

Chan, C. S., & Treacy, M. J. (1996). Resistance in multicultural courses: Student, faculty, and classroom dynamics. In J. Meacham (Ed.),

Multiculturalism and diversity in higher education: Special issue of the American Behavioral Scientist (vol. 40, pp. 212–221). Thousand Oaks, CA: Sage.

Cheatham, H. E. (1991). *Cultural pluralism on campus.* Alexandria, VA: American College Personnel Association (ACPA) Media.

Chen, E. C. (2001). Multicultural counseling supervision: An interactional approach. In J. G. Ponterotto, J. M. Casas, L. A. Suzuki, & C. Alexander (Eds.), *Handbook of multicultural counseling* (2nd ed., pp. 801–824). Thousand Oaks, CA: Sage.

Chesler, M. A. (1994). Organizational development is not the same as multicultural organizational development. In E. Y. Cross, J. H. Katz, F. A. Miller, & E. W. Seashore (Eds.), *The promise of diversity: Over 40 voices discuss strategies for eliminating discrimination in organizations* (pp. 240–251). Boston: McGraw-Hill.

Chickering, A. W., & Reisser, L. (1993). *Education and identity* (2nd ed.). San Francisco: Jossey-Bass.

Choney, S. K., & Behrens, J. T. (1996). Development of the Oklahoma Racial Attitudes Scale—Preliminary Form (ORAS-P). In G. R. Sodowsky & J. Impara (Eds.), *Multicultural assessment in counseling and clinical psychology* (pp. 225–240). Lincoln, NE: Buros Institute of Mental Measurements.

Christensen, C. P. (1989). Cross-cultural awareness: A conceptual model. *Counselor Education and Supervision, 28,* 270–289.

Clement, L. M. (1993). Equality, human dignity, and altruism: The caring concerns. In R. Young (Ed.), *Identifying and implementing the essential values of the profession* (New Directions for Student Services, no. 61, pp. 25–34). San Francisco: Jossey-Bass.

Coleman, H.L.K. (1998). General and multicultural counseling competency: Apples and oranges? *Journal of Multicultural Counseling and Development, 26,* 147–156.

Commission of Professional Development (COPA). (1988). *The COPA handbook.* Washington, DC: Council on Postsecondary Accreditation.

Constantine, M. G. (1997). Facilitating multicultural competency in counselor supervision: Operationalizing a practical framework. In D. B. Pope-Davis and H.L.K. Coleman (Eds.), *Multicultural counseling competencies: Assessment, education and training, and supervision* (pp. 310–324). Thousand Oaks, CA: Sage.

Constantine, M. G., Kindaichi, M., Arorash, T. J., Donnelly, P. C., & Jung, K. K. (2002). Clients' perceptions of multicultural counseling competence: Current status and future directions. *Counseling Psychologist, 30,* 407–416.

Cooper, T. L. (1998). *The responsible administrator: An approach to ethics for the administrative role* (4th ed.). San Francisco: Jossey-Bass.

Copeland, E. J. (1982). Minority populations and traditional counseling programs: Some alternatives. *Counselor Education and Supervision, 21,* 270–289.

Cottone, R. R., & Claus, R. E. (2000). Ethical decision-making models: A review of the literature. *Journal of Counseling and Development, 78,* 275–283.

Council for the Advancement of Standards for Student Services/Development Programs (CAS). (1986). *Council for the Advancement of Standards: Standards and guidelines for student services/development programs.* Washington, DC: Author.

Council for the Advancement of Standards for Student Services/Development Programs (CAS). (1992). *Council for the Advancement of Standards: Standards and guidelines for student services/development programs.* Washington, DC: Author.

Council for the Advancement of Standards for Student Services/Development Programs (CAS). (1997). *Council for the Advancement of Standards: Standards and guidelines for student services/development programs.* Washington, DC: Author.

Council for the Advancement of Standards for Student Services/Development Programs (CAS). (1999). *Council for the Advancement of Standards: Standards and guidelines for student services/development programs.* Washington, DC: Author.

Cox, T. (1993). *Cultural diversity in organizations: Theory, research, and practice.* San Francisco: Berrett-Koehler.

Creamer, D. G., Winston, R. B., & Miller, T. K. (2001). The professional student affairs administrator: Roles and functions. In R. B. Winston, D. G. Creamer, & T. K. Miller (Eds.), *The professional student affairs administrator: Educator, leader, and manager* (pp. 3–38). New York: Brunner-Routledge.

Creamer, D. G., Winston, R. B., Schuh, J. H., Gehring, D., McEwen, M. K., Forney, D. S., et al. (1992). *Quality assurance in college student affairs: A proposal for action by professional associations.* Washington, DC: American College Personnel Association and National Association of Student Personnel Administrators.

Cross, E. Y., Katz, J. H., Miller, F. A., & Seashore, E. W. (Eds.). (1994). *The promise of diversity: Over 40 voices discuss strategies for eliminating discrimination in organizations.* Boston: McGraw-Hill.

Dalton, J. C. (1993). Organizational imperatives for implementing the essential values. In R. Young (Ed.), *Identifying and implementing the essential values of the profession* (New Directions for Student Services, no. 61, pp. 87–96). San Francisco: Jossey-Bass.

Dalton, J. C. (1999). Helping students develop coherent values and ethical standards. In G. S. Blimling & E. J. Whitt (Eds.), *Good practice in student affairs: Principles to foster student learning* (pp. 45–66). San Francisco: Jossey-Bass.

Dana, R. H. (Ed.). (2000). *Handbook of cross-cultural and multicultural personality assessment.* Mahwah, NJ: Erlbaum.

D'Andrea, M., Daniels, J., & Heck, R. (1991). Evaluating the impact of multicultural counseling training. *Journal of Counseling and Development, 70,* 143–150.

Davis, B. G. (1993). *Tools for teaching.* San Francisco: Jossey-Bass.

Dawis, R. V. (1987). Scale construction. *Journal of Counseling and Development, 70,* 143–150.

Delworth, U., & Hansen, G. R. (Eds.). (1989). *Student services: A handbook for the profession* (2nd ed.). San Francisco: Jossey-Bass.

Dixon, B. (2001). Student affairs in an increasingly multicultural world. In R. B. Winston, D. G. Creamer, & T. K. Miller (Eds.), *The professional student affairs administrator: Educator, leader, and manager* (pp. 65–80). New York: Brunner-Routledge.

Drummond, R. J. (2000). *Appraisal procedures for counselors and helping professionals* (4th ed.). Upper Saddle River, NJ: Merrill.

Durst, M., & Schaeffer, E. M. (1987). Using multimethod research techniques to study college student culture. *Journal of the National Association for Women Deans, Administrators, and Counselors, 51,* 22–26.

Ebbers, L. H., & Henry, S. L. (1990). Cultural competence: A new challenge to student affairs professionals. *NASPA Journal, 27,* 319–323.

Elfrink, V. L., & Coldwell, L. L. (1993). Values in decision making: The INVOLVE model. In R. Young (Ed.), *Identifying and implementing the essential values of the profession* (New Directions for Student Services, no. 61, pp. 61–73). San Francisco: Jossey-Bass.

Ern, E. H. (1993). Managing resources strategically. In M. J. Barr (Ed.), *The handbook of student affairs administration* (pp. 439–454). San Francisco: Jossey-Bass.

Erwin, T. D. (1991). *Assessing student learning and development: A guide to the principles, goals, and methods of determining college outcomes.* San Francisco: Jossey-Bass.

Evans, N. J. (1997). Multicultural immersion: Using learning styles to educate about difference. *Journal of College Student Development, 38,* 195–197.

Evans, N. J., Forney, D. S., & Guido-DiBrito, F. (1998). *Student development in college: Theory, research, and practice.* San Francisco: Jossey-Bass.

Evans, N. J., & Wall, V. A. (Eds.). (1991). *Beyond tolerance: Gays, lesbians, and bisexuals on campus.* Alexandria, VA: American College Personnel Association.

Freire, P. (1970). *Pedagogy of the oppressed.* New York: Continuum.

Fried, J. (1995). *Shifting paradigms in student affairs: Culture, context, teaching and learning.* Washington, DC: American College Personnel Association.

Fried, J. (1997). Changing ethical frameworks for a multicultural world. In J. Fried (Ed.), *Ethics for today's campus: New perspectives on education, student development, and institutional management* (New Directions for Student Services, no. 77, pp. 5–22). San Francisco: Jossey-Bass.

Fried, J. (2002). The scholarship of student affairs: Integration and application. *NASPA Journal, 39,* 120–131.

Fried, J. (2003). Ethical standards and principles. In S. R. Komives & D. B. Woodard (Eds.), *Student affairs: A handbook for the profession* (4th ed., pp. 107–127). San Francisco: Jossey-Bass.

Fuertes, J. N., Bartolomeo, M., & Nichols, C. M. (2001). Future directions in the study of counselor multicultural competency. *Journal of Multicultural Counseling and Development, 29,* 3–12.

Fuertes, J. N., & Brobst, K. (2002). Clients' perceptions of counselor multicultural competency. *Cultural Diversity and Ethnic Minority Psychology, 8,* 214–223.

Fulton, C. P. (1994). *The relationship between white racial identity development and multicultural competence among white trainee therapists.* Unpublished doctoral dissertation, California School of Professional Psychology, Los Angeles.

Gay, L. R., & Airasian, P. (2000). *Educational research: Competencies for analysis and application* (6th ed.). Upper Saddle River, NJ: Merrill.

Gehring, D. D. (2001). Legal parameters for student affairs practice. In R. B. Winston, D. G. Creamer, & T. K. Miller (Eds.), *The professional student affairs administrator: Educator, leader, and manager* (pp. 107–152). New York: Brunner-Routledge.

Gibson, G. (1995). Chickering's model of student development and the academic performance of African-American college students on a predominantly white campus. *Dissertations Abstracts International, 56*(10), 3848A.

Gilligan, C. (1982). *In a different voice: Psychological theory and women's development* (2nd ed.). Cambridge, MA: Harvard University Press.

Giroux, H. A. (1983). *Theory and resistance in education: A pedagogy for the opposition.* South Hadley, MA: Bergin and Garvey.

Grieger, I. (1996). A multicultural organizational development checklist for student affairs. *Journal of College Student Development, 37,* 561–573.

Grieger, I., & Toliver, S. (2001). Multiculturalism on predominantly white campuses: Multiple roles and functions for the counselor. In J. G. Ponterotto, J. M. Casas, L. A. Suzuki, & C. M. Alexander (Eds.), *Handbook of multicultural counseling* (2nd ed., pp. 825–848). Thousand Oaks, CA: Sage.

Hamrick, F. A., & Schuh, J. H. (1992). The great books of student affairs: A great conversation? *NASPA Journal, 30,* 66–74.

Hamrick, F. A., & Schuh, J. H. (1997). Great books in student affairs: Use in graduate programs. *NASPA Journal, 35,* 69–84.

Hansen, N. D., Pepitone-Arreola-Rockwell, F., & Greene, A. F. (2000). Multicultural competence: Criteria and case examples. *Professional Psychology: Research and Practice, 31,* 652–660.

Helms, J. E. (1992). *A race is a nice thing to have.* Topeka, KS: Content Communications.

Helms, J. E., & Richardson, T. Q. (1997). How multiculturalism obscures race and culture as differential aspects of counseling competency. In D. B. Pope-Davis & H.L.K. Coleman (Eds.), *Multicultural counseling competencies: Assessment, education and training, and supervision* (pp. 60–82). Thousand Oaks, CA: Sage.

Herrera, R. S., DelCampo, R. L., & Ames, M. (1993). A serial approach for translating family science instrumentation. *Family Relations, 42,* 357–360.

Higginbotham, E. (1996). Getting all students to listen: Analyzing and coping with student resistance. In J. Meacham (Ed.), *Multiculturalism and diversity in higher education: Special issue of the* American Behavioral Scientist (vol. 40, pp. 203–211). Thousand Oaks, CA: Sage.

Hood, A., & Arceneaux, C. (1990). *Key resources on student services.* San Francisco: Jossey-Bass.

hooks, b. (1994). *Teaching to transgress: Education as the practice of freedom.* New York: Routledge.

Hoover, C. (1994). *An investigation of the preparedness of student affairs professionals to work effectively with diverse campus populations.* Unpublished doctoral dissertation, University of Maryland, College Park.

Howard-Hamilton, M. F., Phelps, R. E., & Torres, V. (1998, Summer). Meeting the needs of all students and staff members: The challenge of diversity. New Directions for Student Services, (no. 82, pp. 49–64). San Francisco: Jossey-Bass.

Howard-Hamilton, M. F., Richardson, B. J., & Shuford, B. (1998). Promoting multicultural education: A holistic approach. *College Student Affairs Journal, 18,* 5–17.

Ibrahim, F. A., & Kahn, H. (1987). Assessment of world views. *Psychological Reports, 60,* 163–176.

Illovsky, M. E. (1994). Defining samples in multicultural psychological research. *Journal of Multicultural Counseling and Development, 22,* 253–256.

Ivey, A. E., D'Andrea, M., Ivey, M. B., & Simek-Morgan, L. (2002). *Theories of counseling and psychotherapy: A multicultural perspective* (5th ed.). Boston, MA: Allyn and Bacon.

Jackson, B. W., & Hardiman, R. (1981). *Description of a multicultural organization: A vision.* Unpublished manuscript, University of Massachusetts, Amherst.

Jackson, B. W., & Hardiman, R. (1986). *Oppression: Conceptual and developmental analysis.* Unpublished manuscript, University of Massachusetts, Amherst.

Jackson, B. W., & Hardiman, R. (1994). Multicultural Organizational Development In E. Y. Cross, J. H. Katz, F. A. Miller, & E. W. Seashore (Eds.), *The promise of diversity: Over 40 voices discuss strategies for eliminating discrimination in organizations* (pp. 231–239). Boston: McGraw-Hill.

Jackson, B. W., & Holvino, E. (1988). Developing multicultural organizations. *Journal of Applied Behavioral Science and Religion, 9,* 14–19.

Jackson, M. L. (1995). Multicultural counseling: Historical perspectives. In J. G. Ponterotto, J. M. Casas, L. A. Suzuki, & C. M. Alexander (Eds.), *Handbook of multicultural counseling* (pp. 3–16). Thousand Oaks, CA: Sage.

Jiang, Q. (2002). The general patterns of psychosocial development of Asian American traditional-age undergraduate students. *Dissertation Abstracts International, 63*(05), 1738A. (UMI no. 3052885).

Johnson, S. D. (1990). Toward clarifying culture, race, and ethnicity in the context of multicultural counseling. *Journal of Multicultural Counseling and Development, 18,* 41–50.

Jones, S. R., Arminio, J., Broido, E., & Torres, V. (2002). Adding depth to an expanded horizon. *Journal of College Student Development, 43,* 431–433.

Jones, S. R., & McEwen, M. K. (2000). A conceptual model of multiple dimensions of identity. *Journal of College Student Development, 41,* 405–414.

Jordan-Cox, C. A. (1987). Psychosocial development of students in traditionally black institutions. *Journal of College Student Development, 28,* 504–512.

Josselson, R. (1987). *Finding herself: Pathways to identity development in women.* San Francisco: Jossey-Bass.

Katz, J. H. (1978). *White awareness: Handbook for anti-racism training.* Norman: University of Oklahoma Press.

Katz, J. H. (1985). The sociopolitical nature of counseling. *Counseling Psychologist, 13,* 615–625.

Katz, J. H. (1989). The challenges of diversity. In C. Woolbright (Ed.), *Valuing diversity on campus* (pp. 1–21). Bloomington, IN: Association of College Unions International.

King, P. M., & Howard-Hamilton, M. (2000). Becoming a multiculturally competent student affairs professional. In NASPA (Ed.), *Diversity on campus* (pp. 26–28). Washington DC: NASPA.

King, P. M., & Howard-Hamilton, M. F. (2001). *Becoming a multicultural competent student affairs professional.* Retrieved Feb. 21, 2002, from National Association of Student Affairs Administrators (NASPA) Website (www.naspa.org).

King, P. M., & Kitchener, K. S. (1994). *Developing reflective judgment.* San Francisco: Jossey-Bass.

King, P. M., & Shuford, B. C. (1996). A multicultural view is a more cognitively complex view: Cognitive development and multicultural education. In J. Meacham (Ed.), *Multiculturalism and diversity in higher education: Special issue of the* American Behavioral Scientist (vol. 40, pp. 153–164). Thousand Oaks, CA: Sage.

Kitchener, K. (1985). Ethical principles and ethical decisions in student affairs. In H. Canon & R. Brown (Eds.), *Applied ethics in student services* (New Directions for Student Services, no. 30, pp. 17–30). San Francisco: Jossey-Bass.

Knefelkamp, L. L. (1978). *A reader's guide to student development theory: A framework for understanding, a framework for design.* Unpublished manuscript, University of Maryland, College Park.

Knefelkamp, L. L. (1984). *A workbook for the practice-to-theory-to-practice model.* Alexandria, VA: American College Personnel Association.

Kochman, T. A. (1981). *Black and white styles in conflict.* Chicago: University of Chicago.

Kodama, C. M., McEwen, M. K., Liang, C.T.H., & Lee, S. (2002). An Asian American perspective on psychosocial development theory. In M. K. McEwen, C. M. Kodama, A. N. Alvarez, S. Lee, & C.T.H. Liang (Eds.), *Working with Asian American college students* (New Directions for Student Services, no. 97, pp. 45–59). San Francisco: Jossey-Bass.

Kolb, D. A. (1981). Learning styles and disciplinary differences. In A. W. Chickering (Ed.), *The modern American college: Responding to the new realities of diverse students and a changing society* (pp. 232–255). San Francisco: Jossey-Bass.

Komives, S. R., and Woodard, D. B. (Eds.). (1996). *Student services: A handbook for the profession* (3rd ed.). San Francisco: Jossey-Bass.

Komives, S. R., and Woodard, D. B. (Eds.). (2003). *Student services: A handbook for the profession* (4th ed.). San Francisco: Jossey-Bass.

Kuh, G. D. (1995). The other curriculum: Out-of-class experiences associated with student learning and personal development. *Journal of Higher Education, 66,* 123–155.

Kuh, G. D., Whitt, E. J., & Shedd, J. D. (1987). *Student affairs work, 2001: A paradigmatic odyssey.* Alexandria, VA: American College Personnel Association.

Ladany, N., Brittan-Powell, C., & Pannu, R. (1997). The influence of supervisory racial identity interaction and racial matching on the supervisory working alliance and supervisee multicultural competence. *Counselor Education and Supervision, 36,* 285–305.

LaFromboise, T. D., Coleman, H.L.K., & Hernandez, A. (1991). Development and factor structure of the Cross-Cultural Counseling Inventory-Revised. *Professional Psychology: Research and Practice, 22,* 380–388.

LaFromboise, T. D., & Foster, S. L. (1992). Cross-cultural training: Scientist-practitioner models and methods. *Counseling Psychologist, 20,* 472–489.

Lee, C. C. (1998). Counselors as agents of social change. In C. C. Lee & G. R. Walz (Eds.), *Social action: A mandate for counselors* (pp. 3–14). Alexandria, VA: American Counseling Association and ERIC Counseling and Student Services Clearinghouse.

Levine, A., & Cureton, J. S. (1998). *When hope and fear collide: A portrait of today's college student.* San Francisco: Jossey-Bass.

Lewis, A. C., & Hayes, S. (1991). Multiculturalism and the school counseling curriculum. *Journal of Counseling and Development, 70,* 119–125.

Lopez, S. R., Grover, K. P., Holland, D., Johnson, M. J., Kain, C. D., Kanel, K., et al. (1989). Development of culturally sensitive psychotherapists. *Professional Psychology: Research and Practice, 20,* 369–376.

Lyddon, W. J. (1990). First- and second-order change: Implications for rationalist and constructivist cognitive therapies. *Journal of College Student Development, 69,* 122–127.

Madaus, G. F., Scriven, M., & Stufflebeam, D. L. (1983). *Evaluation models.* Hingham, MA: Kluwer Academic.

Magolda, P. M. (1999). Using ethnographic fieldwork and case studies to guide student affairs practice. *Journal of College Student Development, 40,* 10–21.

Malaney, G. D. (1999). The structure and function of student affairs research offices: A national study. In G. D. Malaney (Ed.), *Student affairs research, evaluation, and assessment: Structure and practice in an era of change* (pp. 11–22). San Francisco: Jossey-Bass.

Malaney, G. D. (2002). Scholarship in student affairs through teaching and research. *NASPA Journal, 39,* 132–146.

Manning, K. (1994a). Liberation theory and student affairs. *Journal of College Student Development, 35,* 94–97.

Manning, K. (1994b). Multicultural theories for multicultural practice. *NASPA Journal, 31,* 176–185.

Manning, K. (1999). *Giving voice to critical campus issues: Qualitative research in student affairs.* Lanham, MD: University Press of America.

Manning, K., & Coleman-Boatwright, P. (1991). Student affairs initiative toward a multicultural university. *Journal of College Student Development, 32,* 367–374.

Marin, G. (1984). Stereotyping Hispanics: The differential effect of research method, label, and degree of contact. *International Journal of Intercultural Relations, 8,* 17–27.

Marin, G., & Marin, B. V. (1991). *Research with Hispanic populations.* Thousand Oaks, CA: Sage.

Martinez, R. P., & Holloway, E. L. (1997). The supervision relationship in multicultural training. In D. B. Pope-Davis and H.L.K. Coleman (Eds.), *Multicultural counseling competencies: Assessment, education and training, and supervision* (pp. 325–349). Thousand Oaks, CA: Sage.

McAdoo, H. P. (Ed.). (1993). *Family ethnicity: Strength in diversity.* Thousand Oaks, CA: Sage.

McEwen, M. K. (1996). The nature and uses of theory. In S. R. Komives & D. B. Woodard, Jr. (Eds.), *Student services: A handbook for the profession* (3rd ed., pp. 147–163). San Francisco: Jossey-Bass.

McEwen, M. K., Kodama, C. M., Alvarez, A. N., Lee, S., & Liang, C.T.H. (2002). *Working with Asian American college students* (New Directions for Student Services, no. 97, pp. 1–104). San Francisco: Jossey-Bass.

McEwen, M. K., & Roper, L. D. (1994a). Incorporating multiculturalism into student affairs preparation programs: Suggestions from the literature. *Journal of College Student Development, 35,* 46–53.

McEwen, M. K., & Roper, L. D. (1994b). Interracial experiences, knowledge and skills of master's degree students in graduate programs in student affairs. *Journal of College Student Development, 35,* 81–87.

McRae, M. B., & Johnson, S. D. (1991). Toward training for competence in multicultural counselor education. *Journal of Counseling and Development, 70,* 131–135.

McWhertor, T. E., & Guthrie, D. S. (1998). Toward an ethic for the profession. In M. J. Amey & L. M. Reesor (Eds.), *Beginning your journey: A guide for new professionals in student affairs* (pp. 21–36). Washington, DC: National Association for Student Personnel Administrators.

Meacham, J. (1996). Interdisciplinary and teaching perspectives on multiculturalism and diversity. In J. Meacham (Ed.), *Multiculturalism and diversity in higher education: Special issue of the* American Behavioral Scientist (vol. 40, pp. 112–122). Thousand Oaks, CA: Sage.

Miller, T. K. (Ed.). (2001). *The CAS book of professional standards for higher education* (2nd rev. ed.). Washington, DC: Council for the Advancement of Standards in Higher Education.

Miller, T. K., & Winston, R. B. (Eds.). (1991). *Administration and leadership in student affairs: Actualizing student development in higher education* (2nd ed.). Muncie, IN: Accelerated Development.

Minnich, E. K. (1990). *Transforming knowledge*. Philadelphia: Temple University Press.

Moore, L. V. (1985). *A model for evaluating job competencies of professional staff*. Unpublished manuscript, Bowling Green State University, Bowling Green, Ohio.

Moore, L. V., & Hamilton, D. H. (1993). The teaching of values. In R. B. Young (Ed.), *Identifying and implementing the essential values of the profession* (New Directions for Student Services, no. 61, pp. 75–85). San Francisco: Jossey-Bass.

Mueller, J. A. (1999). *The relationship between white racial consciousness and multicultural competence among white student affairs practitioners*. Unpublished doctoral dissertation, Teachers College, Columbia University.

Mueller, J. A., & Pope, R. L. (2001). The relationship between multicultural competence and white racial consciousness among student affairs practitioners. *Journal of College Student Development, 42,* 133–144.

Musil, C. M. (1996). The maturing of diversity initiatives on American campuses. In J. Meacham (Ed.), *Multiculturalism and diversity in higher education: Special issue of the* American Behavioral Scientist (vol. 40, pp. 222–232). Thousand Oaks, CA: Sage.

Musil, C. M., Garcia, M., Smith, D., & Moses, Y. (1995). *Diversity in higher education: A work in progress*. Washington, DC: Association for American Colleges and Universities.

National Association of Student Personnel Administrators (NASPA). (1987). *A perspective on student affairs on the 50th anniversary of the* Student Personnel Point of View. Washington, DC: Author.

National Association of Student Personnel Administrators (NASPA). (1993). *NASPA standards of professional practice*. Washington, DC: Author.

National Association of Student Personnel Administrators (NASPA). (1999). Standards of professional practice. In *Member handbook* (pp. 18–19). Washington, DC: Author.

Noddings, N. (1984). *Caring: A feminine approach to ethics and moral education*. Berkeley: University of California Press.

Okun, B. F. (1997). *Effective helping: Interviewing and counseling techniques*. Pacific Grove, CA: Brooks/Cole.

Okun, B. F., Fried, J., & Okun, M. L. (1999). *Understanding diversity: A learning-as-practice primer*. Pacific Grove, CA: Brooks/Cole.

Ottavi, T. M. (1996). *Exploring white racial consciousness attitudes and factors influencing self-reported multicultural counseling competencies.* Unpublished doctoral dissertation, University of Iowa.

Ottavi, T. M., Pope-Davis, D. B., & Dings, J. G. (1994). The relationship between white racial identity attitudes and self-reported multicultural counseling competencies. *Journal of Counseling Psychology, 41,* 149–153.

Padilla, A. M. (2000). Issues in culturally appropriate testing. In L. A. Suzuki, J. G. Ponterotto, & P. J. Meller (Eds.), *The new handbook of multicultural assessment: Clinical, psychological and educational applications* (2nd ed., pp. 5–27). San Francisco: Jossey-Bass.

Parham, T. A. (1999). Diversity and the helping professions: Lessons in understanding, advocacy, and sensitivity. In Y. M. Jenkins (Ed.), *Diversity in college settings: Directives for helping professionals* (pp. 239–246). New York: Routledge.

Parker, C. A. (1977). On modeling reality. *Journal of College Student Personnel, 18,* 419–425.

Parker, C. A. (Ed.). (1978). *Encouraging development in college students.* Minneapolis: University of Minnesota Press.

Pascarella, E. T., & Terrenzi, P. T. (1991). *How college affects students: Findings and insights from twenty years of research.* San Francisco: Jossey-Bass.

Patterson, C. H. (1996). Multicultural counseling: From diversity to universality. *Journal of Counseling and Development, 74,* 227–231.

Pedersen, P. (1988). *A handbook for developing multicultural awareness.* Alexandria, VA: American Association for Counseling and Development.

Pedersen, P. B. (1987). Ten frequent assumptions of cultural bias in counseling. *Journal of Multicultural Counseling and Development, 15,* 16–24.

Ponterotto, J. G. (1988). Racial consciousness development among white counselor trainees: A stage model. *Journal of Multicultural Counseling and Development, 16,* 146–156.

Ponterotto, J. G. (2002). Qualitative research methods: A fifth force in psychology. *Counseling Psychologist, 30,* 394–406.

Ponterotto, J. G., Burkard, A., Rieger, B. P., Grieger, I., D'Onofrio, A. A., Dubuisson, A., et al. (1995). Development and initial validation of the Quick Discrimination Index (QDI). *Education and Psychological Measurement, 55,* 1016–1031.

Ponterotto, J. G., & Casas, J. M. (1991). *Handbook of racial/ethnic minority counseling research.* Springfield, IL: Thomas.

Ponterotto, J. G., Lewis, D. E., & Bullington, R. (Eds.) (1990). *Affirmative action on campus.* San Francisco: Jossey-Bass.

Ponterotto, J. G., & Pedersen, P. (1993). *Preventing prejudice: A guide for counselors and educators.* Thousand Oaks, CA: Sage.

Ponterotto, J. G., Reiger, B. P., Barrett, A., Harris, G., Sparks, R., Sanchez, C. M., & Magids, D. (1993). *Development and initial validation of the Multicultural Counseling Awareness Scale (MCAS-B)*. Paper presented at the Ninth Buros-Nebraska Symposium on Measurement and Testing: Multicultural Assessment, Lincoln.

Ponterotto, J. G., Rieger, B. P., Barrett, A., Harris, G., Sparks, R., Sanchez, C. M., & Magids, D. (1996). Initial development and validation of the Multicultural Counseling Awareness Scale (MCAS-B). In G. R. Sodowsky (Ed.), *Multicultural assessment in counseling and clinical psychology* (pp. 247–282). Lincoln, NE: Buros Institute of Mental Measurements.

Ponterotto, J. G., Rieger, B. P., Barrett, A., & Sparks, R. (1994). Assessing multicultural counseling competence: A review of instrumentation. *Journal of Counseling and Development, 72,* 316–322.

Pope, R. L. (1993a). *An analysis of multiracial change efforts in student affairs*. Unpublished doctoral dissertation, University of Massachusetts, Amherst.

Pope, R. L. (1993b). Multicultural-organization development in student affairs: An introduction. *Journal of College Student Development, 34,* 201–205.

Pope, R. L. (1995). Multicultural organizational development: Implications and applications in student affairs. In J. Fried (Ed.), *Shifting paradigms in student affairs: Culture, context, teaching and learning* (pp. 233–250). Washington, DC: American College Personnel Association.

Pope, R. L. (1998). The relationship between psychosocial development and racial identity among black college students. *Journal of College Student Development, 39,* 273–282.

Pope, R. L. (2000). The relationship between psychosocial development and racial identity of college students of color. *Journal of College Student Development, 41,* 302–312.

Pope, R. L., & Mueller, J. A. (2000). Development and initial validation of the Multicultural Competence in Student Affairs-Preliminary 2 scale. *Journal of College Student Development, 41,* 599–608.

Pope, R. L., & Reynolds, A. L. (1997). Student affairs core competencies: Integrating multicultural awareness, knowledge, and skills. *Journal of College Student Development, 38,* 266–277.

Pope, R. L., Reynolds, A. L., & Cheatham, H. E. (1997). American College Personnel Association (ACPA) strategic initiative on multiculturalism. *Journal of College Student Development, 38,* 62–67.

Pope-Davis, D. B., Breaux, C., & Liu, W. M. (1997). A multicultural immersion experience: Filling a void in multicultural training. In

D. Pope-Davis & H.L.K. Coleman (Eds.), *Multicultural counseling competence: Assessment, education and training, and supervision* (pp. 227–241). Thousand Oaks, CA: Sage.

Pope-Davis, D. B., & Dings, J. G. (1995). The assessment of multicultural counseling competencies. In J. Ponterotto, J. M. Casas, L. A. Suzuki, & C. M. Alexander (Eds.), *Handbook of multicultural counseling* (pp. 287–311). San Francisco: Jossey-Bass.

Pope-Davis, D. B., Dings, J. G., & Ottavi, T. M. (1994). The relationship between demographic and educational variables on multicultural competencies. *Iowa Psychologist, 40,* 12–14.

Pope-Davis, D. B., & Ottavi, T. M. (1995). Examining the association between self-reported multicultural counseling competencies and demographic and educational variables among counselors. *Journal of Counseling and Development, 72,* 651–654.

Pope-Davis, D. B., Reynolds, A. L., & Dings, J. G. (1994). Multicultural competencies of doctoral interns at university counseling centers: An exploratory investigation. *Professional Psychology: Research and Practice, 25,* 466–470.

Pope-Davis, D. B., Reynolds, A. L., Dings, J. G., & Nielsen, D. (1995). Examining multicultural counseling competencies of graduate students in psychology. *Professional Psychology: Research and Practice, 26,* 322–329.

Pope-Davis, D. B., Toporek, R. L., Ortega-Villalobos, L., Ligiero, D. P., Brittan-Powell, C. S., Liu, W. M., et al. (2002). Client perspectives of multicultural counseling competence: A qualitative examination. *Counseling Psychologist, 30,* 355–393.

Porter, N. (1995). Supervision of psychotherapists: Integrating anti-racist, feminist, and multicultural perspectives. In H. Landrine (Ed.), *Bringing cultural diversity to feminist psychology: Theory, research, and practice* (pp. 163–176). Washington, DC: American Psychological Association.

Ramirez, B. C. (1993). Adapting to new student needs and characteristics. In M. J. Barr (Ed.), *The handbook of student affairs administration* (pp. 427–438). San Francisco: Jossey-Bass.

Reagon, B. J. (1983). Coalition building. In B. Smith (Ed.), *Homegirls: A black feminist anthology* (pp. 356–369). New York: Kitchen Table Press.

Reisser, L., & Roper, L. D. (1999). Using resources to achieve institutional missions and goals. In G. S. Blimling and E. J. Whitt (Eds.), *Good practice in student affairs: Principles to foster student learning* (pp. 113–131). San Francisco: Jossey-Bass.

Reynolds, A. L. (1995a). Challenges and strategies for teaching multicultural counseling courses. In J. Ponterotto, M. Casas, L. Suzuki, & C. Alexander (Eds.), *Handbook of multicultural counseling* (pp. 312–330). Thousand Oaks, CA: Sage.

Reynolds, A. L. (1995b). Multiculturalism in counseling and advising. In J. Fried (Ed.), *Shifting paradigms in student affairs: Culture, context, teaching, and learning* (pp. 155–170). Lanham, MD: University Press of America.

Reynolds, A. L. (1997). Using the Multicultural Change Intervention Matrix (MCIM) as a multicultural counseling training model. In D. Pope-Davis & H.L.K. Coleman (Eds.), *Multicultural counseling competence: Assessment, education and training, and supervision* (pp. 209–226). Thousand Oaks, CA: Sage.

Reynolds, A. L. (1999). Working with children and adolescents in the schools: Multicultural counseling implications. In R. H. Sheets & E. R. Hollins (Eds.), *Aspects of human development: Racial and ethnic identity in school practices* (pp. 213–230). Mahwah, NJ: Erlbaum.

Reynolds, A. L. (2001a). Embracing multiculturalism: A journey of self-discovery. In J. Ponterotto, M. Casas, L. Suzuki, & C. Alexander (Eds.), *Handbook of multicultural counseling* (2nd ed., pp. 103–112). Thousand Oaks, CA: Sage.

Reynolds, A. L. (2001b). Multidimensional cultural competence: Providing tools for transforming psychology. *Counseling Psychologist, 29,* 833–841.

Reynolds, A. L. (forthcoming). Illustrative applications in supervision. In R. T. Carter (Ed.), *Handbook of racial cultural counseling and psychology.* New York: Wiley.

Reynolds, A. L., & Pope, R. L. (1991). The complexities of diversity: Exploring multiple oppressions. *Journal of Counseling and Development, 70,* 174–180.

Reynolds, A. L., & Pope, R. L. (1994). Perspectives on creating multicultural campuses. *Journal of American College Health, 42,* 229–233.

Reynolds, A. L., & Pope, R. L. (2003). Multicultural competencies in counseling centers. In D. B. Pope-Davis, H.L.K. Coleman, W. M. Liu, & R. L. Toporek (Eds.), *Handbook of multicultural competencies in counseling and psychology* (pp. 365–382). Thousand Oaks, CA: Sage.

Reynolds, A. L., Pope, R. L., & Wells, G. V. (2002). *Creating a student affairs diversity action plan: Blueprint for success.* Paper presented at the meeting of the American College Personnel Association, Long Beach, CA.

Rhoads, R. A., & Black, M. A. (1995). Student affairs practitioners as transformative educators: Advancing a critical cultural perspective. *Journal of College Student Development, 36,* 413–421.

Rickard, S. T. (1993). Truth, freedom, justice: Academic tradition and the essential values. In R. Young (Ed.), *Identifying and implementing the essential values of the profession* (New Directions for Student Services, no. 61, pp. 15–23). San Francisco: Jossey-Bass.

Ridley, C. R., Espelage, D. L., & Rubinstein, K. J. (1997). Course development in multicultural counseling. In D. Pope-Davis & H.L.K. Coleman (Eds.), *Multicultural counseling competence: Assessment, education and training, and supervision* (pp. 131–158). Thousand Oaks, CA: Sage.

Ridley, C. R., Mendoza, D. W., & Kanitz, B. E. (1994). Multicultural training: Reexamination, operationalization, and integration. *Counseling Psychologist, 22,* 227–289.

Ridley, C. R., & Thompson, C. E. (1999). Managing resistance to diversity training: A social systems perspective. In M. S. Kiselica (Ed.), *Confronting prejudice and racism during multicultural training* (pp. 3–24). Alexandria, VA: American Counseling Association.

Roberts, D. C. (1993). Community: The value of social synergy. In R. Young (Ed.), *Identifying and implementing the essential values of the profession* (New Directions for Student Services, no. 61, pp. 35–46). San Francisco: Jossey-Bass.

Rodgers, R. F. (1990). Recent theories and research underlying student development. In D. G. Creamer (Ed.), *College student development: Theory and practice for the 1990s* (pp. 27–79). Alexandria, VA: American College Personnel Association Media.

Rodgers, R. F. (1991). Using theory in practice in student affairs. In T. K. Miller & R. B. Winston (Eds.), *Administration and leadership in student affairs: Actualizing student development in higher education* (pp. 203–251). Muncie, IN: Accelerated Development.

Rodgers, R. F., & Widick, C. (1980). Theory to practice: Uniting concepts, logic, and creativity. In F. B. Newton & K. L. Ender (Eds.), *Student development practices: Strategies for making a difference* (pp. 3–25). Springfield, IL: Thomas.

Rogers, J. L. (1996). Leadership. In S. R. Komives & D. B. Woodard (Eds.), *Student services: A handbook for the profession* (3rd ed., pp. 299–319). San Francisco: Jossey-Bass.

Roper, L. D. (1996). Teaching and training. In S. R. Komives & D. B. Woodard (Eds.), *Student services: A handbook for the profession* (3rd ed., pp. 320–334). San Francisco: Jossey-Bass.

Rowe, W., Behrens, J. T., & Leach, M. M. (1995). Racial/ethnic identity and racial consciousness: Looking back and looking forward. In J. Ponterotto, J. M. Casas, L. A. Suzuki, & C. M. Alexander (Eds.), *Handbook of multicultural counseling* (pp. 218–235). San Francisco: Jossey-Bass.

Rowe, W., Bennett, S. K., & Atkinson, D. R. (1994). White racial identity models: A critique and alternative proposal. *Counseling Psychologist, 22,* 129–146.

Saltmarsh, J. (1997). Ethics, reflection, purpose, and compassion: Community service learning. In J. Fried (Ed.), *Ethics for today's campus: New perspectives on education, student development, and institutional management* (New Directions for Student Services, no. 77, pp. 81–95). San Francisco: Jossey-Bass.

Sandeen, A. (1991). *The chief student affairs officer: Leader, manager, mediator, educator.* San Francisco: Jossey-Bass.

Sandeen, A. (1993). Organization, functions, and standards of practice. In S. R. Komives & D. B. Woodard (Eds.), *Student services: A handbook for the profession* (3rd ed., pp. 435–457). San Francisco: Jossey-Bass.

Sanford, N. (1967). *Where colleges fail.* San Francisco: Jossey-Bass.

Sanlo, R. (2002). Scholarship in student affairs: Thinking outside the triangle, or Tabasco on the cantaloupe. *NASPA Journal, 39,* 166–180.

Saunders, S. A., & Cooper, D. L. (2001). Programmatic interventions: Translating theory to practice. In R. B. Winston, D. G. Creamer, & T. K. Miller (Eds.), *The professional student affairs administrator: Educator, leader, and manager* (pp. 309–340). New York: Brunner-Routledge.

Schmitz, B. (1992). *Core curriculum and cultural pluralism.* Washington, DC: Association for American Colleges and Universities.

Schuh, J. H. (1994). Education and Identity (2nd ed.). [Review of book]. *Journal of College Student Development, 35,* 310–312.

Schuster, M. R., & Van Dyne, S. R. (1985). Stages of curriculum transformation. In M. R. Schuster & S. R. Van Dyne (Eds.), *Women's place in the academy: Transforming the liberal arts curriculum* (pp. 13–29). Totowa, NJ: Rowman and Allanheld.

Simpson, G. E., & Yinger, J. M. (1985). *Racial and cultural minorities: An analysis of prejudice and discrimination* (5th ed.). New York: Plenum.

Snowden, P. E., & Gorton, R. A. (2002). *School leadership and administration: Important concepts, case studies, and simulations* (6th ed.). Boston: McGraw-Hill.

Sodowsky, G. R., Taffe, R. C., Gutkin, T. B., & Wise, S. L. (1994). Development of the Multicultural Counseling Inventory (MCI): A self-report measure of multicultural competencies. *Journal of Counseling Psychology, 41,* 153–162.

Speigel, J. (1982). An ecological model of ethnic families. In M. McGoldrick, J. K. Pearce, & J. Giordano (Eds.), *Ethnicity and family therapy* (pp. 55–83). New York: Guilford Press.

Speight, S. L., Myers, L. J., Cox, C. I., & Highlen, P. S. (1991). A redefinition of multicultural counseling. *Journal of Counseling and Development, 70,* 29–36.

Stage, F. K. (1992a). The case for flexibility in research and assessment of college students. In F. K. Stage (Ed.), *Diverse methods for research and assessment of college students* (pp. 1–11). Washington, DC: American College Personnel Association.

Stage, F. K. (Ed.). (1992b). *Diverse methods for research and assessment of college students.* Washington, DC: American College Personnel Association.

Stage, F. K., & Associates. (1993). *Linking theory to practice: Case studies for working with college students.* Muncie, IN: Accelerated Development.

Stage, F. S., & Manning, K. (1992). *Enhancing the multicultural campus environment: A cultural brokering approach* (New Directions for Student Services, no. 60, pp. 1–75). San Francisco: Jossey-Bass.

Stage, F. K., & Russell, R. V. (1992). Using method triangulation in college student research. *Journal of College Student Development, 33,* 485–491.

Stamatakos, L. C. (1991). Student affairs administrators as institutional leaders. In T. K. Miller and R. B. Winston (Eds.), *Administration and leadership in student affairs: Actualizing student development in higher education* (2nd ed., pp. 673–705). Muncie, IN: Accelerated Development.

Stewart, J. B. (1991). Planning for cultural diversity: A case study. In H. C. Cheatham (Ed.), *Cultural pluralism on campus* (pp. 161–181). Washington, DC: American College Personnel Association.

Strange, C. (1983). Human development theory and administrative practice in student affairs: Ships passing in the daylight? *NASPA Journal, 21,* 2–8.

Strange, C. (1987). *Bridging the gap between theory and practice in student affairs.* (ERIC Document Reproduction Service, no. ED 292 410).

Strange, C. (1991). Managing college environments: Theory and practice. In T. K. Miller & R. B. Winston (Eds.), *Administration and leadership in student affairs: Actualizing student development in higher education* (pp. 159–199). Muncie, IN: Accelerated Development.

Strange, C., & Alston, L. (1998). Voicing differences: Encouraging multicultural learning. *Journal of College Student Development, 39,* 87–99.

Strange, C. C., & King, P. M. (1990). The professional practice of student development. In D. G. Creamer (Ed.), *College student development: Theory and practice for the 1990s* (pp. 9–24). Alexandria, VA: American College Personnel Association Media.

Sue, D. W. (1981). *Counseling the culturally different: Theory and practice.* New York: Wiley.

Sue, D. W. (1991). A model for cultural diversity training. *Journal of Counseling and Development, 70,* 99–105.

Sue, D. W. (1995). Multicultural organization development: Implications for the counseling profession. In J. G. Ponterotto, J. M. Casas, L. A. Suzuki, & C. M. Alexander (Eds.), *Handbook of multicultural counseling* (pp.474–492). Thousand Oaks, CA: Sage.

Sue, D. W. (2001). Multiple dimensional facets of cultural competence. *Counseling Psychologist, 29,* 790–821.

Sue, D. W., Arredondo, P., & McDavis, R. J. (1992). Multicultural counseling competencies and standards: A call to the profession. *Journal of Counseling and Development, 70,* 477–486.

Sue, D. W., Bernier, J. E., Durran, A., Feinberg, L., Pederson, P., Smith, E. J., & Vasquez-Nuttall, E. (1982). Position paper: Cross-cultural counseling competencies. *Counseling Psychologist, 10,* 45–52.

Sue, D. W., Bingham, R. P., Porche-Burke, L., & Vasquez, M. (1999). The diversification of psychology: A multicultural revolution. *American Psychologist, 54,* 1061–1069.

Sue, D. W., Carter, R. T., Casas, J. M., Fouad, N. A., Ivey, A. E., Jensen, M., et al. (1998). *Multicultural counseling competencies: Individual and organizational development.* Thousand Oaks, CA: Sage.

Sue, D. W., Ivey, A. E., & Pedersen, P. B. (Eds.). (1996). *A theory of multicultural counseling and therapy.* Pacific Grove, CA: Brooks/Cole.

Sue, D. W., & Sue, D. (1999). *Counseling the culturally different: Theory and practice* (3rd ed.). New York: Wiley.

Sue, S. (1998). In search of cultural competence in psychotherapy and counseling. *American Psychologist, 53,* 440–448.

Sue, S., & Zane, N. (1987). The role of culture and cultural techniques in psychotherapy: A critique and reformulation. *American Psychologist, 42,* 37–45.

Sundberg, D. C., & Fried, J. (1997). Ethical dialogues on campus. In J. Fried (Ed.), *Ethics for today's campus: New perspectives on education, student development, and institutional management* (New Directions for Student Services, no. 77, pp. 67–80). San Francisco: Jossey-Bass.

Suzuki, L. A., & Kugler, J. F. (1995). Intelligence and personality assessment: Multicultural perspectives. In L. A. Suzuki, J. G. Ponterotto, & P. J. Meller (Eds.), *Handbook of multicultural assessment: Clinical, psychological and educational applications,* pp. 493–515). San Francisco: Jossey-Bass.

Suzuki, L. A., Ponterotto, J. G., & Meller, P. J. (2000). *Handbook of multicultural assessment: Clinical, psychological, and educational applications* (2nd ed.). San Francisco: Jossey-Bass.

Talbot, D. M. (1992). *A multimethod study of the diversity emphasis in master's degree programs in college student affairs.* Unpublished doctoral dissertation, University of Maryland, College Park.

Talbot, D. M. (1996a). Master's students' perspectives on their graduate education regarding issues of diversity. *NASPA Journal, 33,* 163–178.

Talbot, D. M. (1996b). Multiculturalism. In S. R. Komives & D. B. Woodard (Eds.), *Student services: A handbook for the profession* (3rd ed., pp. 380–396). San Francisco: Jossey-Bass.

Talbot, D. M., & Kocarek, C. (1997). Student affairs graduate faculty members' knowledge, comfort, and behaviors regarding issues of diversity. *Journal of College Student Development, 38,* 278–287.

Tatum, B. D. (1997). *Why are all the black kids sitting together at the lunch table?* New York: Basic Books.

Taub, D. J., & McEwen, M. K. (1991). The relationship of racial identity attitudes to autonomy and mature interpersonal relationships in black and white undergraduate women. *Journal of College Student Development, 33,* 439–446.

Terenzini, P. T., Pascarella, E. T., & Blimling, G. S. (1999). Students' out-of-class experiences and their influence on learning and cognitive development: A literature review. *Journal of College Student Development, 40,* 610–623.

Testa, A. M. (1994). *A study of psychosocial development of African American, Hispanic, and white university students: A comparison of scores between first-year and upper-division students on the Student Development Task and Lifestyle Inventory (SDTLI) at a western university.* Doctoral dissertation, University of Nevada at Reno, 1994. *Dissertation Abstracts International, 55*(07A), 1833.

Thomas, C. (2001). The relationship between psychosocial development and socioeconomic status among black college students. *Dissertation Abstracts International, 62*(05), 1753A. (UMI no. 3014816).

Upcraft, M. L. (1993). Translating theory into practice. In M. J. Barr (Ed.), *The handbook of student affairs administration* (pp. 260–273). San Francisco: Jossey-Bass.

Upcraft, M. L. (1994). The dilemmas of translating theory to practice. *Journal of College Student Development, 35,* 438–443.

Upcraft, M. L., & Poole, T. G. (1991). Ethical issues and administrative politics. In P. L. Moore (Ed.), *Managing the political dimensions of student affairs* (New Directions for Student Services, no. 55, pp. 81–94). San Francisco: Jossey-Bass.

Upcraft, M. L., & Schuh, J. H. (1996). *Assessment in student affairs: A guide for practitioners.* San Francisco: Jossey-Bass.

Utterback, J. W. (1992). Interactive effects of gender and ethnicity on levels of intimacy in college students. Doctoral dissertation, University of Northern Colorado, 1992. *Dissertation Abstracts International, 5,* 53–06A, 1820.

Vazquez, L. A. (1997). A systematic multicultural curriculum model: The pedagogical process. In D. Pope-Davis & H.L.K. Coleman (Eds.), *Multicultural counseling competence: Assessment, education and training, and supervision* (pp. 159–183). Thousand Oaks, CA: Sage.

Vera, E. M., & Speight, S. L. (2003). Multicultural competence, social justice, and counseling psychology: Expanding our roles. *Counseling Psychologist, 31,* 253–272.

Wallace, B. C. (2000). A call for change in multicultural training at graduate schools of education: Educating to end oppression and for social justice. *Teachers College Record, 12,* 1–16.

Walsh, W. B., & Betz, N. E. (1995). *Tests and assessment* (3rd ed.). Upper Saddle River, NJ: Prentice-Hall.

Watzlawick, P., Weakland, J., & Fisch, R. (1974). *Change.* New York: Norton.

Weimer, M. (2001). Learning more from the wisdom of practice. In C. Kreber (Ed.), *Scholarship revisited: Perspectives on the scholarship of teaching* (New Directions for Teaching and Learning, no. 86, pp. 45–56). San Francisco: Jossey-Bass.

White, J. (2002). Student affairs scholarship: Reconsidering questions toward possibilities for collaboration and innovation. *NASPA Journal, 39,* 158–165.

Wilkinson, W. K., & McNeil, K. (1996). *Research for the helping professions.* Cincinnati: Brooks/Cole.

Williams, J. A. (1994). *Classroom in conflict: Teaching controversial subjects in a diverse society.* Albany: State University of New York Press.

Winston, R. B., Creamer, D. G., & Miller, T. K. (Eds.). (2001). *The professional student affairs administrator: Educator, leader, and manager.* New York: Brunner-Routledge.

Winston, R. B., & Dagley, J. C. (1985). Ethical standards statements: Uses and limitations. In H. Canon & R. Brown (Eds.), *Applied ethics in student services* (New Directions for Student Services, no. 30, pp. 49–66). San Francisco: Jossey-Bass.

Wolfe, C. T., & Spencer, S. J. (1996). Stereotypes and prejudice: Their overt and subtle influence in the classroom. In J. Meacham (Ed.), *Multiculturalism and diversity in higher education: Special issue of the* American Behavioral Scientist (vol. 40, pp. 176–185). Thousand Oaks, CA: Sage.

Woolbright, C. (Ed.). (1989). *Valuing diversity on campus.* Bloomington, IN: Association of College Unions International.

Wrenn, C. G. (1962). The culturally encapsulated counselor. *Harvard Educational Review, 32,* 444–449.

Wright, D. J. (1987). Minority students: Developmental beginnings. In D. J. Wright (Ed.), *Responding to the needs of today's minority students* (New Directions for Student Services, no. 38, pp. 5–22). San Francisco: Jossey-Bass.

Young, R. B. (1993). The essential values of the profession. In R. Young (Ed.), *Identifying and implementing the essential values of the profession* (New Directions for Student Services, no. 61, pp. 5–13). San Francisco: Jossey-Bass.

Young, R. B. (2001). Ethics and professional practice. In R. B. Winston, D. G. Creamer, & T. K. Miller (Eds.), *The professional student affairs administrator: Educator, leader, and manager* (pp. 153–178). New York: Brunner-Routledge.

Name Index

Subject Index

A

Administration: as core competency, 8–9; exemplary practices in, 71–75; functions of, 47–50; and Multicultural Change Intervention Matrix (MCIM), 56–62, 176; multicultural competence in, 54–55; and multicultural organization development (MCOD), 55–56; and Multicultural Organization Development Checklist (MODC), 62–63, 180; and Multicultural Organization Development (MCOD) Template, 63–71, 180; problems facing, 46–47; skills needed for, 50–53; summary on, 75, 218

Advising and helping: advocacy skills, 93–94; counseling competence, 82–84; cultural assumptions underlying, 91–92; and cultural concepts, 89; culturally responsive interventions for, 89–90; exemplary practices in, 94–97; and interpersonal dynamics, 90–91; problems encountered in, 76–77; self-awareness for, 86–87; seven competencies for, 85–86; in student affairs, 78–81; summary on, 97, 217; understanding of cultural groups for, 87–88

Advocacy skills, 93–94

American College Personnel Association (ACPA), 8, 125, 126, 143, 223–224

Assessment: defined, 100; research versus, 100–101

Assessment and research: alternate approaches to, 102, 113–115; assumptions in, 102–104; data collection, 102, 111–113; defining population, 102, 105–108; exemplary practices in, 116–118; instrumentation, 102, 108–111; multicultural competence in, 101–102; summary on, 118–119, 218–219

Assumptions, challenging, 220–221

Average white guy case study, 203–207

Awareness, multicultural: and advising, 86–87; as characteristic, 18–19; defined, 216; exemplary, 20–21; in theory and translation, 40–41

C

Case studies: average white guy case study, 203–207; benefits of using, 183; and case exploration activities, 184–190; diversity training case study, 210–213; equal opportunity employer case study, 193–197; hate speech case study, 201–203; "looking for a place to be all of me" case study, 197–200; orientation skit flap, 190–193; reality-based, 184; watching TV case study, 207–209

Characteristics of multiculturally competent professionals, 17–19

Collectivism, 103, 104, 111

Conscientizacào, 102

Core competencies: administrative and management, 8–9; ethical and professional standards, 8, 9; helping and advising, 9; list of seven, 8;

exemplary practices in, 116–118; instrumentation, 108–111; multicultural competence in, 101–102; problems in, 98–99; in student affairs, 100–101; summary on, 118–119, 218–219; and time orientation, 103, 104, 111

S

Self-awareness of advisors, 86–87
Skills, multicultural: as characteristics, 18–19; exemplary, 24–27; in theory and translation, 42
Strategic planning, MCIM tool for, 60–61
Student affairs core competencies: brief description of, 6–9; model of, 1, 9–11, 215–220
Student Learning Imperative, 143
Students, values and ethics of, 132–134

T

Teaching and training: as core competency, 8, 9; and curricular transformation, 61–62, 147–149, 157; exemplary practices in, 156–161; and multicultural competence,

146–147; problems in, 141–142; in student affairs, 144–146; and student affairs preparation programs, 149–154; summary on, 161–162, 219–220; and workshop assessments, 155–156
Theory and translation: cautions for using, 34–35; defined, 8, 9; and multicultural awareness, 40–41; multicultural competence in, 36–40, 217; and multicultural knowledge, 41–42; and multicultural skills, 42; problems with, 29–30; in student affairs work, 31–36; value of, 30–31
Time orientation, 103, 104, 111

V

Values: institutional, 124–125; legal implications of, 125; personal, 124; professional, 124, 125; of students, 132–134

W

White guy case study, just an average, 203–207
White racial consciousness, 172–173